THE TACTICAL
USES OF PASSION

THE TACTICAL
USES OF PASSION

An Essay on Power, Reason, and Reality

F. G. BAILEY

Cornell University Press

ITHACA AND LONDON

Contents

Preface

This book has two themes, one on the surface and one beneath.

The overt question concerns the ways in which displays of passion—anger, grief, hilarity, and so forth—are interpreted, and the ways in which they are used to exert power over other people. The inquiry moves from the relatively primitive arena in which emotions are displayed apparently involuntarily upward to the infinite sophistications of rhetoric. In the concluding part of the book, the narratives of several arguments—parlimentary debates in India, a squabble in a Californian city council, and the (fictional) meeting of a government committee in London—are used to infer some rules for winning (or losing) arguments by the uses of passion.

The deeper theme is the limited capacity of reason to help us understand and therefore manage the world around us. This theme is reached by way of a paradox: in debates and arguments reason must ultimately be trumped by emotion, but at the same time it is upheld as the superior mode. From this observation we come first to the conception of culture as a layered construction, at the top of which is a necessary public "lie" (the noun is Ibsen's). Second, we find that in competition for power, those who know when and how to penetrate the outer cover—the normative integument of culture—win the day. Third, it seems that the passions are tools both for the maintenance of this integument and—paradoxically—for its penetration.

I owe the title to a suggestion from Ernestine McHugh. My colleagues (in particular Roy D'Andrade and Marc Swartz) have chewed over various chapters; so have friends in several places—Stanley Barrett in Canada, and others in seminar gatherings in Suva, Waikato, Sydney, Canberra, Adelaide, Perth, Sambalpur, Bhubaneswar, Swansea, and Aberystwyth. Two anonymous readers provided strikingly constructive comments. The work was begun while I held a Guggenheim Fellowship. The Senate Research Committee of this campus gave indispensable financial aid, and the manuscript was prepared, impeccably, by Barbara Boyer and Marian Payne. I thank them all.

F. G. BAILEY

University of California, San Diego

THE TACTICAL
USES OF PASSION

Introduction

Nescis, mi fili, quantilla ratione mundus regatur [You do not understand, my son, how small a part reason plays in governing the world].

> —Count Axel Gustafsson Oxenstierna
> (1583–1654), chancellor of Sweden,
> to his son, 1648

What did Oxenstierna oppose to reason? If by "reason" he meant "prudence," its opposite could perhaps be "stupidity" —*stultitia*. If he had results in mind, it could be "accident"— for want of good reasoning, things are allowed to happen without the ruler's intending them, and what is intended does not come to pass. I have chosen a third interpretation: that in the exercise of government it is necessary to address the non-reasoning side of human nature—feelings and sentiments and emotions. To do so is to adopt the categorization of human motivation that has prevailed in our culture since Plato: reason is opposed to passion. Displays of passion signal that reason (prudence) is in abeyance; and those who lack prudence have a diminished capacity to plan realistically and to foresee and so prevent an undesirable eventuality.

The spectacle of thoughtless actions, especially when taken by those in power, is unnerving. We like to believe that our rulers are in touch with reality. Rulers, in turn, prefer subjects who have "realistic" expectations. If rulers and subjects are to be anchored in reality, and if reality is accessible only to reason and if reason is occluded by emotion, then those who display passion are a cause for concern. As Platonists we mistrust such people.

But it may work the other way, for we are also romantics who long for contact with "real" persons. Displays of emotion can be reassuring, having a power that reason lacks. Living now among colleagues who have both feet in psychological anthropology, I find my faith in reason's capacity has much diminished. One also learns about "real" persons, for, living in a strange culture, which is (perhaps marginally) more romantic and more demonstrative than that of the English—a culture in which grown men are allowed to weep in public and to let their voices break as they come before the television cameras to confess their own disgrace—one notices this lack of reserve and asks what it means. How are others expected to respond to these displays? Certainly they pick up a message. Certainly, also, this message may be conditioned by inferences about sincerity and insincerity. Is he really moved or is he putting it on? Certainly they make distinctions between what is an appropriate display and what is inappropriate. In asking such questions, they are making a *reasoned* judgment about behavior that is (apparently, at least) *not* controlled by reason. From the emotional behavior they can read a message. If their judgments are favorable, the message will carry conviction and be persuasive and therefore be a way of exercising power. In short, displays of emotion are (among other things) also ways of eliciting trust. They are devices for persuasion, and if Oxenstierna is right, they play a much larger part than does reason in governing people.

But how can displays of passion excite both trust and mistrust? The answer lies in that elusive concept, reality, and in the way in which reality is simplified by culture, and in our need for such simplification.

People say one thing and do something different, and are ready to present what they have done as being precisely what they said. I am not referring only to "straightforward" deception. We shall come to that later. The sentence has more disturbing implications, for its meaning is rooted in the way in which we make sense of and cope with the world around us and the people in it. We cope, to put it briefly, by falsifying experience.

In the common-sense description of how we cope, however, there is no hint of falsification. The common-sense model is composed of five elements: body, mind, culture (beliefs and values), that part of culture which concerns interactions with others (society), and, finally, experience.

The pieces fit together in the following way. The body has needs, not only physiological requirements for sustenance and shelter, but also psychological needs, which are made apparent to others through the *display* of emotions and to oneself through *feeling* emotions. The mind translates these needs into actions that will satisfy them. But the mind does not respond blindly: it chooses and decides and reconciles, selecting the "real" needs, those that by the seventeenth century had come to be called "interests" (Hirschman, 1977:31–42), from mere harmful appetites. The mind is trained for and guided in this task in two ways: by culture and by experience. Culture is an ordered array of beliefs and values that reveal how the world is and how it should be, how people are and how they should be. Thus one may think of a culture as a set of rules for interpreting experience and shaping action. These rules are learned from other people, so that, in a sense, all culture grows out of social interaction, out of communication. But the interaction is not merely the product of a particular culture. It can take place also between people who may apply different and contradictory beliefs and values to a situation and thus enter into a competition to define what is appropriate in that situation. In this way we learn from the experience of interaction; and our culture is continuously being modified and adapted in the light of experience. So beliefs and values guide action and, since we learn from experience, are themselves shaped by action.

This is a neat cybernetic model, the inputs coming from the body, from culture, and from interactions with other people. The mind is the black box in the center processing the inputs and issuing adaptive commands. The picture is one of a relatively well-adjusted organism, able to take care of itself in a welter of changing environments. It is a very reassuring model: just keep your head and you will be able to cope. The world, too, becomes a secure place, for the behavior of others is predictable because it is rational and governed by interest (Hirschman, 1977:48–56).

But there are failures. Sometimes the outcome is not what we intended or expected. That puts a dent in *our* reasoning, or perhaps in the accuracy of the information from which we made our calculations, but it leaves unharmed the principle of rationality itself. Now suppose that someone else takes an action we think is not appropriate in the circumstances. We may be gracious enough to say that he was misinformed, or that he made an error of judgment. Alternatively, we may say that he must have been "out of his mind." It can be even worse: suppose we detect *ourselves* failing to do what we knew was appropriate or even what we intended. The body (that is, the emotions) somehow has bypassed the mind and hooked itself straight into action.

This is far from reassuring. There are occasions when the emotions are welcomed into a position of dominance, as when someone is urged to "have a good cry." But when we wish to act purposefully, we intend to use our minds and, failing to do so, we are disturbed. There are two common lines of defense. The first is to restore rationality by rationalizing: by finding (after the event) some superior force that compelled us to do the distressing thing. We punish a child and, inside ourselves, know that we have yielded to anger and have been cruel. But it was only to be kind: chastisement is proof of love. In this way we rewrite the experience after the event, and so deny its apparent meaning. Second, we can plead a breakdown. We were too angry, worried, frightened, indolent, absent-minded, or whatever to know what we were doing. Thus we preserve the rational image of our "normal" self by making the lapse an exception. In short, the common-sense model of the rational self becomes a pretense ("life's lie," in Ibsen's words), a facade or a shield erected to conceal what we know is behind it— continuing disagreeable evidence that we, in the form of mind, are not as much in control as we would like—of ourselves, let alone of our world.

Something similar emerges when we look at the process that in the common-sense model connects culture with actions and events. Common sense suggests that the patterns found in culture and the patterns found in action must tend to conform with one another. They must do so if ideas shape action and if action produces experience, which in turn shapes ideas. Certainly there may be a gap, a delay while culture catches up with a changing world or while it takes the initiative and reshapes the world to fit its own image. But even if the delay is always there, inevitably culture and action, even if they never converge, are forever moving along the same track in the same direction.

This model, like that of the "rational self," gives us the reassurance of an orderly world. But when it is examined more closely, it fails.

In the first place, the model treats culture as a unitary thing. It is indeed possible to abstract *a* culture so as to make it a unity, but when one looks at the people who practice that culture, one finds large elements of diversity. They are likely to interact, as we noticed earlier, with people who bear a different culture. Moreover, they are themselves likely to "practice" a variety of cultures—one with parents, another with peers, a third on the job, and so on. So if there are several culture "tracks," we are left with the thought that a particular form of action may be duly following along one culture track, but if we locate it on a different track, it may be all set for a collision.

Second, as I have ready noted, there is ample evidence that people say they do one thing and in fact do something different. The cultural rules that are supposed to guide behavior turn out to have little in common with behavior. Let us look at some examples, and then consider again the question of falsification.

The Tuareg, Robert Murphy tells us (1971:220–22), insist that they marry their maternal cross-cousins. But at the same time they are quite hazy about genealogical reckoning and the reality seems to be that any woman they marry, by the very fact of marriage, gets to be defined as belonging to the category of maternal cross-cousin. They claim to be guided by one rule of marriage preference and in fact can be shown to do something different.

The Nuer are described by E. E. Evans-Pritchard as being extravagantly egalitarian. "The Nuer is a product of hard and egalitarian upbringing, is deeply democratic, and easily roused to violence. His turbulent spirit finds any restraint irksome and no man recognizes a superior. Wealth makes no difference. . . . Birth makes no difference" (Evans-Pritchard, 1940: 181). Certainly there is no formal ranking through which power could be allocated. Nor is there a system of stratified classes based on wealth. Nevertheless some come to dominate others, who receive food and protection and become as clients to a patron. The patrons are (1951:27) "persons not only of age, wealth and character, but also members of the dominant clan of the tribe—tribal aristocrats." It seems that wealth and birth do make a difference. A similar discrepancy emerges when one looks at another Nuer value: that of patrilineal descent. This principle provides a model of how Nuer society works: territories are divided from each other and relations between people are organized by the fact that (notionally) each territory is manned by a group of agnates. But in practice in each territory there is a wide range of people not connected by agnation. Evans-Pritchard (1951:28) explains that the agnatic principle is so strong that no confusion is caused by its obvious and frequent breaching.

Evans-Pritchard apparently saw no problem in this manifest gap between principle and action. "However much the actual configurations of kinship clusters may vary and change, the lineage structure is invariable and stable" (1951:28). "Structure" inheres, it seems, in the intellectual maps that people have of what they do or should do, and not in what they at least sometimes must know they actually do. Ideas, moreover, are sealed against experience.

Louis Dumont, confronted in his *Homo Hierarchicus* with a

similar situation, fails to display the same effortless astigmatism. His concern is with "a system of ideas and values" (1970:35). But he grants that investigations into ideology leave some things unexplored. There remains a "residue" apparent in the "confrontation of ideology with observation" (1970:77).

His subject is the Indian caste system. In this structure there is a separation of status and power. Status is necessarily hierarchical, being based on an opposition between pure and impure, purity being superior and impurity inferior. "To adopt a value is to introduce hierarchy, and a certain consensus of values, a certain hierarchy of ideas, things and people, is indispensable to social life" (1970:20). This hierarchy belongs to the world of the sacred, to religion, which calls for "a classification of beings according to their degree of dignity" (1970:65).

Power, on the other hand, belongs to the secular world. It is subordinated to hierarchy: "Hierarchy cannot give place to power as such, without contradicting its own principle. Therefore it must give a place to power without saying so, and it is obliged to close its eyes on this point on pain of destroying itself" (1970:77).

But there remain behavioral awkwardnesses, the "residues." In the "interstitial levels" of the caste system power does indeed seem to subordinate hierarchy to itself: particular castes go up and down the hierarchy as they gain or lose wealth and power, or at the decree of secular authorities. Dumont's explanation is that power "surreptitiously makes itself the equal of status in the interstitial levels" (1970:153). (Why "equal"? Evidently he could not bring himself to write "superior.") This is a transparent example of the working of "life's lie." It is a falsification to preserve simplicity and comprehension, in this case through the word "surreptitiously." In this "delightful" fashion (his adjective—see 1970:76), he sweeps a problem out of sight to save his model. We all do: only the degree of arrogance varies.

Neither Evans-Pritchard nor Dumont brings to the foreground the element of falsification required to impose a system on the flow of events. The patterns of residence of the Nuer are described, but the considerable discrepancy between them and the agnatic ideology seems to raise questions neither about the latter's continued unmodified existence nor about its descriptive adequacy. Dumont recognizes a difficulty, but "words" it out of the way. Why do people do this?

One answer is given in Ibsen's *Wild Duck*. It is a necessary self-deception. We need to feel that we understand what is going on. To do so we abstract, following the suggestions given us by our culture. We focus on some things and ignore others; we impose a pattern on the flow of events, and thus "falsify" them if only by simplifying the diversity and the complexity; thus we provide ourselves with "the illusion of a superior, but simpler order" and so make the real world "palatable and comprehensible" (Murphy 1971:114-5).

All thinking is an act of simplification. It is a kind of necessary make-believe. It is the act of "holding other things equal" because to include all those other things would be to make computation impossible. But I am saying more than that. We disregard things that we know could, with effort, be built into the computation. Our simplification, in other words, is the product not of a technical but of a psychological necessity. It goes beyond what is inevitable; it is willful, and it can therefore, to some extent, be undone: our subject is the political advantage to be gained from doing so with skill.

This discussion suggests an alternative to the notion of an inevitable, if delayed, homology between culture and the world of action. The gap is not in the form of a lag: rather it is a gap across which opposites confront each other. We are seeing not a procrastinating homology but rather a continuing and unmerging opposition: the reality denies and is denied by the culture. One thing is enjoined, but its opposite is practiced. Murphy suggests this.

But there are difficulties. The clear distinction between culture and practice is misleading. If the "natives" are aware of their practice, is that practice not itself part of their culture? Perhaps we should place the confrontation *within* the realm of culture.

We can do so first by going beyond the notion of knowledge suppressed into the unconscious to protect "life's lie" and considering *deliberate* falsification. Such lies are part of everyone's experience. Nobody, for example, is publicly more vociferous in the cause of justice than the racketeering politician. Nor do the defenders of free enterprise and of the unfettered play of market forces find it difficult to close their eyes to government intervention and regulation when it is to their own benefit. (Polanyi, 1968:chaps. 6 and 12).

As this last example suggests, there can also be partial falsification by omission and concealment. At first glance it seems clear that to maintain a contradiction between culture and practice people must close their eyes to the practice. But do they? Or do they sometimes only close their mouths? There are indeed cases in which people are quite unaware of the significance of what they are doing or saying (like the young missionary lady who enlivened a clerical breakfast table where I was a guest with an account of her dreams about a large snake that visited her bed and inexplicably caused her to feel not terror but warmth and happiness). But in other cases there must be knowledge of that part of the experience which is not allowed *public* structuring and endorsement. It follows that if people have knowledge of that "hidden" sector, they must have been able to structure it by abstraction and pattern making. If they can do that, then the covert sector too must be part of culture, and in place of culture versus practice there emerges an opposition between the overt and covert parts of culture.

When I use the phrase "covert sector" I am thinking neither of statistical regularities nor of that deeper structure which is said to underlie both the conscious models and the statistical patterns (Lévi-Strauss, 1963:chap. 15). Rather I am talking about "alternative" structures of which some people are aware, but which they do not parade. They can, however, be articulate about these structures and can communicate them to selected other people. Furthermore, their conscious models include propositions about how to bring the overt and the covert sectors of the culture into connection with one another, so as to achieve particular goals in particular situations.

Just as overt cultures are not shared equally by all those who interact, so also knowledge of covert cultures is differentially distributed. It will be part of my argument that the resulting differential capacity to make use of what "officially" is deemed not to exist and therefore is "officially" not available for use is *one* of the factors regulating relative power.

At this point we need a further clarification of "reality." I have implied, in the discussion of "life's lie" and of the shield of falsification by which we make reality "palatable and comprehensible," that there is a reality lying beneath both the overt and the covert levels of culture.

Such a reality is one that by definition can play no part in our examination of a culture's rules for persuasion, because it exists in that part of the "material flow" (D'Andrade, n.d.) which is beyond even the covert sector of culture. Here is an example. Actions have consequences. When you impose a definition of the situation on someone, your immediate intention is to provoke him into taking an action, but your goal is the consequence of this action. The consequence may turn out to be other than what you calculated, because some factor of which you were unaware influenced the outcome. Just as there are brute facts in nature—such as water flowing downhill (even that is not without ambiguity, as we will see later)—so there are brute facts in social interaction which may lie beneath a particular culture (albeit known in some cultures) and yet may influence the outcomes of actions enjoined by that culture. How many Gandhians were able to build into their nonviolence the brute fact that the restraint that comes easily to the few is fragile in a crowd? Population densities, disease transmission, the wastage of natural resources, the effects of diet, and a thousand other things, at various times and in various places, have been hidden influences on the outcomes of culturally directed action. Since we intend to describe a culture rather than to write a history, however, this "objective" reality is not at the center of our interest.

There is another kind of "reality" that is subjective, is part of culture itself, and must be factored into an attempt to understand techniques of persuasion. Culture, as is often remarked, achieves a kind of reality. Those definitions that are widely accepted gain "objectivity" through subjective agreement. "Truth" is the outcome of consensus: if everyone says it is so, it is so. "A collective representation presents guarantees of objectivity by the fact that it is collective . . ." (Durkheim, 1957:437). One questions such definitions at one's peril, for society reacts with "violence" against "attempted dissidents" (1957:208).

But this picture is too stark and too simple. It fails in two ways. First, there are things that cannot be made objectively true by consensus. That is exactly what "objective" means. "Fifty million Frenchmen can't be wrong" in matters of rights, duties, tastes, and such; but their consensus does not establish the existence of God or the correctness of the principle of phlogiston or make it possible to prolong life indefinitely without nourishment. Such "subjective truths" of course have objective consequences, as we noted earlier in the case of Gandhian nonviolence. But they are not themselves made objectively true by consensus. Second, the inviolability of collective representations (assuming that this phrase refers to the overt segments of culture) is too strongly asserted. Only if one fails to take account of the covert sector can one conclude that questioning the overt sector of culture invariably is perilous. It all depends on how one attempts the dissidence, and the key is contained in the rules that regulate the use of items in the covert sector.

Now we can understand why a display of passion excites both trust and mistrust. We believe that there is a reality—that "material flow"—and we desire to view it, understand it in its entirety, confront it, and so control it. But we also know that this is impossible. The vision that we have of it is filtered and distorted through our culture. This vision, pretending to completeness and therefore comforting, is cathected. It is sustained by emotion. Reason cannot help, because its analytical scrutiny would destroy the vision, revealing its incompleteness. So the passions comfort us and excite trust. But we are aware also that they stand in the way of reason, which alone can give us better access to reality. Therefore they also make us uneasy.

This brings us to the next topic: power and persuasion, and

how these two things are connected in the light of the preceding remarks about reality.

We have many words to indicate categories of power (which is the capacity to have another person do something, willing or not): force, authority, manipulation, influence, control, privilege, dominance, clout; brainwash, spellbind, outmaneuver, bluff; and literally hundreds of others. Despite this abundance, most writing in political anthropology (because it concentrates on distribution—who holds power over whom) seldom categorizes more ambitiously than the distinction between force and legitimate power.

My field invites a richer categorization. I am interested in formal organizations (bureaucracies) and such highly regulated political arenas as parliaments and assemblies. They have two attractive characteristics: first, little use is made of naked force; second, they develop highly sophisticated rules for competitive interaction.

These are rules that tell you how to make your definition of the situation prevail. They are part of culture, many of them—those in which I am most interested—lying in the covert sector. It follows that they generally have to be inferred from what other people do rather than from what they admit to doing. These inferences, however, need not be ours alone, the products of an outsider's analysis: people also will talk freely about the hidden tactical intentions behind moves made by other people, especially by their opponents.

How do you persuade another person? Our culture distinguishes two ways. The first is the Platonic way, the use of reason. This method is possible when the persuader can find some value that the other person accepts, and that can serve as the premise from which to lead an argument. The persuader then works from the accepted value, showing logically that other values can be derived from it and coming eventually to a definition of the situation which, he hopes, will lead to the appropriate action. Alternatively the persuader may proceed by demonstrating that certain forms of action stand in the way of achieving some desirable goal. Such reasoning implicitly uses the notion of opportunity cost: "If you do *this,* you will inevitably forfeit *that.*" It is causal in form: "The pursuit of money inhibits good family relations." Such arguments invite the use of the head and a critical examination of the steps by which one gets from a life focused on moneymaking to domestic discontent.

The other form of persuasion (direct use of the passions) seeks to eliminate the mind and the critical faculties. It provokes feeling rather than thought. It is employed when the persuader suspects that the logical steps in the argument will not survive critical examination, or when he can find no shared value that will serve as the premise for an argument by reason. The appeal to emotion may be designed either to create such a shared value or to provoke a direct connection between feeling and action without the intervention of mind and its capacities for criticism.

Let us illustrate the relationship between reason and the passions by considering (after Simmel) how reticence about the self is connected with power. We are very cautious about showing anything but "fragments" of our inner selves. These fragments are never "a representative selection" but "a transformation of this inner reality, teleologically directed, reduced and recomposed" (Simmel, 1969:312). There are, this argument implies, alternative structures of the self, just as there are alternative cultures.

What is the purpose to which Simmel refers in the phrase "teleologically directed"? The "editing" must be directed toward communication, toward conveying a particular impression, perhaps to oneself as well as to the other person: toward creating the "palatable and comprehensible." But power too may be a consideration. The person who knows the "truth" about you, who can command a "representative selection" of your "psychological-real whole" (Simmel, 1969:312), has power over you: keep the "truth" to yourself and you avoid subjection.

Conversely, the more you can reach into the "inner self" of another, the more you have control. To reach into the "inner self" of another is to know his feelings and desires, that is, his emotions. By playing on these emotions you can regulate his receptivity to information and his capacity to see, examine, criticize, and test. In other words, this notion of the head-and-heart-as-contraries implies that by knowing how to manipulate emotions we can inhibit the working of another's mind and make a direct connection between body and action. The passions, in these circumstances, are a route to power.

The dichotomy between reason and emotion is part of our overt culture; that is, it is part of the shield of falsification by which we make life comprehensible. Reason and emotion are seen as practical contraries: the rise of one means the fall of the other. But what is the reality that lies in the covert sector behind this facade? Here reason and the passions are not practical contraries, mutually exclusive, nor are they evenly balanced. The passions rule. There can be no purposive activity without emotion, for purpose implies goal, and goal, in the end, entails passion: the final goal must always be cathected. Reason has no power to move: without passion, one remains inert, unmoved oneself and unable to move others. So if reason and emotion were really in complementary distribution, an act of persuasion in which reason dominated absolutely would be an impossibility, because persuasion entails goal-directed activity, and that in turn entails in the end a nonreasoning attachment (an emotional attachment) to the goal. In the covert sector of culture it is "known" that there can be no persuasive transaction without the presence, at least in some degree, of the passions. Overtly, in certain cultures, the necessity of this connection is denied.

A similar argument can be made in the opposite direction. There are cultures that elevate the passions and dispense with reason, or at least make reason very subordinate. Hitler ignored his experts and specialists. He had a horror of "rational classifications" and "structural arrangements" (Fest, 1975: 674–75). There was a "craving to escape from ideas, concepts and systems into some uncomplicated sense of belonging" (1975:428). But though the passions provide the nonreasoning attachment to a goal, they cannot bring about its attainment; only reason can show the way. This fact was certainly part of the covert culture of National Socialism.

In brief, reason and passions are not, at the covert level of culture, seen to be in complementary distribution; rather they are complementary.

The overt denial that passions have a significant part to play appears in that particular segment of our political culture with which I am concerned—bureaucracy, committees, parliaments, and the like. The denial is made by establishing a priority. Reason and emotion are not only distinguished as contraries but also arranged in a hierarchy, with reason on the top. Rationality is the proper mode, *overtly* dominant in the committee world (just as the heart should be dominant in, say, our present-day version of the marital relationship). The situation is of of the same form as among the Nuer: one value (equality and agnation) is dominant while the other (hierarchy and the bilateral connections) is officially submerged but lived out in action. Rationality is like Dumont's "status"—the religion: the passions intrude "surreptitiously." But without knowing how this intrusion can be managed, we cannot begin to comprehend the range of tactics available for persuasion. Mishandled, a display of passion only excites distrust or derision.

So we are looking for rules that advise on the tactical use of displays of passion by oneself and of the provocation of such displays in other people. To do that we must ask first what meanings are attached to displays of passion.

The design of this book is first to identify those behavioral (including verbal) signs that in our culture are taken to indicate emotions or their absence. Then we have to find out what meanings are attached to such displays. There is a range of meaning from, at the simplest level, a psychological state (Chapter 1) upward through the increasing complexity of a whole "character" (Chapter 2) to meanings provided by various institutional settings and norms (Chapters 3 and 4).

The second part of the book raises its sights from relatively primitive displays of emotion to the more sophisticated arena of rehetoric. Up to that point we have asked: What is the persuasive significance of various displays of passion? Now we reverse the question and ask: What kinds of persuasive devices are available, and what part is played in them by displays of passion? Chapter 6 is about assertive rhetoric; Chapter 7 about the rhetoric of compromise; and Chapter 8 about the rational discourse used in solving problems.

The third part of the book (Chapter 9) uses extended examples to take up again the central question: What are the rules in bureaucratic-political cultures for making tactical use of the passions? More generally expressed, the question is: What are the rules in bureaucratic-political cultures for making tactical use of items in the covert sectors of those cultures?

The reader should remember throughout that my aim is to describe cultures and *their* assumptions about human nature and human society. My concern is with the facade (comprising both overt and covert sectors of cultures). I do not wish anywhere to imply that I know—or anyone else knows—what human nature is "really" or "universally" like: but words being what they are, the reader is asked to make allowance for lapses and to remember that, despite ambiguities of phrasing, my analytical perspective is from the audience and not from inside the heads and hearts of the performers.

PART I

DISPLAYS OF EMOTION

CHAPTER 1

Emotions, Discontinuity, and Commitment

In this chapter we examine two common interpretations of displays of emotion as indicators of a frame of mind.

The first interpretation (which looks backward) is that the person moved by passion has encountered some kind of discontinuity: something has happened which is unexpected and probably (but not necessarily) disagreeable. The display of emotion is thus an expression of anger and frustration and uncertainty or of surprise and pleasure (if the event is agreeable).

A different interpretation, looking forward, is that the message conveyed is more than just *present* reaction. It can also express a psychological commitment that transcends rationality: a refusal or an inability to listen to any reasoned argument that would undermine the position cathected.

I had a colleague, an Englishman born into the upper reaches of the middle class, somewhat reserved, proper almost to the point of primness, and in committees a most irascible man. When confronted with a proposal with which he did not agree, he would say "This makes me angry!" Then, with his lank brown hair drooping over his forehead, two bright pink spots appearing in his very pale cheeks, and his fists clenched in front of him on the table, he would say loudly and forcefully that the proposal was a disgrace, that it violated every principle on which the institution depended, and that he felt himself bound to resist it to the utmost of his powers. He could not in conscience give way to any colleague who was misguided enough to support the proposal.

But his contributions were not simply splutterings of rage. In between the expressions of condemnation came quite lucid and logically ordered descriptions of the consequences of adopting the proposal, and it was not long before his colleagues schooled themselves to listen to these parts of his discourses and to bracket away such phrases as "I am angry" and "This is a disgrace." It was usually not difficult to set aside the physical evidence (the clenched fists and the reddened cheeks and the harshly assertive voice) and avoid reflexive reaction, for the anger was never directed at a colleague who was present. We were a small committee and we knew one another well, and the angry man himself usually acknowledged this by ending his outburst with the smallest of self-deprecating smiles, as if to say, "do not be disturbed by the display. I just like making it."

Nevertheless, despite the bracketing away and the apologetic smile, these displays conveyed several messages. I never asked my colleagues directly, but it seemed that we were all agreed that this was a man of principle, a man who had standards and kept to them. To me it also seemed that he was peremptory and dictatorial, giving orders rather than persuading. He was so convinced that he was right on these occasions that he saw himself standing above those who disagreed or even might disagree. "Authoritarian" might be the word: since he accepted rules and regulations and the principles that lay behind them without question, others should be just as ready to accept commands.

In my second example the display of emotion is more complex, for it was compounded of anger, grief, frustration, anxiety, and depression. The perpetrator of this display we shall call Sadsack.

He was a slightly built man with eyes like a beagle's, kindly but sad, long in service with the institution, much respected, a man of deep feelings for principles and even deeper ones for people, having all the markings, as someone said rather sentimentally, of a saint.

The occasion for the display was a meeting of a committee that assembled each week and was small enough for everyone to know everyone else. The first five or ten minutes of every meeting were spent in a ritual display of amity. From a practical point of view, of course, the members were waiting for latecomers to arrive: the time was spent in frivolity, in making ridiculous suggestions about matters on the agenda, in teasing one another and doing other nonsensical things before the serious business of the meeting began. The performance in some way resembles the swimmer shaking his limbs loose before he begins the race. This behavior will be examined in Chapter 4.

Just before this period ended and the meeting was to begin, the chairman made some jocular remark to Sadsack. Sadsack did not smile and did not return the joke, but said very clearly, albeit in a low voice, that he could see no point in talking about that or about anything else, for whatever they discussed in committee, whatever they decided, had no effect whatsoever on the administrators, who just went ahead and did what they wanted, what they had decided to do anyway before the meeting. He then launched into a discourse that was a cross between a diatribe and a dirge, asking how he could be expected to do his job when the administrators never listened, when they had no idea and never took the trouble to find out what his needs were, and how thankless and hopeless was his task. He did not descend to tears, but he was clearly very upset. From time to time there was a hint of anger in his voice, but nothing resembling the ruddy-cheeked fist-clenching display of the Englishman in the previous example.

When he stopped, there was silence, complete silence, the silence of embarrassment. Given the stage of the meeting, and given that the cue for the lament was a joke from the chairman, possibly someone might have broken the silence with humor. Eventually the chairman said, "But this is very serious! I had no idea. Let us get together after the meeting and find out just what can be done. But I think we should now deal with our agenda."

So they started work and soon seemed to have dispelled the embarrassment What are we to make of this display of emotion?

Clearly there are other ways of making complaints. It is conceivable that Sadsack, who on other occasions had performed much like everyone else in the ten-minute opening period of irresponsibility, could have made his point as a joke or taunt, for the incompetence of the administrators (some of whom were present) was a favorite joking topic. He could also have made formal arrangements to put the matter on the agenda and have it discussed in, one hopes, a rational fashion, so that solutions would be found. But Sadsack did neither of these things. He let his feelings show, he gave a lament rather than an itemized list of complaints, and the feelings he expressed were entirely out of accord with that stage of the meeting.

The story of Sadsack is a gloomy one, and in case it seems that the light emotions have been forgotten—certain enthusiasms, some kinds of laughter, various displays of pleasure—the figure I choose for the third example is Messianic Man, encountered while I was making the rounds at an academic conference in England. One cannot call him the Messiah, for that honor was held by an abstraction: the liberator of oppressed people (in this case housewives) was to be the study of English local history.

He gave a splendid performance, stage and pulpit fruitfully conjoined in ten uplifting minutes of discourse. First our hearts were invited to bleed for those poor women, young and not so young, caught between the stove and the sink and the washtub, their potentially fine minds coarsened by the daily wash of journalistic sensation and soap operas, yearning to find the way to self-respect and intellectual preservation. The answer was the study of local history. Our parishes were full of records and local government offices were filled with archives only waiting to be devoured by the hungry minds of British housewives. The history of the common people lay unknown, unexplored, unsystematized. It was a duty to our ancestors and our posterity alike to preserve the riches of historical knowledge, and in a surprisingly short time all of England, perhaps all of Britain, from the earliest records down to the Great Depression of the 1930s, would be enshrined in books—volumes indeed—researched by British housewives and written by Messianic Man and his colleagues.

Such a dream! It would be nice to report that the audience rose as one man and headed off to the suburbs to proposition housewives, but the meetings of learned scholars are not like that. A few, of the same breed as Messianic Man, spoke their enthusiasm; others, less excitable, asked where the money was and if anyone had found out how much time and energy housewives had to spare. I have forgotten most of the audience, but I have not forgotten Messianic Man: small beads of perspiration on his forehead, shining eyes, a voice and a diction and the cadences of a Welsh nonconformist preacher at the top of his form. He believed; and he conveyed this belief not through the strength of the proposals he made (I think they were mostly nonsense) but through the way he used his voice and his body and his face to radiate (there is no other word) enthusiasm.

The final example is less straightforward. During World War II a company of American artillerymen, some of Italian descent and others of a category later called WASP, was commanded by a captain who held their respect and loyalty. Receiving notice of a posting elsewhere, he called the men together and made a brief speech of farewell, congratulating them on their discipline and their performance, thanking them and wishing them well. He was a stern man, somewhat aloof, and not in the least given to displays of sentiment. Nevertheless, the Italians were heard asking one another after the speech, "Did you notice how moved he was? How hard he found it to hold back his tears!" My informant, a WASP, saw no sign of tears and said that for such a man to weep in public would have been quite out of character.

This informant no doubt had been brought up to regard blubbering as an indication of weakness, an inability to master oneself and the situation, qualities certainly not desired in a leader. For the Italians, on the other hand, respect and loyalty

33

between a leader and his men were forms of affection properly indicated, at the moment of parting, by a display of sorrow. The judgments are simple enough and are adequately expressed in such terms as "warmhearted" (for the Italians) and "clearheaded" (for the WASPs). Notice that we are no longer seeing a display of emotion and then observing the inferences that people make about the displayer's character. The inferences go in the other direction: both parties have a firm idea of the character and situation, and from that idea they reason the level of emotional arousal they must have observed. (So much for objectivity.)

Out of this situation we have a language-like connection: emotional displays indicate mood or character. People believe that if they get a look at one, they can make a guess about the other. Now let us see what inferences can be drawn from these vignettes.

A display of emotion is not only a window onto a person's character or mood: it is also said to reveal how we interpret events around us. These events "cause" emotion.

One category of events that gives rise to displays of emotion is said to be that of "interruption" or "discontinuity": emotions are associated with the unexpected, the incongruous, the sensation of "What does this mean?" or "What is to be done?" Sadsack, feeling frustrated, vents emotion. Let us now examine this idea as it appears in cognitive psychology, social anthropology, and one type of psychological history.

Emotions are displayed, it is said, when we are disturbed in some routine that we are following to achieve a particular goal. This is a very intellectualist outlook on human existence. Life is a series of efforts to solve problems. We are continually faced with alternative possibilities, both between goals and between strategies for achieving goals, and only by making the correct choices do we become masters of the situation and masters of our own destinies. Faced with the problem, not knowing what to do, we experience emotion. Knowing what to do, putting the routine into action and then discovering that it does not work, we experience emotion. Being without a plan, or discovering that our plan does not work, we experience that horror of meaninglessness, of being unable to domesticate intellectually what is happening.

Such assertions as "the interruption of highly organized activities generates autonomic arousal" and "novel and unusual events generate states of arousal" (Mandler, 1975:153) are so much more than merely plausible that one is hard put to imagine a situation in which they were not true. When the pig flies past the window and the farmer says, "Ho hum!" and registers zero arousal on our instruments, we are likely to hang on to the proposition that "novel and unusual events generate states of arousal" by remarking that this is not a normal farmer.

In short, we are in the presence of one of those useful tautologies such as "Every man has his price." But just as prices vary from one situation to another, so also what constitutes an interruption, what "highly organized" means, and what is "novel and unusual" are variously defined in various contexts and cultures. Though I do not deny the usefulness of the perspective that sees life portrayed in "a key sticking in a lock, a pellet not found in the food cup, or a brake failing in a car" (Mandler, 1975:54), it will suit our comparative purpose better to look at examples in which the priority of culture is more in evidence.

Consider funerals and their customary displays of grief. A death is an interruption, not just the final rupture of the dead person's cognitive endeavors, but also of established routines performed by and for him. There has to be readjustment, probably in the affective states of the bereaved, and certainly in the roles—rights and duties—which are redistributed through succession and inheritance. All these are public events and they are generally accompanied by displays of emotion. Indeed, most cultures have quite firm rules about the proper intensity of feeling to be displayed, and those persons who go beyond the limit, no less than those who fall short, are reprimanded. The visceral, so to speak, is controlled and subordinated, so that in the case of hired mourners an extravagant display of grief may presumably be accompanied by no

35

arousal whatsoever. In such a situation the frustrated individual of cognitive psychology becomes little more than an allegory. The general proposition, however, that emotional *displays* are connected with interruptions in established procedures (in the case of the funeral, social rather than only cognitive procedures) remains intact.

The framework of the third set of ideas—those of the psychological historian (Barbu, 1960)—is attractive in its simplicity and breathtaking in its scope. Certain periods in the history of civilizations are marked by extravagance and exuberance, by brightness, loudness, a liking for extremes; passions and feelings run high, unrestrained by reason and moderation and calculating self-control. Sixth-century Athens had these characteristics; so did the waning Middle Ages; also the Roman Empire in its decline; and Elizabethan England.

These are also the times in which a new order of society, a new culture, is being evolved, but has not yet, so to speak, found itself. The sequence seems to be this. First the established ways of ordering social life are seen to be inadequate, for whatever reason—perhaps famine, population growth, conquest, racial enmities, prolonged warfare, or some continuing natural disaster. There follows a period of *uncertainty* (which is the outcome of discontinuity) and of experiment, in which people attempt to redefine their goals and to find ways of attaining them.

At such times values are made very simple and are stated without qualification (as is the tendency in any advocacy situation), and life's goals are seen always as polarized, never as the mean. We destroy the middle ground. Heaven and hell, angels and devils, pious altruistic men and unspeakable greedy bestial men of unfathomable cruelty, saintly virgins and scabrous whores—and in between nothing of significance is to be found. You may aim for the highest, for perfection: but you are unlikely to succeed and the penalty for failure is total degradation, for any compromise is deemed failure. Life is defined through its extremes, where passions reign: there is no middle ground of reason. Indeed, in a sense, there is no civilization.

Then order may return. The ferocious blood feuds of sixth-century Athens are curbed by Draconian laws, a term that has come to indicate the extreme of severity; Draco's code is amended and softened and made more civilized (in a quite literal sense of centering it on the "citizen" rather than on the corporate kin group) by Solon, and his in turn by the reforms of Cleisthenes, until in fifth-century Athens we have a society and a life-style that stand for refinement of thought, delicacy in artistic expression, catharsis not through the orgy of carnival but in the tragedies of Aeschylus, Sophocles, and Euripides, a way of living summarized in that famous phrase *mēden agan*, "nothing too much."

Certainly this is the grandest form of that theory which links displays of emotion with discontinuity: not the key sticking in a lock or the rat wondering where the food pellet has gone, not the community temporarily thrown from its course by the death of a leader or the rise to adulthood of a new generation, but entire civilizations collapsing into displays of passion, cleaving to the extremes because, for the time at least, they have not the capacity to reason their way toward the compromises of the middle ground.

Common to all these analyses—psychological, social, and historical—is the notion of discontinuity, of a break in some established routine that has been shown to be no longer practical. There are some comments to be made about this theory. First, it seems to account better for the dark emotions (anger, grief, or fear, and the deeper, slower, and more lasting manifestations of anxiety and depression) than it does for such lighter emotions as joy and serenity or the active transports of love. These emotions suggest to us not discontinuity but the reverse. The quiet satisfactions got from a well-turned sentence, an engine that is running well, a movement neatly carried out, a point of view clearly and elegantly stated—all these give rise to a feeling of pleasure that owes nothing to discontinuity. Certainly my messianic historian displayed strong feelings, but they had no roots in discontinuity or frustration.

The theory is also less than satisfactory in accounting for meanings attributed to some of the dark emotions. It is not so much wrong as incomplete, for the display of emotion may indicate not only "Things are falling apart" but also—and in political interaction this is clearly significant—"I intend to stand firm." Anger may be the anger of frustration, but it can also convey resolution and inflexibility. My Englishman's displays of temper signified commitment to fundamental values, about which he would brook no argument, still less come to a compromise. In a similar way, Sadsack's display of feeling conveyed a deep and serious attachment to the goals that neglectful administrators prevented him from attaining. A display of emotion, therefore, may be a way of affirming faith.

There is a pervasive connection between emotion, faith, and suffering, as the several meanings of the word "passion" suggest. To attain or demonstrate faith a visionary subjects his body to abuse. He starves himself, drugs himself, sits for days on end in a place that symbolizes his removal from the world and is, by preference, acutely uncomfortable; he may mutilate himself, like the Plains Indians who hacked off bits of a finger to induce visions; anything, in short, that a man in his senses would never do. The Sanyasi practices a regime of ascetic denial of his body's needs for food and shelter and comfort, until he eliminates not only the body's needs but also normal human feelings. Nothing that arouses ordinary people should excite him, not love or fear or hatred. His total tranquillity signals his union with the divinity.

Faith may also be tested through mental anguish, as when a person is said to come through some ordeal with faith intact or restored. Such tests may be institutionally ordained. The novice nun, eating filth, is like the Sanyasi, denying her ordinary emotions in order to testify to a higher passion (Goffman, 1961:31). One tests and affirms faith in a higher value by exciting emotions of disgust or fear, and insisting that they be suppressed.

There are more commonplace ways of affirming faith, which in fact include the notion of sacrifice. A contract or a deposit demonstrate willingness to incur a loss, to suffer a penalty, if one fails to live up to one's word.

Displays of emotion likewise may indicate commitment.

Words used to yield to a threat will be the more convincing if they are accompanied by displays of fear, less convincing if they are framed by signs of amusement. A threat calls for a display of present anger or some indication of the capacity for future anger. Various kinds of laughter indicate insincerity, that "one's heart is not in it" or that one is "going through the motions."

All these ways of affirming faith involve sacrifice, either inflicting suffering on one's body or enduring without complaint assaults on one's self-respect. The victim must also sacrifice the relief of a normal display of emotion. The Plains Indian who chops off a knuckle and hops around telling everyone how much it hurts, or the ascetic who licks his lips at the sight of food and complains of hunger, shows himself as yet unable to move mountains. The recruit or novice who loses self-control needs further training. The elimination of normal displays of emotions on these occasions is not to be taken as evidence that feeling and emotion have given place to reason. On the contrary, the lesser emotions are sacrificed to make room for a display of an ultimate passion for the divinity or an ultimate and mindless loyalty to the institution.

Any display of emotion carries a similar idea of sacrifice, for in the display reason and calculation are forgone. The word "sacrifice" may seem somewhat metaphorical, but if one reflects, in all these cases the person offers up some part of himself, his property, his body, his reputation, or his self-respect. In emotional displays he gives up the faculty of reason. The basic meaning is simple: he is locked in a course toward or away from a particular action, and he cannot be shifted by reasoned argument. To frame a threat or a promise with a display of anger, with tears, or with transports of joy is to indicate the absence of doubt, an unwillingness to compromise or to change one's mind. The display resembles a handshake at the end of bargaining or the auctioneer's hammer: the deed cannot be undone. It signals that whatever is framed by the display of emotion *has become an end in itself, an intrinsic value.* Thus it resembles that sensuous or aesthetic enjoyment, the satisfaction got from a job going well, which I described earlier.

These suggestions are not inconsistent with discontinuity theories. The display of emotion, when one is unexpectedly halted in one's progress toward a goal, measures (other things being equal) the value attached to that goal. The more it is an end in itself (assuming the interruption is seen as a genuine threat to its attainment), the more we expect to see a display of emotion.

When we see or hear a display of emotion of the kind so far discussed, the major inference to be made is commitment, in the sense that reasoned counterargument will no longer be an effective persuasion. This seems to cover all the situations: the novice nun, the recruit being put through an ordeal, mortification of the flesh, annoyance or fear at the interruption of an established routine (whether problem solving or rearranging roles or at the grander levels of historical watersheds), the choleric Englishman, the messianic historian, Sadsack at the end of his tether, and the captain who should have shed a tear—all signify that those who display emotion (or restrain one feeling to make room for a higher one) are attending to (or are being trained to attend to) verities that have been placed beyond argument and beyond compromise or to problems that they know will not yield to a reasoned solution. They are making a peremptory assertion of an "indisputable" truth.

The psychological states are inferred, according to cultural rules for interpretation, from behavior. But the inference is not simple: a flush can arise from anger or shame; a laugh can mean pleasure or contempt; tears run the whole range from joy to anger to misery. If we cannot get beyond this first hurdle of translating bodily and verbal signals into basic emotions, how can we get to such interpretations as "recognition of discontinuity" or "commitment"?

The answer is clear. We find meaning not by perceiving the item of behavior (such as a blush or a smile) but by perceiving also the context in which it occurs. These combinations of item and context are, of course, given to us by our culture. It is by watching the setting in which fists are clenched, a plaintive note creeps into the voice, volume intensifies or dwindles in vocal delivery, and so forth that we judge whether a person is taken aback or deeply committed or whatever.

But the brush strokes of this analysis are too broad: the picture could contain more detail. It is true that manifested anger may convey attachment to a principle and through it one's need for certainty and order. It is true also that a display of frustration may indicate a high value set upon whatever has been denied. But the displays do more than that: they tell us also about the performer and what he is likely to do next. Both Sadsack and the choleric Englishman indicate that their claim is beyond dispute and the value they are upholding is not to be compromised, but their performances signal different characters and different intended actions. The choleric fellow is confident and ready to fight: Sadsack is spent, his spring unwound, at the moment a threat to nothing more than other people's peace of mind—at least that is what his demeanor conveys.

In short, displays signal not only feeling—commitment, frustration, enthusiasm, and so forth—but also likely performance. The performances with which we are concerned are those involved in interactions with other people. These interactions may be characterized by a sense of duty, by trust, by competitiveness, or by a variety of other modes. Our first argument will be that displays of emotion (or their absence) indicate what kind of "self" (dutiful, competitive, irresponsible, and so forth) is being offered to another person or to an audience at large.

CHAPTER 2

The Colony of Selves

Georg Simmel, as we noted earlier, remarks on the way we present only "edited" versions of our whole selves: "a transformation of this inner reality, teleologically directed, reduced and re-composed" (1969:312). In this chapter we look at a repertoire of selves available in our culture for use in particular situations. We also consider the idea of a "true" self and the part it plays in the tactics of persuasion.

If we argue that displays of emotion mean nothing more than "Here I stand and I will not be shifted," we will not be able to understand certain displays that proclaim, "I do not know where I should stand" or "I am at the end of my tether." We would also be on the way to embracing an argument that seems contrary to experience: that displays of emotion can never be used to soften a position and to open the way to compromise. Clearly they can be used in that way, depending on the direction in which the emotion is pointed, as when we decide we would rather lose an argument than lose a friend. To understand this we should look for other kinds of messages in the displays.

So far we have discussed displays of emotion as indicators of mood and attitude—frustration or determination or faith. But such displays can also be seen as clues about likely performance in social roles: the displays indicate what kind of self the performer is bringing into action, what character he is adopting, and what responses he expects from others. To be successful, of course, the performer must convince his audience that he *is* that kind of person: to give the impression that one has chosen a character to suit the occasion is generally to disqualify oneself. Sincerity, however, is not our question: only an acceptable display of sincerity. Our main interest is in setting up and analyzing a range of characters that can be used "teleologically" in persuasive interactions with others.

The term "character" folds within itself the distinction we have made between the facade and the reality. The character found in a novel or a play is a construct, like a mask, an appearance stripped of the many-sided complexity of any real individual, artificially simplified so as to point a moral. On the other hand; we also use the word "character," sometimes marking it by the adjective "true," when we penetrate the appearances and arrive at the fundamental distinctive reality of that particular individual. Stressing distinctiveness, we say of someone, "He's quite a character!" When used in this sense, "character" does not suggest appearance, the mask on the surface, but rather some deep level of personality: the "true self" as distinct from the presentation that that individual may choose to make in different contexts.

We make a similar contrast (between appearances and reality) when, interacting with other people, we speculate about the firmness or the sincerity or the "credibility" of their judgments, promises, and threats. There are various ways to make this assessment, and one of them, as we have seen, is to look for a display of emotion. A promise or a threat marked by tears or a hand placed on the heart constitutes a claim that the statement comes from the "real self" and not from one of its appearances. Obvious nonarousal—apathy or boredom—has the same effect. Displays of emotion, to this way of thinking, are a window on some kind of "true self": displays of reason draw a blind across the "true self." If we accept Simmel's argument, of course, the "true self" (in the sense of the whole self) can never be conveyed.

So the distinction between the "true self" and insincerity is itself a dimension measuring other selves. The colony of selves contains more members than just "the true self" and its opposite. In this chapter we shall discuss five varieties: the moral self—the person in a relationship that is its own reward; the civic self and the tactical self—the individual in the world of action and purpose: the divine self—the person possessed; and the silly self—the person cutting loose. Each will qualify as a "true" self, if the audience grants that it is.

Let us first examine that form of self which we will call silly, an adjective that suggests but does not precisely parallel its German counterpart *selig*, meaning "blessed."

A figure for satire (comical when described but not when encountered) is the mild, apparently well-mannered man who, placed behind the wheel of a motor car, becomes a foul-mouthed, uncontrollable ruffian, quick to take and anxious to give offense alike to pedestrians and to other motorists. Such behavior is, of course, deplored—but it is also expected that people will let off steam. Motor cars in many countries are places where drivers assert their individuality. They show a side of themselves that would be cause for severe embarrassment if it were displayed at the office, in church, or even (in some cases) within the family.

A collective exercise of a similar kind is carried out in England on "outings," day trips in a charabanc—a tour bus—to a seaside resort or some other place where bodily indulgences may be had. The nature of such occasions is beautifully caught (for Wales) by Dylan Thomas (1954:47–48) as his uncle takes off his spectacles "so that he could read" and surveys the list of prospective trippers.

> "Enoch Davies. Aye. He's good with his fists. You never know. Little Gerwain. Very melodious bass. Mr. Cadwalladwr. That's right. He can tell opening time better than my watch. Mr. Weazley. Of course. He's been to Paris. Pity he suffers so much in the charabanc. Stopped us nine times last year between the Beehive and the Red Dragon. Noah Bowen. Ah, very peaceable. He's got a tongue like a turtle dove. Never an argument with Noah Bowen. Jenkins Loughor. Keep him off economics. It cost us a plate glass window. And ten pints for the Sergeant. Mr. Jervis. Very tidy."

"He tried to put a pig in the charra," Will Sentry said.
"Live and let live," said my uncle.

The people who take the ride usually know one another already, perhaps being members of a sporting club or the regular clientele of a public house. Often, too, only men go on the trips, leaving their wives behind. ("It's me or the outing, Mr. Thomas," said his wife, and he replied, "Well, then, Sarah, it's the outing, my love.") The comedy of these occasions is standard: an organizer worrying whether they have stacked enough crates of bottled beer to last the trip; an itinerary including sufficient stops at public houses to let the connoisseurs tank up on draft beer instead of the gassy stuff; a pell-mell race for the public urinal when the bus stops or free elimination along a hedge in the countryside; there are songs, smutty or sentimental, and funny stories about people getting left behind, and angry or apprehensive publicans, and not so funny stories about what you do on a charabanc with those who cannot hold the liquor down. In short, it is, as someone told me, an occasion for men to "get the silly out of them."

Another method of letting oneself loose in a way that would normally be reprehensible is to go as a spectator to a sporting event, especially one that involves bodily contact. A soccer match once a week gets the silly out of the men in the crowd. At all-in wrestling matches old ladies scream for a kill and, with one wrestler identified as hero and the other as villain, the audience enjoys maximum involvement.

There are many other occasions for an apparently unrestrained display of feelings normally kept under control. The Holi festival in India sends those modest, decorous, face-hiding ladies into the streets armed with brass syringes that they hold erect and use to squirt colored liquids over the high and mighty males. Deciphering the symbolism should not be hard. On that day the young and the humble are permitted to insult and degrade those who on other days are their superiors (Marriott, 1968). At carnival time, in European countries, people wear masks and behind this cover cram themselves with excesses of food and drink and go hunting for sexual contacts normally forbidden them. Once upon a time in European villages the young men lived through, as it were, an age of carnival. There were "companies of fools" that practiced irresponsibility (certainly in stereotyped ways) all the year round. They were expected to do foolish things, to carry them to excess, to be improvident, objectionable, and disrespectful (Milano, 1925).

What do car driving, "outings," the behavior of crowds at sporting matches, carnivals, and the permitted irresponsibility of the young have in common? First, these are not occasions for displays of reason and moderation. On the contrary, people are "soft in the head" or they do it to "get the silly out of them." They are given a chance to vent their anger. They are encouraged to be extravagantly joyful. They can eat and drink and sing and dance and pursue irresponsible sex. In short, these are proper occasions for the indulgence and display of certain passions.

The second characteristic is anonymity. Sometimes this is formally arranged, as when participants at carnivals wear masks. The person in a crowd, even without a mask, is almost indistinguishable from others. A similar sense of losing oneself within the crowd is felt on outings and, one supposes, among the companies of young men. Finally the motor car, with glass or steel above and below and in all four directions (together with its capacity to go somewhere else quickly) resembles a mask; for that reason the authorities seek to diminish its anonymity by means of license tags and number plates.

The third characteristic is the consequent lack of responsibility: all those occasions allow a person to get involved (even if only by swearing at another motorist) without taking on the responsibilities of involvement. Where the anonymity is effective, it ensures lack of responsibility, for there is no way to punish a miscreant who cannot be identified. But the lack of responsibility and the refusal to hold people accountable goes further than the mechanical devices that prevent detection. Irresponsible behavior (so long as it stays within customary bounds) is not only allowed but even encouraged, at least to the extent of acknowledging its inevitability. It was in exactly that resigned, indulgent, perhaps mildly scornful tone that I heard the lady say about the men gone on a charabanc trip, "It will get the silly out of them." She implied that it was better to get the silly out at one time and all together, rather than have it dribbling out here and there in places where there might be no arrangements to have the mess cleaned up. Her attitude was very plain, although not put in these words: we need outings for the same reasons that we need water closets.

When President Carter received the votes that finally gave him his party's nomination in 1976, he stood before the television cameras and he was seen to wipe a furtive tear from his cheek. My feeling was one of regret that he had joined the band of American politicians who weep in public. But evidently there were other messages in that incident. Until that time Carter had seemed—although he did not emphasize this side of himself and subsequent events put it somewhat in doubt—the calmest and most calculating of men, efficient, successful, capable of self-control, cool and reasonable even in adversity. So far from being admirable—as it seemed to me— for some people this great self-discipline marked Carter as a political android, without feelings, without the capacity for human relationships. Then he wept and all was well: a human being after all, *a moral person,* and that much the more deserving of trust.

Think about morality and trust. Certain relationships require us to suspend calculation. Neither friends nor family members should count the cost of their connection. It is improper to ask ourselves if such a relationship is profitable in terms of money or prestige or power, because the relationship itself is its own reward. The partners, so to speak, grant one another an infinity of credit, and they trust each other not to exploit any temporary advantage. In a word, each ceases to hold the other accountable and makes it possible for both to lower their defenses and to leave exposed their own "true selves," abandoning the masks and the shield of formality still needed in the world outside.

Such a relationship becomes, to an important extent, an exchange of displays of emotion. Because the partners love one

47

another, they weep for each other, they laugh with each other, and they may display anger together against outsiders. They are expected to disregard rules thrust upon them by the larger society, for these rules demand an improper accountability. The son-in-law gets special treatment in the business because he is a relative. Paradoxically, even the offer of a bribe is an attempt at morality, an effort to transform an official into a moral person, someone with whom one can have a more complete relationship than that allowed by the rules of his office.

Those involved in such relationships tend to build a wall around themselves and to exclude others. They experience "intimacy" (Simmel, 1969:127–28). Their attention is concentrated on one another, as if emotion broadcast too widely is liable to dissipate and to lose its force. Consequently they have no concern for the larger society in which they live, and, focused entirely on each other, they acknowledge no responsibility to it, for, as they see the situation, it can get along without them. In the beautiful words of Donne:

> For love all love of other sights controls,
> And makes one little room an everywhere.

Hatred has similar features. To hate a person for what he is (rather than to calculate what he has done and decide to punish him for it) is to have passed beyond calculation of one's own or society's best interest. The hated person is given an infinity not of credit but of discredit (nothing he does can improve the image); the rules of the larger society lie in abeyance and the hatred pushes into the background relationships with other people. Once again there is a large element of emotion in the transactions that make up the relationship, only this time one grieves for the person's existence, laughs at him or vents one's rage upon him.

The moral self is not a bearer of specific rights and duties, for these things imply accountability and calculation. There is no directive beyond the generalized instruction to love or to hate. By virtue of its simplicity and exclusiveness, the moral tie is like the tie with God. Of course in practice there are few relationships between human beings that cannot be construed, to some extent, as a set of rights and duties. But in the case of a moral relationship, such a description leaves most of the tale untold. It leaves out of account the intrinsic value of the relationship, which is expressed in emotions. That is the difference (we suppose) between a family and a business; father and son compared with boss and worker.

We set a strangely strong and positive value on knowing the moral self, even when the other person turns out to be hateful. It is not difficult to see why this should be so, although there are two quite contradictory reasons. First we have a need for faith, an aversion to endlessly calculating profit-and-loss accounts: a desire to believe and a refusal to question. We are lazy: when we can, we avoid questioning and calculating. In other words, we like our "life's lie." Alternatively we are ambitious and are out to exercise power, to own and to control. Even if we are not, that may be the message conveyed, and is one reason why love can turn so easily into hatred.

One form of love is safe from this risk. It is the love of God and it is manifested in the *divine self*, the person possessed, an association of the divine with the simple. We have made it ourselves in finding an element of divinity in the simplicity of moral relationships, love and hatred, their absence of itemizing and accounting. There is a special affinity in our culture between the divine and the innocence of children or of some creatures. The divine, it seems, belongs in the heart and not in the head.

Some cultures see the extreme form of emotion, the ultimate suspension of reason which is manifested in trance, as evidence of the presence of a divinity. The person is "possessed" by a spirit, a devil or a god. What is supposed to happen to the self on these occasions?

A person in a trance is expected neither to carry out the duties and be entitled to the rights that he has in his normal state nor to exercise normal initiatives. There are similarities with the moral self: both the person in trance and the person in the trance of love or hatred are infused with some divine spirit—at least that is how our language and our poetry encourage us to think.

But there are also differences. The person in a trance has ceased to be a "self." He is nothing more than a vehicle, an instrument of communication through which others may learn of the divine will. In that condition he is anything but a civic self (see below); nor is he a moral self, purportedly a whole rounded person; he is simply an instrument of the divine purpose. Alternatively (in other cultures) he is sick.

The person in a trance, giving the ultimate display of emotion, may symbolize the ultimate values of his culture. In a sense this is an apotheosis of the civic self transformed and raised to the level of religious values: not sets of rights and duties but the final values that guide them—loyalty, honor, purity, charity, or whatever provides the fuel in that particular culture. In a sense also, as we noted, this "divine" self is an apotheosis of the moral self, inasmuch as it is a transcendent, wholly intrinsic relationship with the divinity.

Like other selves, the divine self is a mask. Someone given the right to wear the mask portraying a divinity is no longer a human being, but the divinity itself.

Certain phrases reveal another member of the colony of selves. We say *"in vino veritas,"* meaning that when drunk a person displays a part of himself which he conceals or controls when sober. We accuse people of getting "above themselves." We also say (often ironically) that someone "has excelled himself" in the performance of a task. When a person is rendered helpless by hilarity or is transported by rage, he is said to be "beside himself." If he fails to exhibit an appropriate emotion, we say that "he must not be feeling himself today." It is clear that in these phrases the display of emotion (or its inappropriate absence) is indeed considered a window on some "true self." But the phrases also point to two further kinds of self, *civic* and *tactical*.

The judgment on a person's behavior implied in such phrases as "beside himself" or "not himself" employs two kinds of criteria. First, people look for an average of a person's past performances. Projecting from the way he has behaved in similar situations in the past, he is "beside himself" or "not himself" or "unlike his normal self" if he conducts himself as others would not have predicted: the calm man who flies into a rage, the irascible woman who remains passive when provoked, the bold person who shows fear, or the coward who confronts danger. (Of course, if such displays happen often enough, then the definition of that particular "true self" is likely to be modified.) Second, we may look not at the person and his unique and individual history, but at the status he occupies. Profanity from the headmistress and sentimental tears from the sergeant major are evidence that these people are "beside themselves" or "not themselves."

The moral self excludes, we argued, ideas of right and duty. But it is evident that such phrases as "not oneself" and "above oneself" make sense only if we measure performance against the rights and duties expected of the person. In some of these cases displays of emotion (for example, being "beside oneself") indicate a flaw in the self, an inadequacy. A person who is beside himself is unable to undertake the responsibilities that normally attach to his status. Often the judgment means that he is absolved from guilt: "He could not help it." Evidently this self, unlike the moral self, is validated by accounting procedures. It is the "civic" self and it includes an element that is apart from emotions, either dominating them as a control or standing as a rival for the use of available avenues of expression. In other words, the "civic" self signals that a mind is at work. Let us look at situations in which this idea of the self controlling emotion (rather than being revealed in displays of emotion) appears.

Anyone who has been recruited into an army has experienced systematic official attempts to degrade him, to depersonalize him. I do not know if such practices still go on, although by the logic of my argument they must. His individuality is diminished by a uniform. His name is lessened by the addition of a number, and if he happens to have a common name such as Smith or Jones or Williams he will probably be addressed by the number alone. Army numbers identify the human item, so to speak, but not the individual person. In the British army even the nicknames are curiously impersonal in their uniformity: all Smiths are "Smudger"; Millers are "Dusty"; Jones or Evans or Williams or Hughes is "Taffy." One way or another individuality is removed. There are also *rites de passage* designed to wipe away the civilian identity that a person brought with him into the army. So far as is possible, all signs of uniqueness are forbidden. The recruit has a standard haircut: he can wear a moustache (standard patterns only) but not a beard; the possessions he is required to display—his uniform, bedding, and equipment—are set out every day for inspection, the same way for everyone. If he does have a few personal things that mark him out from the others, they are kept in a locker, out of sight.

Particular care is taken to eliminate spontaneous individual displays of emotion. There are rationalizations for this concern: efficient warfare requires the elimination of excessive fear and excessive impetuosity and is better conducted by concerted action than by individual initiatives. Consequently the soldier is trained to become a creature without feeling and emotion (except collective emotions toward the Queen, the Country, the Regiment, and the enemy) and therefore the more effective.

The first steps toward this objective are taken on the drill square. It is a tradition, at least in the British army and I presume in others, that the drill sergeant should taunt the recruits, heap abuse upon them, and so conduct himself that, off the drill square, any normal person would reward him with a black eye. Recruits are compared to pregnant ducks. They are told that if the Queen saw them, she would certainly abdicate. The trooper whose hair is the length of toothbrush bristles is asked if his head hurts, and, compelled to reply loudly and clearly that it does not, is told that it should, because the sergeant is standing on his hair. All these things are formalized provocations, and the individual must learn not to fight back, not to get angry, not to show himself as an individual. The training is generally effective. Very few people do fight back (at least openly—there are all kinds of interesting ways of

doing so covertly), and those who fight back openly are heavily punished and generally judged by their peers to be stupid
rather than brave. A great majority learn the lesson that the
only self that matters is not the individual with his own peculiar needs and desires, or the moral self (the moral self is covertly permitted in the "mate" or "buddy" system, overtly in
the idealized relationship between Indian soldier and British
officer [Masters, 1956], and, in a subtle way, is encouraged in
the regimental *esprit de corps*), but that self which is nothing
more than a vehicle for rights and duties, in other words, the
civic self. In this performance not one iota of emotion is encouraged, unless it is collective and stage-managed. For example, a drill was used at the funerals of important persons. At
the command "Rest on your arms reversed!" one placed the
muzzle of the rifle on one's toe, bowing one's head. We were
told, "Look sad, you buggers!" We were like hired mourners
at a funeral, and no one expected us to *feel* sad. There was also
a drill for giving three cheers, laying down where the cap
should be grasped (easier with the old peaked cap than the
floppy forage hat), where it should be held during the "Hip!
Hip!," and the appropriate duration of the "Hurrah!" The
only occasions on which "genuine" emotion was enjoined
were simulated encounters with an enemy: when thrusting a
bayonet into a sandbag, one was required to shout with anger
and exultation.

In these examples there is a clear equation between a display
of emotion and the existence of an individualized self. The
suppression of emotions is seen as a condition for creating a
"civic self," one that bears rights and duties, and takes only
those initiatives that are appropriate to that status.

The control of emotions has other aspects besides that of
suppressing the individualized self. Eskimos hold song contests, in which the singers insult one another. In order to win,
two things are required. First, one must have the wit to produce a song that is constructed according to the rules of the
game and that is more insulting than the one delivered by the
opponent. Second, the singer must keep cool. If he loses his

temper, he loses the game. He loses not only according to the rules, but also because, having lost his temper, he may no longer have the capacity (so our culture tells us) to remember or to extemporize an appropriate reply. The same thing goes on in the game of "dozens" played by American blacks, who hurl unspeakable insults at one another about where mother distributes her sexual favors: once again, to lose control of oneself is to lose the game (Rainwater, 1970).

These games have a significance different from that of the drill square. The song contest and the "dozens" do not eliminate a person's individuality so as to make him fit to bear a burden of duties to the collectivity; rather they intensify it. They emphasize the individual as a competitor and innovator. They also bring out again that idea of a complementary distribution between reason and the passions. If a person can be provoked to display emotion, he has lost the capacity to exercise reason and so conduct a winning campaign. He can exercise reason—by thinking out or recalling a more insulting rejoinder—only if he succeeds in controlling his emotions and ignoring the insults that have been heaped upon him. In short, these games oppose emotion to a "tactical self" (unless of course it is *simulated* emotion intended to mislead others).

To summarize: In the song contest emotion is suppressed in order to keep the intellect in working order. This we call the "tactical self." In the context of the drill square, emotion is suppressed not to make room for the intellect, which is suppressed, but in order to leave the carrier free to assume duties put upon him by the collectivity. This is the "civic" self. What these selves have in common is rational activity directed toward a goal (a question we shall consider later).

To conclude this chapter, let us consider briefly three questions: first, let us go again to the facade; second, to the different significance of displays of emotion as criteria for each different self; and, third, to what is being signaled through each self.

Drawing mainly from our own culture, we have had no difficulty in identifying five different kinds of self. No doubt other selections are possible, both in our own and certainly in other cultures. There is nothing surprising about this. We may fall short of being all things to all people (not everyone can present all even of those five versions), but we are certainly *not* one consistent thing to all people at all times. That is what our experience tells us; that is what Simmel claimed.

Nevertheless, despite experience and despite Simmel, we penalize those we judge to be concealing their "true" selves behind the mask of a different self. They are deemed insincere and their capacity to persuade is thereby much diminished. Why do we do so? It is the shield again. We insist, in the overt rules governing persuasiveness, that the persuader should be all of a piece, thus making our world simpler, more comprehensible, and therefore (an illusion, of course) more manageable. It is a kind of timidity. We do not want to look at the hidden interests and deliberately concealed motives: we want to be able to trust.

The covert sector, at first sight, suggests a being that is at once more robust and more realistic. Guided by our knowledge of the covert sector, we can reject the appeal that is on the lips and try to penetrate to the heart. But notice the paradox. Knowledge of the covert reality (that people put on whatever mask they think suits the occasion) heightens the critical examination to which the persuader is subjected; but the goal is to get back to the haven of identifying a "true" self, by eliminating the masks. The goal is to suspend doubt.

Why suspend doubt? Because doubt inhibits action, induces inertia, and the inert organism is soon dead.

So the consequences of accepting (or being able to impose) a particular version of the "true" self is to reduce the area of questioning and doubt. The range of possible behavioral responses is also reduced, for by accepting another person's definition of the situation proffered in the "self," we bind ourselves to behave appropriately. On the other hand, we can keep our options open by refusing to accept this as a "true" self. We can say directly that this is a tactical self masquerading as a moral self (cupboard love, for example) or as a divine self. Alternatively we can offer our own version of the appropriate situation by responding to an invitation to love (moral self) with a stern, albeit regretful, lecture on duty (civic self); or to a would-be clever fellow (tactical self) with mockery (silly self).

None of the selves can be imposed *initially* except through a display of emotion. They require an assertion and not an argument. This is true even in the two cases, the civic and the tactical self, in which *subsequent* persuasion is conducted by means of reasoned argument. From time to time, as we shall see in a later chapter, the definition may have to be reasserted by a further exhibition of the appropriate self.

What messages do the different selves convey about the situation? We shall take each in turn. The essential message of the *silly* self is: "I am not at work. I am not engaged in a task. I have no obligations and I am not accountable. I am indulging *myself*. I am letting off steam.". In other words, the silly self is *ostensibly* (this qualification will be explained in a later chapter) not instrumental, not designed to change the world or anything in it. It is assumed only for one's own psychological gratification.

The *divine* self and the *civic* self stand together at the opposite pole. They proclaim altruism in the form of a concern for society, for the common good, or for the divinity. They differ from each other in that the civic self, once the definition is accepted, is ready to discuss and argue about appropriate means: the divine self pronounces (or relays) authoritative definitions *ex cathedra* and does not allow rational discussion. Unlike the silly self, both are out to get things done in the world.

The *moral* self is not instrumental: a moral relationship is its own reward and is apt to dissolve if used for extrinsic purposes. Therefore, by definition, it has no concern for the common good. We have already asserted this; nevertheless, since the claim seems to run so patently against the usual meaning of morality, the reader is asked to withhold judgment until a fuller discussion is presented in the next chapter. To anticipate briefly, my argument will be that no morality can exist without exclusion: you can treat some people as ends in themselves only at the cost of treating others as instruments. Finally the moral self is not a reasoning and calculating self. In this it re-

sembles both the divine self and the silly self, and differs from
the civic self and the tactical self.

The *tactical* self is not altruistic but self-concerned; in that
respect it is like the silly self. But the relationship it establishes
is instrumental, the extrinsic aim being to acquire power in
one or another form. It is not, like the civic self, guided by
the normative rules of the collectivity, but will evade them or
manipulate them for its own purposes.

These are the simplest meanings (in the sense of predicted
behavior) to be derived from the five selves. But they are very
simple and as yet a long way from behavior. They are like the
roots of words: not used by themselves in speech and—a paradox—stiff with meaning and yet useless to convey meaning
outside the lexicon until they have been inflected, equipped
with prefixes and suffixes, and strung together into sentences.

In the next chapter we begin to deal with larger units:
sequences of behavior in which the various selves (together
with more specific presentations called "postures") follow one
upon the other and influence each other's meaning. This procedure will allow us to build in the variable of power.

CHAPTER 3

Selves and Postures

In this chapter, by means of short narratives rather than vignettes, we place some of the selves into a context of interaction. We begin to examine "situations." The interaction has to do with the attempted exercise of power, that is, with persuading another person to agree to see the situation as you define it and to act appropriately.

The principal actors to be considered in this chapter are only two of the selves. Since all of the instances involve committees or administrative interchanges in a university setting, it is not surprising that the lead is taken by the civic self: the one that takes for granted that the major values and goals are beyond dispute and that, given such agreement, rational argument will result in correct decisions about how to act so as best to achieve the institution's goals. One of these goals, however, is collegiality: a moral relationship (in its aspect of amity; it is not supposed to include the dark side, hostility). It will be seen that rationality (the presentation of the civic self) is in continual danger of being hustled off the stage by one or the other versions of the moral self.

Displays of emotion (or their lack) signify postures. That term, as I intend to use it, is a metaphor, and its meaning is best made clear in such phrases as "defensive posture," "a posture of aggression," "a posture of readiness." The word connotes *intention* and therefore *rationality,* but it is important to remember where I intend the rationality to lie. A display of emotion carries a message about posture. These displays may be rational (that is, purposeful and therefore by definition faked, like hired mourners at a funeral) or they may be the products of genuine feeling. Similarly, the message may be read reflexively—anger for anger or laughter's contagion—or it may give rise to calculations (about character, appropriate response, and so on) that go beyond the mere act of recognizing the display as emotion and identifying its type.

Our present interest is *not* in whether the display in fact arises from genuine feelings or is faked, *nor* is it in "knee-jerk" or spontaneous (i.e., uncalculated and thoughtless) responses, but rather in *rational* interpretations. These are the interpretations for which one can give a reason: "Why did you do that?" "Because I saw he was losing his temper." "How did you know he was angry?" "Because he was pounding the desk and stamping his feet." Such explanations draw on cultural rules that tell one how to identify the emotion, the appropriate response, and so forth.

Such rules, it seems to me, must also direct at least to some extent the apparently spontaneous reactions themselves, in the sense that people tend to respond in this manner—anger to anger and laughter to laughter—only in situations that their culture deems appropriate. People are said to display their madness in culturally prescribed ways; so must they display emotion. Both madness and emotion proclaim removal from reality. Indeed, what is emotion but a lesser form of madness? Certainly cultural rules cover anticipation of reflexive displays: everyone knows what is supposed to happen when you shout "Fire!" (no doubt with the appropriate emotional conviction in your voice) in a crowded theater.

Postures, like the presentation of a self but with more specificity, are indicators (through displays of emotion and by other means) of what a person is likely to do and therefore of the range of appropriate responses. Postures, in other words, can be construed as claims or assertions (whether intended or not), which, if effective, both inform and constrain the other person.

Nowadays many faculty committees have student members. Often this innovation was accepted less than gladly by the faculty, who felt themselves under one or another form of duress. The resultant tension—if not bad feeling—sometimes erupts in the course of a meeting, and such emotional outbursts, I suspect, are regretted more by faculty than by students, because they dissipate the myth of collegiality, of moral solidarity, and above all of rationality. At the back of these difficulties lies the unresolved question of whether student members of faculty committees are still students (*in statu pupillari*) or are colleagues and therefore entitled, at least *pro tem,* to the privilege of collegial treatment.

One such committee, a small one, was dealing with the allocation of rooms in a new building. Since the matter was slightly complicated, the chairman set up a matrix on the blackboard and was filling in the spaces as suggestions came from the committee members. First an entry was made, then the committee discussed possible difficulties and inequities. One of the two student members made a number of suggestions. But the chairman, standing by the blackboard, kept his back to the students and appeared not to hear what was said. Twice this happened, and then a faculty member of the committee drew the chairman's attention to the student and his suggestion. The chairman at once apologized, somewhat lengthily and with just enough effusiveness to produce a whiff of irony, and from that point onward was careful not only to pay attention to what the students said but also to do so with a pronounced air of collegial cordiality.

My second example involves only faculty members, this time a committee engaged in allocating rather small amounts of research funds among faculty applicants. At a previous meeting they had returned an application, saying that the project appeared to be the same one they had supported—supposedly to the point of completion—two years before. They got back an extremely irate response, pointing out that when one professed a subject, its name was attached to the research, but only someone stupid or malicious could pretend that all research projects in a given discipline were therefore the same.

It was not a tactful reply and the writer's friends on the committee braced themselves for battle with the chairman, well known to be on very bad terms with the applicant. The chairman ignored the remainder of the letter, which went on, after the diatribe, to explain rather precisely how the present research differed from that which had been supported earlier. He asserted that it was really the same project, that the applicant was trying to trick them, and, his face darkening with anger, said, "What I cannot stand is a liar!"

Such vehement emotion, the members evidently felt, and in particular that unvarnished description, was intolerable. One member rebuked the chairman; the rest looked embarrassed. The chairman, evidently realizing that he had gone too far and would not be able to make a rational case for denying the award, conceded without grace and without apology and moved quickly on to the next item of business.

My third case concerns a dean of the social sciences. Deans come in many shapes and sizes and it is important to understand the scope of this man's enterprise. I met him at a time when resources, even in England, were plentiful, and this dean had been very successfully engaged in building up an extensive teaching and research empire. Compared with the stereotype of an English academic, this man was gifted with an unusual warmth of personality, a rare sensitivity in his dealings with others, and a quite un-English ability to use displays of emotion—both the light and the dark emotions—to bring people to his side. Lastly, although he had the final power of decision in all academic matters, he relished the forms of democracy and made a practice of reaching important decisions with the advice of faculty committees. Being skillful in his dealings with people, he rarely had to refuse a committee's recommendation.

His Achilles' heel was called "interdisciplinary studies," an activity he loved and promoted beyond reason, and he found himself locked in a continuing conflict with the heads of departments, who grieved to see so much money diverted into what they considered a form of academic prostitution.

The dean had proposed a chair in interdisciplinary social science and had gone so far as to invite an old acquaintance to take the position. Only then did he remember his faculty advisers. When he consulted them, putting forward both the chair and the prospective occupant, the advisory committee asked for more time to think about establishing the chair, but quite flatly rejected the candidate—for any position at all— saying that this jack of all trades was master of nothing except the art of self-promotion. The vehement tone of their report no doubt reflected some annoyance at the dean's procedural lapses.

The day after he received their written report, the dean sent for the chairman of his advisory committee and the following scene—an appropriate word—took place. The dean said, in a calm and rather matter-of-fact way, somewhat in the manner in which expert testimony is delivered in a court of law, that he had great respect for the chairman, had much enjoyed their cooperation, hoped that it would long continue, and trusted that what he was about to say would not spoil their future relationship. Then he exploded into a torrent of angry accusation. The committee was biased; its members had not made their case; they had been moved by emotion(!) rather than by reason; they just wanted to make him trample over them. After about half a minute of this, the chairman of the advisory committee suddenly brought his fist down on the table and said very sharply, "Don't talk to me like that! Control yourself!" The chairman, too, appeared to be extremely angry.

The dean seemed surprised at this outburst, possibly also at his own behavior. He said nothing. His antagonist, still very angry, then said that if what he needed was a more reasoned statement, he would certainly produce one, and it would not only confirm the incompetence of the candidate but would also make it impossible for anyone to continue with the proposal to establish a chair in interdisciplinary studies. He would be pleased to write such a report, and it was a mistake not to have done so the first time.

The dean still sat there, saying nothing, his head bowed, not taking up what appeared to be a challenge.

The scene ends with the subdean, who had evidently been

placed in the room by a benevolent providence, picking up the pieces, blaming both men impartially but without rancor, and suggesting some further discussions another day. At that point, when the meeting closed, the dean walked round the table and shook the chairman's hand—an odd gesture, particularly for an Englishman, except perhaps in the boxing ring.

My fourth and last case is a brief one and takes us back to the battleground of student–faculty relationships. In the mid-1960s at a university where the students were just beginning to flex their muscles, the graduate students presented the head of a department with a written request that they might participate in some departmental decisions, especially those that concerned their own course of studies. The wording of the request was careful, reasoned, and far removed from the provocations and downright insults that later became common. They pointed out that those who completed their course successfully would become professionals like their own teachers, and that a collegial opportunity to share in the responsibilities would be not only welcome but also appropriate. But the head did not take kindly to the suggestion of near-equality. He replied firmly—also in writing—that students, including graduate students, were not qualified, were not experienced, and above all did not have to be around long enough to take the responsibility for their decisions. The faculty, he said, had no intention of yielding up its responsibilities to those who were not qualified to bear them. The tone of the letter, as well as the content, was certainly intended to put the young people in their place. But the students were not so much cowed as puzzled—or at least that was how they chose to present themselves. The vehement tone of the head's reply, they insisted, must betoken some deep personal insecurity, for in no way could any rational person see the students as a real threat to faculty power.

So there are four cases: the student whose suggestions were at first overlooked, the man who called a colleague a liar, the emotion-displaying dean, and the head who was branded as insecure because he responded with heat to a cool request. From these cases what postures can we derive? There are two parts to this question. First, what positions are people claiming to occupy toward each other? What versions of the self are they offering? Second, what movements are made between positions?

Three of the four cases indicate positions that are identified by relative *power*. The chairman who at first failed to register the student's suggestions, apparently deliberately, signaled not (as he might have claimed) the obtuseness of the suggestion but the insignificance (and therefore powerlessness) of the suggester. He asserted, in effect, that the student was not qualified to present a civic self. In the other case involving students, the issue was exactly whether or not they were in some situations to be accepted as the collegial equals of the faculty. The hard-of-hearing chairman, after he had been reminded by his colleague, went out of his way to signal equality and amity with the student members of his committee. He did so by the presentation of a moral self, exuding friendliness and esteem for them as individuals. (Thus he preserved his original position, evading the issue of their fitness to bear civic responsibility.) There are other situations in the cases given above where people are concerned, openly or covertly, with equality, superiority and inferiority, and we shall come to them later in the discussion. These few instances are enough to show that one dimension along which positions may be arranged is relative power: higher, lower, or equal.

The second dimension is *solidarity*. The extreme negative position is that indicated by the sentence "What I cannot stand is a liar!" This is the presentation of a moral self (hatred) and it signals the suspension of reasoned discourse and any concern for the common good. The outburst of violent anger on the part of the dean and his antagonist in my third case falls into the same category (but, as we shall see, in that case the positions are perhaps less significant than is the anticipation of movement between them). The positive value of solidarity appears in the effusive attention that the committee chairman bestowed on his student members, once he had been reminded to do so. It would be wrong to characterize his first stance—

treating students as persons of no consequence—as hostility; for hostility, it seems to me, involves some recognition that the rival can (or perhaps could) be strong enough to do harm. The departmental head who rejected student requests to be represented on faculty committees, and did so, apparently, with unseemly vehemence, was exhibiting hostility and, perhaps despite himself, saying something equivalent to "What I can't stand is an uppity student!" The committee chairman, on the other hand, loftily disdainful of student opinion, was not so much hostile as concerned with the task, not with persons. We shall call this posture "indifference," meaning "indifference to personal relationships." Here again we mark off three positions on the dimension: the three values for solidarity are alliance or friendliness, indifference to persons, and rivalry or hostility.

In some instances it is very evident that both dimensions are being used to locate a position. The committee chairman sees himself as higher than the students whom he is ignoring and at the same time is indifferent, as the verb "ignoring" implies. Once reformed, he signals not only equality with those students, but also a collegial friendliness, a warmth of manner that should tell them that he sets an intrinsic value on his association with them. The departmental head asserts superiority and at the same time reveals (so the students say) hostility. Even when, at least on the surface, the relationship is one simply of hostility and relative power appears not to be of immediate concern—as in the case of the man who couldn't stand a liar—only a short way beneath the surface it becomes obvious that power is also an issue. The applicant feels he is being pushed around by his intellectual inferiors; the chairman certainly felt that his committee was not being treated with the respect due to it from a supplicant for research funds. Moral considerations break through the surface of rational task-oriented activity (the civic self).

If these two dimensions, power and solidarity, are taken together, they serve to identify the nine positions that are indicated in Diagram 1. It is important to remember that these nine positions are not descriptions of actual relationships;

Diagram 1

Power	Solidarity		
	Hostile	Indifferent	Friendly
Superior	1	2	3
Equal	4	5	6
Inferior	7	8	9

rather they represent *claims* by one party to define a relationship. The departmental head and the students whose request for representation he rejected clearly had opposed views of their appropriate relationship, and (if we accept student speculations about the significance of his irrational display of hostility) they did not even have the same view of the actual distribution of power between them. Only if both parties agree in their claims can we say that this is (for example) a symmetrical alliance between equals (position 6), or an asymmetrical relationship between superior and subordinate allies (positions 3 and 9).

If each party has a different account—say that one asserts equal alliance (position 6) while the other acknowledges alliance but claims superiority (position 3)—then we should expect a series of exchanges (claims) as a result of which the disagreement may be either intensified or resolved. This brings us to the subject of movement between positions.

Let us begin by recalling some examples of movement. The committee chairman who ignored his student members conveyed a message about their inferiority and faculty superiority; that is, he occupied position 2. His faculty colleague then reminded him (although not in so many words) that membership on the committee implied equality and that the proper position for him should be at least position 5, preferably position 6. He then moved to position 6.

The man who "couldn't stand a liar" thereby occupied position 4, possibly position 1 by reason of the implicit claim to greater righteousness. The embarrassment of his colleagues and the rebuke from one of them reminded him of the collegial ethic and of his obligation to treat a fellow scholar as a colleague and a friend: in this case, position 6. Several pressures—his colleagues' evident embarrassment, the rebuke, and perhaps above all the entirely rational arguments advanced by the applicant (once he had got the bile out of his system)—made position 4 untenable, and the chairman retreated. But he did not go to position 6, which would have called for some kind of withdrawal of the accusation of dishonesty, perhaps directly and openly or perhaps (so often the way) through some self-deprecating humorous remark. He shifted instead ostensibly into position 2, in effect—although not in so many words—asserting that the applicant and his affairs and his honesty were of small importance and to give more attention to them would be to waste time. His colleagues on the committee in fact saw him rather in position 8, defeated by his evident incapacity to counter the applicant's rational arguments in support of the project. It was not a graceful performance, and it served also to indicate that position 4 (or position 1) would be resumed, vis-à-vis that applicant, at the first available opportunity.

A more elaborate and therefore more interesting pattern of movement is to be seen in the case of the emotion-displaying dean and his antagonist. You will remember that the dean began with a plainly stated testimony ostensibly offering a moral self, position 6 (equality and friendship) and avoiding position 3, which he might, as the dean, have been entitled to claim without giving offense. Notice that I have made clear the plain factual nature of this statement, its rational tone, the absence of any accompanying display of emotion or warmth. Remember also that this man was in the habit of displaying his feelings. In those circumstances the tone was to some extent a denial of the statement's content. It was a statement rather of position 2 than of position 3. If he really had those sentiments of amity, he would have framed them in a display of emotion. Clearly, if one thinks about it, the tone of that statement was preparing the way for what was to follow immediately.

This, you will recall, was an extravagant outburst of anger. The report that his advisers had given him, he said, denied the proposed appointment without giving any good reason for the denial. If the dean had said the same thing in a more controlled manner, and if he had gone on to detail the report's inadequacies, both men might have remained within reach of position 6 or of position 5. Instead the dean attacked the men and left the argument aside: they were emotional and biased and malicious. These personal attacks, and the vigor with which they were delivered, signaled that the dean claimed position 1 and put his adviser in position 7. In effect he was saying, "I am the boss! Remember that! Remember also that I have no cause to like you!" This is the dark side of the moral self.

At the third stage of the encounter, after the antagonist had made his angry and threatening response, the dean sat silent and with his head bowed, leaving his subdean to put their small social world together again. This withdrawal from the combat signals position 2, or possibly position 5, since the dean tacitly admits a degree of equality with his antagonist by allowing the subdean to stand as arbiter (and therefore as the voice of reason) over both of them. You will remember that the man who "couldn't stand a liar" also shifted to the central column (position 2) when rebuked; but I see a difference. His anger apparently spent, the dean's posture indicated exhaustion and grief; the other man was unrepentant, eager to get back at least to position 4 if not to position 1. The plausibility of this interpretation is increased by the dean's final move, which was to shake hands with his somewhat astonished antagonist, a display of the moral self, certainly intended to put them both back into position 6.

Now consider the antagonist. He shouted back at the dean; then, threateningly, he offered to fill out the indictment and so make it even more damning, for that first report was in fact restrained. The first angry retort, "Control yourself!" means something like this: "I reject your claim to occupy position one. You may be hostile but you are not my superior. So we are in position four. Moreover, unless you behave yourself, I'll write another report that will embarrass you even more. That would put *you* in position seven and *me* in position one." Note how an assertion of rationality (the threat to write a more detailed report) is inflected in such a way that it becomes a presentation of the moral self.

One might conclude that it was this threat that silenced the dean. I doubt it, for the dean's opening in position 6 (a rather thin version, admittedly) and his full-blooded assertion of that position through the handshake at the end affirm that he is not aiming to crush his antagonist, but simply to vent his emotion and get back to position 6 as gracefully as possible. Moreover, it seems to me that the antagonist was in collusion, for the apparent threat also contains the message "I too would like to be in position 6, and for that reason my report on the candidate was much more restrained than it might have been. As things stand, you will get away with disregarding our advice. Force me to make our message clearer, and you will be able to disregard it only at the cost of very great embarrassment."

From that point, until the final handshake, the subdean took control, both parties having had a chance to vent their anger and so get the silly out of them. The antagonist accepted the handshake, a reflex, possibly, rather than a calculated action, but nonetheless an overt acceptance of position 6.

Because it is convenient to express oneself that way, I have from time to time talked as if I had a window into the minds and hearts of my characters. The man who "couldn't stand a liar" was moved by an unshiftable hostility; the dean was not intimidated when the antagonist shouted back, but moved to restrain himself by his desire to restore amicable relations. You may also be curious about the extent to which each character is following a conscious strategy. Did the dean deliberately open with a thin and rational statement of position 6 in order to pave the way for the subsequent outburst of temper? Did his antagonist plan to fold a rational statement of cooperation within the display of anger?

Let me say again that it is not my intention to probe within any individual psyche. I do not have the tools. Rather my interest is what is on the surface. What, in a particular culture, is the meaning of emotional displays? What messages are being transmitted? The dean's posture when his anger was met by equal anger—head down and silent—signals that his anger is spent or at least controlled. It also signals that he has not been intimidated, for then he would have moved to position 6 by displaying repentance or, in a compensatory way, to position 9 by showing abject repentance. Whether the dean had genuinely purged his anger or was simply controlling it I have no means of knowing. Nor do I need to know, for my interest is in the meanings of emotional displays rather than in the psychological or physiological realities. In the same way, I do not know how deliberately the dean thought out his strategy when he coded his initial statement of position 6 in cold language. But neither do I know, when someone utters a grammatical sentence in English, whether he worked it out beforehand. Indeed, put that way, it seems what it is: not a question for someone whose first interest is in the analysis of grammar. In other words, the movements we have traced exhibit something like the rules of grammar: there are correct and incorrect ways of making them.

Another way of putting the point is this: to some extent we can predict moves from one position to another, both because each subsequent move is affected by its predecessors and because each posture signals not only present position but also a limited range of next likely moves, and also, ultimately, because in each context there are only a limited number of "grammatically correct" moves to be made. (The "grammar" is that of persuasion: the "correct utterance" is the one that persuades.) Let me make this clearer by returning to Diagram I and to the examples.

Consider some of the rejected options. The apparently hard-of-hearing chairman began in position 2. When his faculty colleague reminded him (indirectly) of the ethic of collegial equality, he might have met him only halfway by moving to position 5. He could have recorded the suggestions he received from the student, but not, as he did, compensate for his earlier indifference by a display of friendliness. Once again, I do not know what went on inside his mind; I hinted earlier that the display may have had a touch of irony in it, but without greater knowledge of his normal way of conducting himself, I cannot tell. But I do know the consequences of adopting a posture that signaled position 6. By doing that he also signaled his intention not to revert to position 2. Had he gone to position 2 or position 5, he would have left that option open. Position 6, in comparison with those in the central column, is relatively *sealed* (and I wish that word to have the connotations of confirmed or ratified or bonded or made secure), and the sealing is done by the display of emotion—in this case friendliness. Emotion, we see again, signals commitment.

Now contrast this behavior with that of the man who "couldn't stand a liar." He begins by sealing himself into position 4 (or perhaps position 1). The members of his committee, embarrassed or offended, remind him of his collegial responsibilities toward the applicant, and implicitly invite him to move to position 6 (or to forget the man and address himself rationally to the issue). He does neither; he moves ostensibly to position 2, one of indifference, but refrains from producing arguments and thus runs the risk of appearing to be in position 8, a person who makes no move because he lacks the capacity. I have two comments here. It may be that it is very difficult—or, if you wish, "ungrammatical"—to move directly from a sealed position to its sealed opposite; a transitional posture in the column of indifference (that is, of rationality and of emotional neutrality) may be a requirement. To have gone straight from the left- to the right-hand column (from hostility to friendliness) possibly damages the "sealed" quality of both positions. It jeopardizes the image of the "true" self. In other words, one's sincerity is put in doubt. The second comment is less suggestive and repeats what we learned from the first case. A position in the central column might have allowed the chairman to use rational argument, and then switch to position 6. Not choosing or being unable to muster arguments, he signaled the probability that the next encounter with this applicant would see him back in position 1.

The suggestion that to move from one sealed column to the other requires a stopover in the central, unsealed column of indifference and a demonstration of readiness for rational discourse is somewhat supported by the case of the impassioned dean. In this instance I have little doubt that the dean intended the whole affair to end—perhaps not on that day—with both him and his antagonist acknowledging position 6. It fits with his political style and it also makes good political sense, for if one must have advisers, it is better that they should not be hostile. That may be the reason he felt compelled to begin with a statement of amity. But it was merely a statement, *unsealed by those displays of feeling that were normal with him.* Knowing or feeling that he was about to launch into an extravagant position 1, he had no other way of conducting himself "grammatically."

We can draw similar conclusions from the postures of the dean's antagonist. Just before the intervention of the subdean, the antagonist was claiming position 1: "If you continue to abuse me, I'll let loose the full power of the inescapable logic of our case, and then you'll be sorry because you'll be worse off than you are now." Such a statement is a threat. Certainly it expresses hostility and some contempt, for it implicitly says that the dean is a fool not to have worked out the consequences of his anger. He should at least have paused in the central column and thought ahead before letting fly. But at the same time the antagonist's outburst contains a covert stream of rationality. The words of the threat make clear a message that the antagonist evidently expected the dean to have heard for himself: that the report, although adverse, by its very restraint allowed him to make the appointment, if he felt that he must. Behind this posture lies the more general message that the antagonist, too, expects them both to land eventually in position 6 again. There is a curious inverted symmetry between this message and the dean's opening statement. Given the larger context, the very threat, so far from being an expression of mindless hatred, of feeling alone, is instead a method of *unsealing* position 1 and allowing for a future return to position 6. It resembles the dean's opening statement in that both are factual *unsealed* statements of position 6 submerged subsequently or simultaneously in *sealed* statements of position 1.

That is as far as we shall take the analysis for the moment. Let us see what we have.

We have a way to examine politics (persuasive actions) in organizational life which takes account *both* of rational purposive activity directed toward some agreed end *and* of displays of emotion which assert some intrinsic quality of a truth or a relationship or a self. We distinguished sealed from unsealed positions, the former marked by displays of emotions and by postures that signify unwillingness to compromise. We suggested that it may be "ungrammatical" (that is, confusing or unconvincing) to move immediately from one sealed position to its opposite, such a move requiring a stopover in the area of indifference (the unsealed position). In adducing evidence in favor of this argument, we began to notice the complexity and subtlety of postures: how they can signal, at one and the same time, both a sealed position and, subliminally, the unsealed detachment required for a compromise.

The moral self (in both versions—amity and hostility) is placed in the left- and right-hand columns of the chart. The central column is, so to speak, the exit route into rationality, into task-oriented activity, and is the location for both the civic self and the tactical self. The left- and right-hand columns make statements, through displays of emotion, about relationships: they are expressive. The central column, from which feeling is absent, has to do with getting work done in a "real" world.

The contrast between the central column and its two wings is the key to understanding both the rules we have for persuasion and why our attempts to get things done in the world by persuading others to accept our opinion often fail. There is, of course, also an opposition between the left and right columns, between amity and hostility; but we shall treat this as secondary. Diagram 1, in fact, should be construed horizontally not as a statement of (from left to right, for example) "no solidarity—some solidarity—most solidarity," but rather as a hierarchy of contraries: at the lower level, enmity is opposed to solidarity; at the higher level, they are put together as feelings

73

about persons and set in opposition to (feelings about and) rea-soning about tasks. We must insert the bracketed phrase be-cause, as argued earlier, without feeling there is no will to move at all: witness in later chapters examples of emotive statements about the value of reason. We leave it in brackets, however, because it is very much a submerged theme in the central column: from the standpoint of a civic self the need to sing the glories of reason is a sign that chaos may not be far away.

For a civic self this chaos is defined as inattention to the goals of the institution and failure to take action to attain them. The chaos is caused by the human proclivity to get wrapped up in relationships with other people: "So much in love, she is, that there's never a day when the dinner doesn't come burnt to the table!"

If anything deserves to be called "the human dilemma," this is it. We are human because we plan and organize and think ahead about how to control the world around us. We have a vision of what should be masquerading as what is: the facade, the shield, life's lie. But we also know that in order to create even a simulacrum of that facade, we must penetrate into the disorderly reality that lies behind it. This we can do only by the application of doubt, the use of questioning, adopting the posture of a scientific investigator and believing that there is an objective world that is the same for all people (at least, all *sane* people—more on this later), a world where only facts count and opinions can be disregarded, where no amount of opinion will make fire burn without air, a world where a temper tan-trum cannot turn off the rain. The objects of investigation in the real world may indeed be other people; but that does not lessen the need for objectivity. To serve the ends of the institu-tion or the collectivity—or whatever it is on which the civic self is cathected—these people must be reduced to bundles of relevant characteristics, objects for scientific scrutiny rather than subjects for whom one feels.

But such compartmenting is impossible. That is where the dilemma lies. First, as we have said, the scientific endeavor is left unmoving without the fuel of enthusiasm. This enthusiasm, by the definition of a rational investigation, is, of course, for rationality itself and is not directed toward people. But how can it not be so directed? The human endeavor generally is to some degree a collective endeavor. In persuasive action—convincing others to accept your definition of what "really" lies behind the facade—by definition interaction is involved. How, then, can one fail to warm toward those who accept the definition and be unfriendly toward those who do not? From there it is a short step to fostering feelings of solidarity or enmity *in order to* influence intellectual judgments: "Respect me, then respect my statements!" is a common tool in argument. The step beyond that is to accept the feelings as ends in themselves. At that point rationality, along with the civic self, has vanished. "The boundless giving of oneself is as radical as possible in its opposition to all functionality, rationality, and generality" (Weber, 1957:347).

Generalized objective judgments about the relative strength of reason and passion, of the civic self and the moral self (that is, the central column and its two wings), are not easy to make. If we narrow the judgment to our chosen field of bureaucratic endeavors, the verdict seems to be for entropy: the civic self is what should prevail, but its supremacy is precarious and achieved only through constant vigilance. In other words, it seems to be much easier to slip into the outer columns than it is to get back into the central column.

Why is this? The answer brings us to a discussion, promised earlier, about the excluding tendencies of a moral relationship. That lovers put themselves out of the everyday world is asserted not only in the sentence from Weber quoted above, but also by Freud ("Two people coming together . . . in so far as they seek for solitude, are making a demonstration against . . . the group feeling. The more they are in love, the more completely they suffice for each other"—in Richman, 1957:206, quoted from *Group Psychology and the Analysis of the Ego*). It is also a commonplace of everyday folk wisdom: nothing fouls up rational bureaucratic activity more efficiently than an injection of libido. All imperatives yield before—this is Iris Murdoch's neat irony—the "categorical imperative of Eros."

But, it may be objected, it is a long step from sexual involvement to collegiality. Can one really argue that the tender-
ness one is supposed to feel for a colleague, the willingness to
shield him from the impersonal rigors of accounting procedures, the pleasure one takes in his accomplishments, the for-
bearance granted his misdemeanors, the sympathetic pity
bestowed on him for his failures, the willingness to accept him
for himself as a whole being (and not just as another instrument in the service of the institution) and above all the sense of
being the same kind of person, all of which seem to be what
collegiality means—can one argue that there is something here
in common with love? I have no doubt that one can. Nor does
one need to postulate a genetic connection, a common pre-
cultural determinant for both love and collegiality. Such a connection may well be there. But for our purposes it is enough
to point out the behavioral similarities: the refusal to apply the
standards of the institution to that other person and the insistence on treating him not as a means to an end but as an end in
himself.

A similar argument, with the adjectives reversed where necessary, can be made for the colleague in the left-hand column,
the one who is hated. One may hold him accountable in the
sense of digging up whatever dirt one can find to use against
him, but this is not done impersonally so as to benefit the institution (indeed, the scandals may do it harm). Rather the aim
is to hurt the individual, and to this end the institution and its
needs become a mere instrument.

But why should this make it difficult, once one has fallen
into one of the outer columns, to get back to the center line of
rational task-oriented activity? Why the entropic tendencies?
Why should rationality be presented in this model as so much
more fragile than the passions?

That they are so presented can be inferred from the rigors of
institutional discipline described in the previous chapter. You
have to be trained, first, to accept the institution's definition of
itself and its goals, and to eliminate any feelings toward others
(whether institutions or persons) which are not consistent with
the institution's needs; and then, second, to use rationality to

decide how to work upon resources so as to fulfill the institution's goals. It is a long apprenticeship. There are no lessons in how to bring on those irrelevant or harmful passions, only in how to suppress them. Obviously the assumption is that they will come unbidden.

What reasons could be advanced to justify such an image of the weakness of rationality and the strength of passion? First the moral self carries its own defenses in that it is rooted in the passions and is therefore immune to rational arguments. It has a facility for twisting and rendering unintelligible negative messages from outside the relationship: a jamming device, so to speak. This, too, is a kind of facade: a pretense that the real world can be left to go its own way. It is also a shield keeping away what Weber calls "the cold skeletal hands of rational orders" and "the banality of everyday routine" (1957:347).

Second, rational activity is weak just because it is receptive, because its business is to penetrate the facade and find out what is "really" there, to doubt, to question, and to criticize. It therefore continually runs the risk of encountering a world that is neither "palatable" nor "comprehensible" and of finding itself so overloaded with discordant information that it runs for relief into the simpler region of the passions. This is why people often get the blame, when in fact the system is at fault.

Third, the civic self is weak because, other than in a few instances of dubious merit (for example, those sons of empire who sacrificed health and family life to serve devotedly in some distant and insalubrious outpost), it is recognized that even the truest of civic selves must share their "host" with other selves, whereas the moral self is thought to be a total and exclusive occupant. The civic self has always to be thinking about compromise—for example, with a tactical self and sometimes with a silly self (which turns out to have some quite rational aspects, as will be seen in the next chapter). The moral self, on the other hand, is apt to be more robustly persuasive (other things being equal, and what these other things are will emerge as the book continues) than the civic self for the same reason that one is more inclined to follow someone "who knows his own mind" than to follow a ditherer. The civic self, in short, lacks force because its image includes other selves lurking in the background, because it betrays its own complexity, and therefore it falls short of achieving the stark simplicity of a "true" self.

Fourth, and last, the civic self is weakened by an internal contradiction that repeats the "human dilemma," described earlier. A bureaucracy runs on the rule that all problems yield to reason: it has the Cartesian foundation that we will discuss in a later chapter. But this very belief is itself a facade, something for which there can be no *reasoned* foundation. It is a heuristic defense against an unpalatable complexity. But there are many problems, particularly those involving value judgments on human interaction, which can be solved (in the sense of coming to a decision as to what should be done) only by the use of the passions. Not all problems yield to reason: many problems are beyond the capacities of a civic self.

After this defense of entropy (the notion that unprotected rationality easily dissolves into feelings) the reader may be wondering how, given the rules of our culture, positions ever get unsealed.

In those brief narratives, I have not gone further than to suggest that, *usually prompted by others,* people do manage to step back into the central column (if only, sometimes, as a way station to a contrary sealed position).

In the next chapter we look at one of the ways of prompting. It involves a version of the silly self: joking. This is not a simple activity. In the form to be described it belongs in the left-hand column: joking at the expense of individuals by definition always carries some hostility, and in the present case this hostility is accentuated. But the tactic belies the form: it is intended to push contestants (or likely contestants) into realizing either that they have collegial responsibilities (that is, they should be friends—right-hand column) or that they have a job to do (central column), or, paradoxically, it makes use of a collegial appeal (a moral relationship) to evoke a civic self ("If we are friends, we must have common interests").

We shall see that, when one shifts attention from the individual actor to the activities of a group, the stopover in the central column is no longer a requirement for movement between the outer columns. It follows that messages conveyed by the different selves can change as their contexts change. The context, in the next chapter, is presented in the form neither of vignettes nor of narratives, but as generalized accounts of the working of certain kinds of committee.

CHAPTER 4

Persuasion and Play

My intention in this chapter is to demonstrate that ostensible irresponsibility (presentation of the silly self) can be used for the serious purpose of facilitating a return to or preventing a fall from the central column, that is, from rational purposive activity. In order to make this demonstration we identify two further kinds of activity that are analogous to but not the same as the two outer columns of Diagram 1 in the previous chapter. One of these, corresponding to the left-hand column, is hostility revealed in an act of aggression or an altercation. The other is solidarity. The framework for modeling these activities remains the same: hostility is opposed to solidarity, and both together, as displays of emotion, stand against the central column of rational purposive activity.

How do these three terms (rational activity, solidarity, and hostility) correspond to what has gone before? The solidarity is brought about by a version of the silly self. Rational purposive activity—in the case of committees it takes the form of debate—is an activity of the civic self. Hostility is manifested in altercations and it is complicated. First, although the distinction between debate and altercation is clear enough in principle (the former addresses the problem and the latter addresses the person), in practice it may be difficult to separate them, and the aggressor will surely claim to be a debater acting in the mode of the civic self. His opponents, however, see him as a moral self, blinded to the common good by his antipathies. Others will see him as a tactical self, well aware of the common good that guides a civic self, but intent upon furthering his own interests, which are not those of the collectivity. His capacity to persuade will clearly depend on which interpretation wins the day.

How does Diagram 2 (see below) differ from Diagram 1? The latter is an inventory of postures, claims that can be made by *individuals* about power and solidary in a *dyadic relationship,* cross-cut by the dimension (reason or passion) of the mode used to make those claims. Diagram 2 uses the same modes (reason and passion) but its purpose is to provide a chart of the behavior of a *collectivity* and to furnish a means of describing movement between one collective posture and another. The collective postures are more complicated than the individual postures discussed in the previous chapter, for they include,

Diagram 2

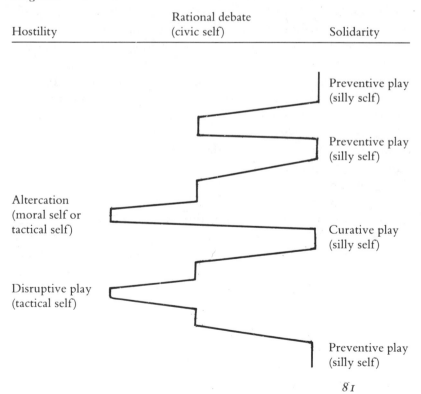

Hostility   Rational debate (civic self)   Solidarity

Preventive play (silly self)

Preventive play (silly self)

Altercation (moral self or tactical self)

Curative play (silly self)

Disruptive play (tactical self)

Preventive play (silly self)

besides power and solidarity, statements about the urgency
and importance of the task in hand.

I shall give generalized accounts of behavior in three kinds
of committee. Let us identify them as *A, B,* and *C* and concentrate first on the opening phase of a meeting.

The opening phase is that period of five or ten minutes
spent settling down, waiting for the unpunctual, and it is ter-
minated when the chairman calls the meeting to order.

The model I have in mind for Type *A* is an ad hoc committee that meets only once to examine a personnel file and recommend for or against promotion. There is no single meeting
place for these ad hoc committees and there is usually a five- or
ten-minute delay while those members not gifted with path-
finder skills search for the designated room. In the meantime
those who have arrived converse. The nature of this conversa-
tion varies according to the extent to which individuals already
know one another or of one another and of one another's affairs, and according to whether or not anything of general
concern to the university is going on at the moment. Not in-
frequently there are also exchanges about the case they are to
discuss. Everyone has had the opportunity to read the file before and I suspect that most people have already partially
(sometimes wholly) closed their minds to all but one decision.
These exchanges about the file, before the chairman formally
opens the meeting, have a tactical purpose: to find out beforehand how others think about the case and so have a chance to
work out persuasive lines of argument.

The salient feature of this initial exchange, if it happens to
be about the file, is that many things are not said. Opinions
are expressed with a studied impersonality. One should never
push a private preference openly and directly: it is not done.
Rather one speaks on an analytic plane about the principles involved; one may even speculate about the probable outcome,
deriving hypotheses not only from the principles of the case,
but also from an analysis of committee behavior in general. In
short, the five members are expected to behave as if this is not

an adversary situation, but one that will be settled impersonally by correct reasoning from agreed principles: disagreement
would indicate that someone is in logical error. The truth will
become self-evident in the debate.

Type *B* and Type *C* committees meet regularly and are engaged in the management and allocation of resources. Unlike
the members of ad hoc committees, these committeemen
know one another and have in mind a history of past meetings
and a prospect of future meetings.

Type *B* I have elsewhere called an elite committee (Bailey,
1965). Its members are not severally answerable to outside
constituencies. They are *collectively* answerable to some higher
entity—to God, to themselves and their interests, to a principle, or to the collectivity that they govern. In short, they see
themselves as "guardians." This type of committee will be
discussed more fully in a later chapter.

I have served on several such committees and have been
struck by the members' continuing and effortless assumption
of their own superiority. They are castelike in their arrogation
of distinctiveness (and, of course, distinction) and, when chal-
lenged, they conduct themselves as if faced with some horrendous act of sacrilege. Marked internal dissension is a cause for
great distress, and the violent expression of disagreement is
discouraged. Nor is it expected. Elite committees always rest
upon at least one fundamental agreed axiom from which to
begin their debate and their reasoning: their own superior
status.

Such committees may have formal opening ceremonies at
each meeting: a prayer, perhaps, or (in England) the fraternal
glass of sherry (not beer or gin) symbolizing donnish civility.
Whether such a ritual is practiced or not, the opening moments while the members are assembling and perhaps looking
over their papers seem to be indistinguishable from the rest of
the meeting. Those who want to talk to their neighbors or to
the room at large about an item on the agenda do so in the
way that they will talk later: they may be analytic or they may
express their feelings openly and directly. (They are unlikely

to speculate about their own future and behavior as a committee, as sometimes happens in the case of Type *A;* that would be faintly blasphemous, at least lese majesty.)

Type *C* is the arena committee (Bailey, 1965). Its members, either individually or in (sometimes shifting) alliances, are representatives severally answerable to outside constituencies. As the name indicates, these committees are cockpits, where champions fight over resources.

The behavior expected and usually exhibited during the opening phase of such committee meetings seemed to anticipate contentiousness, at least at those meetings I attended. The period of five or ten minutes before the latecomers arrived and the meeting was formally opened (and extending sometimes into ribald asides on the minutes) was marked by extravagant displays of familiarity. If a member had done something of note since they last met—published a book, made a strong speech at the Senate, won a prize, directed a play, bought a car or a house or a bicycle, or been seen jogging, and so on—he became the target of loud and public congratulations, occasionally straightforward, more usually barbed with a covert insult. Newcomers to the committee, providing they are old members of the institution, are welcomed with a barrage of insults and are expected to indicate their acceptance of this welcome with a suitably insulting rejoinder. The joking, in the examples I recall, was sometimes pursued to the point of coarseness, but it was clear that no one was expected to take offense.

It is likely that a number of covert strategies were being followed in this activity, including the establishment of rank (the loser failing to respond suitably, or failing to keep his temper—as in the "dozens"—or overstepping the mark). But the collective activity seems to me to symbolize a rather frantic camaraderie, an assertion of total familiarity, an attempt to anticipate and render less divisive the serious quarreling over resources which the members knew would follow later. By exchanging insults in play, and not losing their tempers, they demonstrate, it is supposed, sufficient interpersonal trust (and even, in an odd way, affection) to form the basis for orderly debate and reasoned compromise and to hold themselves back from a fight to the finish. They also demonstrate that they are capable of self-restraint and not easily moved by emotion. The entire performance recalls the "loosening up" that an athlete practices before committing himself to serious effort: stretches and passes beforehand lessen the chance of strain or injury later.

Notice, finally, that this anticipatory display takes no direct notice of what is to come on the agenda: it is not at all directed toward particular decisions, but rather toward reminding the arena committee members that, given the necessity of making decisions, there is a level of cooperation and compromise and mutual trust below which they must not fall.

Let us now look at sequential patterns of behavior during the course of a meeting. In all three types of committee—indeed, in all committees—the "proper" framework of procedure is the same: a problem is put forward, its solutions are discussed, and a decision is reached. Committees beat their way like a pulse through the diastole of discussion and the coming together of decision. But the metaphor is a poor one, for it suggests a regularity that is seldom achieved. Decisions may go through "on the nod," the chairman offering the answer as he phrases the question—no diastole. On the other hand, the discussion may become a debate and may be so extended and perhaps become so acrimonious that no decision is reached—no systole.

If there are no short cuts and no total stoppages, and the meeting runs normally, this normality does not mean that the members employ themselves exclusively in rational debate and in reaching decisions. The sequence of modes in an arena committee might take place as in Diagram 2.

The diagram can be translated into narrative form. The meeting opens with an episode of joking, of the kind I described earlier in this chapter. It passes then to discussion of serious matters and reaches a decision. This is signified by the first vertical line in the central column. The members then mark an interlude (literally, if we regard debate-with-decision as constituting an act in the drama) by another bout of play. They then return to serious business, and in the course of the discussion someone loses his temper, being either genuinely impassioned (moral self) or finding it expedient to appear to be so (tactical self). The argument becomes heated enough to direct attention away from business and the participants become more intent on winning than on finding the proper decision.

One way (not the only way) of ending this situation is for someone to initiate a play episode. That is why the line passes directly through the central column, indicating that there is no intervening period of rational argument, to the right-hand column. This is called, for obvious reasons, curative play.

If this is successfully done, then the members get back into the central column and pursue a rational discussion, as indicated by the vertical line.

But before they can reach a decision and move into the right-hand column for a period of relaxation and fence mending in preventive play, there is another shift to the left and a suspension of rational activity. This is caused by disruptive play, the nature of which I shall describe shortly.

The cure is less likely to be a move into the right-hand column—curative play—than a straight authoritative assertion by someone (it should be the chairman) of the civic self: the value of rationality.

If this move succeeds in bringing the members back to business and they reach a decision, then there will be another celebratory episode of preventive play, bringing our imaginary meeting to an end.

Before we consider the other types of committee in the light of this imaginary sequence, I shall describe some of the markers that initiate and define the various episodes.

Rationality, in the kind of committees we are considering, needs no strong rhetoric to mark it (except perhaps when choking off disruptive play) because it is the accepted and official norm. A few standard phrases seem to suffice:

"Time to get down to business. . . ."

"The task that faces us is . . ."

"As a reasonable man, I must say . . ."

or the ubiquitous and often deceptive: "It stands to reason that . . ."

I have distinguished three kinds of play: preventive, curative, and disruptive. More subtle distinctions are perhaps possible. For example, the preventive play that takes place between episodes is likely to be different in content from that with which the meeting opens. The latter is relatively more free, more random, purposefully directed away from the context of the agenda and centered on personalities. The interlude play may take this form but is also likely to include remarks that refer directly to the business that has just been transacted. It can therefore have in it a curative element (as in the third example below):

"I thought we did that rather well. . . ."

"We're on form today. Maybe we should tackle the parking problem next."

"That's one in the eye for you, George. You should try losing your temper more often."

Paradoxically, the curative play that follows immediately upon a burst of bad feeling may studiously direct attention elsewhere. Someone must break the tension with a joke. If he is skilled and fortunate enough to have others collude with him, they launch into a play session, ridiculing each other and perhaps the protagonists. There is no set way of doing it:

"I can't stand the sight of blood."

"This is getting like the House of Commons."

I have heard it done very effectively in a long-winded phrase-repetitive allegory that coded the word, without actually using it, "bullshit." Such play reasserts in symbolic behavior that all the members really like one another. It also directly addresses itself to the recent contretemps in two ways. First, it says to the protagonists: "You are ridiculous to be so serious. The proper frame for this matter is a joke." Having drawn the teeth of the altercation by treating it as a joke, the members can get back to their civic selves. Second, there may be an attempt at putting the frame in place *after* the event: inviting the protagonists to agree that they were joking all the time, and that what seemed to be altercation was in fact play; thus faces may be saved and principled differences pushed out of sight.

So far everything concerned with play has had the pleasant Panglossian ring of structural-functionalist solidarity at its blithest: what looked like hostility turns out to be a means of cohesion. But disruptive play brings us back to the nasty world of political entrepreneurs. One form of persuasion is ridicule. You may attack the premise of rationality not by an outright denial of its validity but by so behaving that you signal its triviality. Sarcasm will serve; so will paying conspicuous inattention and talking to your neighbor or, even better, across the table; so will entering into a joking-and-insulting session with anyone who is willing to collude.

Disruptive play is not direct altercation. The difference is that although in play there may be the appearance of antagonism, the form itself insists on unity, on being undivided. Offering play against play (even in the form of trading insults) is, willy-nilly, a collusion that serves to mark withdrawal from work. Disruptive play indicates the same withdrawal. In the central column the definition of "This is work!" is accepted. Disruptive play cannot be answered with curative play, for that would only perpetuate the disruption. The cure must be an authoritative assertion of a different mode, that of the civic self. One can only say: "This is *not* an occasion for play!" thus rejecting the mode.

The assertion, as a counter to disruptive play, is likely to be sealed by a display of emotion:

"I do wish people would stop playing the fool," or

"It grieves me to see this important matter taken so lightly."

The contrast between the two kinds of nonrational activity "play" and "serious hostility" (the right- and left-hand columns) forecasts subsequent behavior. If I call my colleague "a hustling son of a bitch" and manage to do it in the framework of curative or preventive play, I may still be expected to further his ambitions on another occasion (and he mine). If I am seen to be serious ("What I cannot stand is a liar!") it will be assumed that I will block his advance if I can. The markers between the different types of play vary from one culture to another and even between persons. Their ambiguity gives disruptive play its strength, and the very real possibility of misreading a clue, or having one misread, is one way in which altercations are produced.

Straightforward altercations arise because someone chooses to make clear that not everyone is agreed on the premise that is supposed to be guiding the debate:

"It is generally agreed that we are here to mold character as much as to impart knowledge, and therefore . . ."

"I don't agree. Universities exist to advance knowledge. Undergraduate teaching bores me."

This sort of statement can pass to: "It's less than honest to take a job teaching and then refuse to do what you are paid for," answered by "Anyone with half a mind has to be frustrated by undergraduate teaching. Why don't you go take a job in a place that matches your lack of intellectual interests?"

At that point they could come to blows and the meeting, no doubt, would be adjourned. But I know of only one such instance among academics. Otherwise the chairman may assert himself: "Behavior like that will get us nowhere." Alternatively, the day may be saved by a recourse to curative joking.

Having discussed the markers for play, hostile activity, and rational activity, now let us turn to questions of context and compare the three types of committee.

The various moves in Diagram 2 which committees make collectively or their individual members make severally are persuasive techniques for advancing claims both about patterns of social relations and about the task in hand. Thus those who use preventive or curative play are saying that some level of mutual trust is required, and that differences of principle should not be allowed to destroy that mutual trust. Disruptive play proclaims both that the matter in hand or the argument being currently advanced is trivial and that those who take it seriously are themselves lightweight people. The civic self is a continuing reminder that there are problems to be faced in dealing with the outside world and an assertion that there must be an agreed premise for the reasoning that will provide the answers to those problems.

The definition and redefinition of a committee's nature and activity go on, to a greater or lesser degree, through the succession of claims and counterclaims during a meeting and over a series of meetings. No committee, however, starts from the open ground upward. Committees are generally subordinate things (they are so by definition, but their degree of actual autonomy in practice varies greatly) and they begin and continue through life with a mandate or a charge, a set of statutes or regulations defining their power, their task, and often the principle to be used in recruiting members, sometimes even selecting the actual members. Thus claims made in the course of a particular meeting, if they are to be taken seriously by others, must bear some relation to the committee's constitutional position: claims subsequent to the mandate must be presented as matters of increment and amendment to the mandate, preserving its intention.

Claimants are also constrained by the fact that committee members may have allegiances elsewhere. We have already noticed this in the case of the arena committee, where the members are answerable to their constituents. Let us call these "allegiance" constraints.

It should follow that if we look at the constitutional and allegiance constraints and their variations among different kinds of committees, we should be able to correlate them with and so account for differences among committees in their use of expressive behavior (the left- and right-hand columns—hostility and amity) and, at the same time, understand differences in the ratio of expressive to rational behavior (the central column). I think we can also look from the other direction and think of the expressive behavior as, in some way, an enabling device, perhaps even determining whether, given that constitution and that set of allegiances, the committee is likely to do the job given to it. Let us take each type of committee—ad hoc (A), elite (B), and arena (C)—in turn.

Type *A,* the ad hoc personnel committee, is the best example of the expected use of logic, reasoning from an agreed premise, and the expected execution of a task. What are the features of its expressive performances?

All forms of play (the silly self) are excluded. The opening phase, as I described, substitutes for play a form of intellectual chit-chat, sometimes probing, but addressed always to issues and not to persons. If members do get into an altercation, they can be brought back to rational debate only by a direct reiteration of the constitutional requirement, which enjoins rationality.

All this is in accordance both with the constitution and with the short life of the committee. The members do not meet regularly and cannot therefore acquire a sense of the value of their own existence. They do not need any such sense of solidarity and mutual respect in order to make compromise possible, because their task is conceived, in the regulations, as an entirely logical application of rules to a defined situation. There is a right answer and a wrong answer, and disagreement represents errors in logic rather than conflicts of belief and value. So there is no need for compromise; so there is no need for play.

But experience often turns out to be different. First, in all but the most straightforward cases of promotion and appointment, the regulations are not clear. Distinction in research may compensate for poor teaching and vice versa, but the extent of the trade-off is a matter of judgment, not of regulation. Ensuring that equity is practiced as between different ranks and different disciplines is complicated enough to leave room for doubt, and in any case there are unwritten rules about charity to one's colleagues, as we have noticed, which conflict with the other, supposedly absolute, rules about excellence. Second, despite strident enjoinders to be impersonal and objective, the members of these committees belong to the same institution and may have personal likes and dislikes for each other or for the candidate, which put them into the partisan condition of the members of an arena committee and diminish their objectivity and their concern for logic. Third, every man has the constituency at least of his *amour propre* and some are tempted, despite the constitutional rules (or because these rules leave gaps) to argue passionately about first principles. Others, with an uncontrollable propensity to clown, give a nonstop performance of disruptive play; but such people are not often selected. In short, for these and other reasons, the expected orderly progression through chitchat, debate, and decision may not happen, and the members of the Type *A* committee may find their moral selves locked in altercation. Compromise is discouraged by the regulations and anything other than a unanimous report is discouraged by custom. The regulations, backed by the transient nature of the group and its incapacity for play, usually prevail and, in the case of altercation, there emerge one or more minority reports, which of course reflect the absence of an agreed premise without which rational discussion (the civic self) cannot be maintained.

The elite committee (Type *B*), unlike the ad hoc committee, has a continued existence that the members value. They are familiar with one another, and the value they set on mutual trust is symbolized in a variety of subtle interpersonal ways (good manners, for example) and sometimes in ceremonial robes, special chambers, special forms of speech, and so on.

Expressive behavior (to the left or the right of the central column) is discouraged except in the context of external adversaries. The ridiculing performance of disruptive play or the solemn affirmation of a moral self (negative) are reserved for those who cast doubt on the wisdom and authority of the elite council, such attacks being considered, as noted earlier, to be sacrilege.

Play in any form is uncharacteristic of elite committees. It is not just that such bodies tend to take themselves with solemnity, but also because *internal* adversary relationships are neither expected nor countenanced. Preventive play, for example, makes no sense without some element of anticipated overt internal hostility, at least of ambivalence. But the members of an elite committee must behave toward one another as if they have no such feelings. It follows that their expressions of solidarity do not take the form of play.

Nor is curative play readily available. The only safe route

out of the unwelcome impasse of impassioned altercation (members disputing heatedly about first principles) is the use (or perversion) of logic to demonstrate that either one or both of the premises represented in the quarrel is out of line with the ruling premise that this is an *elite* committee. It need not, of course, be done in those crude words. One can say: "The responsibility is ours, and we alone must exercise it, undiminished by the compromises that have been suggested." An attempt to clear the impasse by the use of curative joking would be to admit the inadmissible in two ways: first, that there are deep-seated differences, and second, that the ruling premise ("our superiority") is not strong enough to resolve those differences.

How often should one expect such altercations to occur in elite committees? The controlling premise (their own effortless superiority) is sufficiently general to cope with most situations, and the elite committee, unlike the Type C committee, should not frequently be faced with an unresolvable clash of principles. The second source of discord, partisanship outside the committee, is by definition excluded. The third source of trouble, *amour propre* and the wayward personality, is lessened by the fact that the members of Type B committees are usually selected with great care, awkward people being excluded. If a mistake is made and such a person is selected, the subsequent dilemmas will be resolved, if the newcomer does not learn to mend his ways, not by play but simply by getting rid of him. Like the Type A committee, but for different reasons, the elite committee does not have play in its repertoire. If for any reason altercations cannot be handled by "elite logic" or by "surgery," then the committee cannot go on.

Unlike the other two types of committee, the members of an arena committee (Type C) may be found in all the expressive positions on Diagram 2. Their capacity for play is a sign that the members have no single controlling premise to guide their debate. (They will pay lip service to rationality in the abstract—claiming it is not they who are out of their minds—but in the next breath assert with passion a nonnegotiable position.) Play is, second, a sign of their diverse partisanship.

Third, play signals, underneath the enmities, the acknowledgment that some level of cooperation will be necessary.

In a Type C committee, like Type B but in contrast with the ad hoc committee, the same set of people meet regularly. They get to know one another and they learn to accommodate one another to some extent, having come to realize that without such give and take, no decisions and therefore no allocations are possible, and opportunities may be lost, everyone thereby suffering.

Such committees, in short, sit astride the incubus of ambiguity. The members meet to make decisions and work out policies. But they also meet as adversaries and, despite the frequent use of apparent rationality as a ploy and a weapon, they know that many of their decisions cannot be reached by logic, for there is often no agreed principle from which to begin reasoning. On the other hand, frequent encounters, the prospect of future encounters and the knowledge that some compromises must be made, produce some of the characteristics of an elite committee: at least they know they have to show sufficient solidarity to allow compromises.

A further reason for restraint on conflict, at least in an institutional setting like that of a university, is that the members know they may meet—may have to meet—outside the confines of that particular committee and be ready to cooperate with one another.

We have identified two kinds of context—the matter in hand and the nature of the group—of which the positions on Diagram 2 are an expression. Let me recapitulate the several overlapping contrasts.

One contrast is the degree to which internal *contention* is anticipated: the arena committee anticipates internal contention while the other two do not.

This situation in turn is linked partly with the *task in hand*. Type A committees deal (theoretically at least) with a problem that should yield to a logical solution: the premises are given, and from these premises reasonable men should be able to argue to the correct solution. In practice, of course, the premises never are that clear and comprehensive.

The contrast in the degree to which contention is anticipated is also linked with the *group's definition of itself.* All three cases are different. (1) The elite committee has no distinctive anticipatory phase because the members have no need to define themselves and their own status; they already know who they are and they need informal reminders neither of their solidarity and of their trust in one another nor of the saving axiom of their own superiority. (2) The ad hoc committee, by contrast, seems to be reminding itself of the incidental nature of its own existence and the entire subordination of itself, as a group, to the logical exercise required of it. Questions of solidarity are beside the point, because neither within the committee nor between it and outsiders are adversary relations anticipated. (3) Finally, the arena committee is structured for contention, being composed of representatives of outside interests, and yet the members know they must hold to a minimum of cooperative behavior among themselves.

The most general connection we can make, taking us back to the first chapter, is between the absence of uncertainty (of values, of authority) and the absence of displays of emotion. If a committee meeting is conventionally defined as without conflict (as in the case of Type *A,* the ad hoc committee), displays of emotion and other rhetorical exhibitions will not be expected. Conversely, the anticipation of contention (about values or about authority) should go along with the anticipation of displays of passion and assertive rhetoric.

What are the costs and benefits of play, as we have described it?

The main benefit is the obvious one. Given the structured partisanship that is characteristic of many institutions and given differences in fundamental values, without the minimal cooperation symbolized and reinforced in play there can be no compromises and therefore no decisions made, and therefore an institution can swiftly be made extinct for the lack of a capacity to adjust itself to its surroundings.

The main cost is also obvious: play is not work. Time and energy spent in play are time and energy used to get oneself into a position to deal with problems in the real world—not in dealing with them. Sometimes it is not even that: play becomes an end in itself. Debating societies—the Oxford Union between the wars was a famous example—having no responsibilities, encourage their members to score points off one another, not to find the best solution. The highest prize goes to the successful proposer of the most outrageous and nonsensical motion, and success is got by skill at rhetoric. In short, play diminishes accountability and members become too much concerned with reputations and too little concerned with their responsibilities.

There are, of course, levels of intensity in play just as there are in other forms of persuasion. The rather wild performances described earlier are no doubt the product of a particular culture wider than the university—a culture where grown men embrace and slap each other on the back and play practical jokes—and such behavior would seem very bizarre in universities in more reserved cultures. But in these cultures, too, there are forms of play—delicate contests in erudition; the scandalous tale about a colleague told, so the manner conveys, not for its juiciness but rather to exhibit the refinements stylistically possible in ironic exposition; the abstruse joke, left unexplained so that those who understand count themselves in and those for whom it remains abstruse know that they are excluded. Even the phrase "With respect . . ." is a form of play, an indirect assertion of solidarity. It means: "I am saying that I respect you and wish our relationship to continue despite the absurdity of your statements and I do not wish what I am about to say to be construed as a personal attack." All these forms of behavior, and many others, indicate a value placed on the solidarity of the group and mutual respect among its members (that is, these expressions assert that this *should* be the case). In doing so they make a distinction between the committee as an instrument and the committee as a moral group. The first is a doer, a performer of tasks, and the successful performance of those tasks justifies its existence. The second is not a doer but something that exists for its own sake, something intrinsically valued.

The continuing problem is that of explaining the survival of any rationality at all. How do the debaters get back into, or how do they avoid falling out of, the central column? How does a committee ever manage to control expressive behavior, and get things done in a rational manner? The outer columns have a "sealed" quality, we have said, and a sojourn in them enhances an incapacity to listen to reason. It appears to be a world of entropy. The penchant for living behind facades and the persuasive and indispensable force of the passions (a force that comes partly from their capacity to disregard reality and to push doubts aside) together make the survival of rationality precarious.

We have argued in this chapter that play, preventive and curative, facilitates the retention of or a return to rationality. Despite its appearance in the form of hostile joking, play asserts solidarity and collegiality and mutual trust; in short, it asserts a moral relationship.

But then, it might be said, the argument is in trouble. It does not show how play leads to solidarity, and still less does it show how solidarity is conducive to rationality. The previous chapter insisted that collegiality has all the characteristics of a love relationship: indifference to the collective good, exclusiveness, rejection of rationality—those very features that are antipathetic (not merely logically opposed) to the open-minded examination of all possibilities to find what is best for the institution or the collectivity. How (the objection is) can a moral self possibly prepare the way for a return to the civic self? If in fact it does function in this way, then surely moral relationships cannot have the characteristics that have been attributed to them. Otherwise the argument would be as nonsensical as saying that only those with tunnel vision can properly take in a panoramic view.

Is this objection valid? One line of defense is to argue as follows. The moral relationship that exists in the solidarity of a group (such as a committee) is similar in content to that found between lovers (it is exclusive and it implicitly rejects or transcends reason) but it is not between two individuals: on the contrary, it includes the entire committee and to that extent cannot be called exclusive, because it embraces the relevant *universe* of actors. Moreover, in recognizing collegiality, the members are thereby recognizing not only mutual concern but also common concerns and common *interests*. Once they become aware of common interests, they have a premise from which to conduct rational argument and so they can make their return to the central column.

As it stands, this defense will not hold. We have in fact described the conditions under which emerges a "senile" committee (to be described in the next chapter): one that is exclusively concerned with itself and is out of touch with the real world. Exclusiveness still blocks this particular defense, for the civic self should cathect not upon a committee but upon the institution, and, being thereby equipped with the required premises, can proceed to debate on how best to manage the world outside.

The second part of the argument—the shift from mutual concern to common concerns—has more promise. But before we can follow that lead, we should consider a second line of defense.

I begin by remarking that there is no entry in the right-hand column of Diagram 2 that is not in the category of play. Play, as we have noticed, comes equipped with ambiguity. Play, so to speak, is always prefaced by a statement: "This is not the real thing." To bite means to clamp your teeth into something, and if that something is animate and conscious, the result is pain. To inflict pain is a hostile act. But there are also love bites, apparently the very reverse of a hostile act and designed to give not pain but pleasure.

But now we run close to another danger. If the assertion of solidarity is made through play, and play is always labeled "not the real thing," then how can it both deny its own reality and at the same time produce solidarity? We know it does (sometimes). But how do we explain that fact? The first answer is simple: the label "not the real thing" attaches only to the element of hostility, and thereby converts the entire act to an assertion of solidarity.

But we are still left with the task of explaining how that assertion of solidarity allows a transition into rationality. To do so we require the following somewhat convoluted, but I think correct, argument. We do not have to show that moral solidarity automatically and necessarily opens the way for a civic self; indeed it does not, as has just been argued. It is enough if we can demonstrate that an assertion of solidarity that is in the mode of play has a lower degree of "sealing" than such a position straightforwardly asserted. The way is then cleared, so to speak, for other forces (like the assertion of civic responsibility or even the calculation of interest made by a tactical self) to lead the committee members back to rational debate.

A straightforward assertion of a moral relationship (for example, protestations of love and devotion) should be absolutely unambiguous. If it is not, and the adoration is seen to be halfhearted, then it is deemed not to come from a "true" self and, as an act of persuasion, it is likely to fail.

But an assertion of solidarity through play is ambiguous. Despite the fact that its overt hostility is inflected to mean "This is not the real thing," there remains an ambivalence. A love bite is still a bite: it is not a kiss or a caress. That is exactly where the ambiguity lies: some residue of hostility remains in the act, like sediment in wine. The silly self, at play, is not a whole "true" self, and therefore a position asserted by play is less sealed than one asserted seriously. In other words, if the hostility is labeled "This is not the real thing," there is also a label attached to the solidarity itself: "This is not my main preoccupation. I have other things in mind too."

At this point we pick up again the glide from mutual concern to common concerns. Strictly there is no reason why one should be equated with the other. I may be concerned for my children and they for me, but the greater part of our lives may run along quite different tracks: we may have few concerns in common. It is also the case that a shared passion for collecting stamps can lead to the marriage bed; but the connection is by no means a necessary one.

The point is that if the connection is to be made, the persuader can assume neither that it is self-evident nor that he will be able to make a convincing open argument by logic alone.

He must use other means, which from the point of view of reason are somewhat devious and indirect. The message that we have been discussing and that is delivered through play—"I feel solidarity with you, not hostility for you, and we are now ready to get back to the business that lies before us"—has exactly that devious and indirect quality. The code is far from plain.

This suggests that if we are to understand movement between the use of reason and the use of passion, and how rationality can survive, we need an inventory of codes and a description of how one code differs from another. Our concern, however, is still with the balance of passion and reason, and with the meanings that are attached in particular cultural settings to displays of emotion, and with the capacity to deal with a real world behind the facade. But the notion of a "display of emotion" begins, at this stage of the argument, to give place to something that is in essence of the same kind (that is, it transcends reason) but is more complex, more codified, more sophisticated, and has a rather peripheral place in our covert culture: the art of rhetoric.

PART II

CODES OF RHETORIC

CHAPTER 5

Undercoding and Overcoding

The purpose of this chapter is to identify persuasive styles, which I shall call codes. The criterion for distinguishing one code from another is the degree to which use is made of passion rather than reason. We begin with occasions on which a display of emotion virtually alone is the means of communication, and then move to instances in which the passions are muted and at least the forms of reason begin to emerge.

The chapter is again set in committee life. It will provide a pattern for the following three chapters, which cover similar ground—from passion to pseudo-reason to reason—but against the wider background of public affairs and political life beyond, as well as within, committees. I shall describe different capacities for communication among committee members, identify persuasive styles that are linked with different capacities, and correlate both with phases in the maturation of committees. We are not, as in the preceding chapter, concerned with the dynamic possibilities of a single meeting, but rather, from a more distant perspective, with the alternative paths available for a committee "career." I shall identify three kinds of communication code but not attempt to examine in detail differences in their content. That comes later. My present intention is to describe stages in a committee's life (or types of committee), to say what conditions favor one or another stage, and to identify persuasive styles (codes of rhetoric) found at each stage.

The life of a committee is divided into three periods: immaturity, adulthood, and senility. Its capacity to perform work (to remain in the central column of Diagram 2) is weak during the first and third stages, as the analogy suggests. Each stage is marked by a characteristic expressive style. In the first stage the members have difficulty communicating with one another and do little more than grunt and grimace, conveying large internally undiscriminated gobs of information about attitudes and feelings. They can convey to each other that they hate Mr. X or they love Mr. X, but not that Mr. X, although a sophisticated rhetorician inebriated with the exuberance of his own verbosity, nevertheless deserves a limited degree of support on specified occasions. Messages are likely to be simple, unqualified, and emphatically delivered. They convey attitudes and feelings about people and things rather than information or plans to get work done.

The period of maturity is characterized by a capacity for making fine discriminations, thus allowing messages to be precise and to convey a point somewhere along a continuum rather than simply the two absolute ends; for example, to distinguish between love, liking, affection, respect, and reluctant cooperation rather than just opposition or support. But since messages can be finely qualified in this fashion, they can also be ambiguous, marked by double meanings, conveying several messages that may not be consistent with one another. Nevertheless, despite the risk of breakdown in communication because the signaling apparatus is so intricate, a committee that has at its disposal a well-developed code is usually better able than an immature committee to deal with real problems. The members have the capacity for recognizing (and communicating to one another about) the complexity of the real world with which they have to deal.

By senility I mean that stage in a committee's life when the members have got to know one another so well that they think they can read each other's mind; that it has all been seen and done before anyway; that nothing is new, and therefore there is no point in communicating with an external world. All that needs to be known by the members, whether about the world outside or about one another, is already available in the body of custom and precedent and folklore accumulated over the years of the committee's life.

There is clearly no necessity that every committee should go through these three stages. Some never grow up, the members never learning to communicate with subtlety and remaining arrested, so to speak, in a world of grunts and snarls and embraces. Others not only reach maturity, but defy the metaphor and, by means of periodical rejuvenations, stave off senility indefinitely. Moreover, as is the case with human beings, it is likely that any one committee will in the behavior of the members exhibit all three stages at the same time, being mature in some respects, juvenile and impetuous and crude in others, and on other occasions going through the tired routines of senility.

Let us now look at these possibilities in more detail to see which forms of persuasion go along with each stage.

When a new member joins an old-established committee—I have in mind a small group of not more than about twenty people—there are certain characteristic ways of behaving. The exact behavior will of course depend on several things, an important factor being the personality of the newcomer. But whatever the variation caused by personality, behavior is expected to follow certain conventions.

The boundaries are set by two opposed forms of behavior and there is sometimes an oscillation between the two. One end is apologetic and seems to be an intimation of a civic self: "Of course I am not familiar with how things are done here, but it does seem to me that given these circumstances . . ." The other end is not apologetic. It is less easily captured in a single characteristic phrase, like the apology given above, and is often conveyed by the newcomer's behavior as well as by the words he uses. In a crude phrase I once heard, "He's trying to tell us he's got balls." There is a marked assertiveness, a willingness—almost an eagerness—to have the chance to stand firm, to make one's point and defend it with vigor, to show that one is not a nonentity even if "not familiar with how things are done here." It foreshadows a readiness for altercation. In the committee I have in mind, the members being highly concerned with getting a job done, such behavior seldom lasted beyond the second meeting. By that time the newcomer had usually taken on the prevailing ethos of getting problems solved rather than winning debates.

How is one to interpret this bellicosity? At one level the explanation already given—that the newcomer wants to show that he is someone with whom they must reckon—is correct. But more can be said, and it is the other end of the oscillation—"I am not familiar with how you do things here"— which gives a clue to the code. The newcomer presumably has been briefed beforehand and has read the constitutional directives that guide the committee's actions. But he does not know the ground rules, that set of unwritten customary rules which the committee members use to interpret and to fill the gaps in the written rules. Not knowing the conventions and therefore lacking the communicative skills that the other members possess, he is a little like a child among adults, able to convey only simple messages that concern where he stands rather than the task in hand. He is driven to assert himself. He is, so to speak, throwing a tantrum to make sure that he gets attention. Certainly the conventional response from the established members agrees with that interpretation: they are expected to humor him, perhaps conceding the point, addressing themselves more to the task of helping him to find his feet than directly to the substance of what he has said. Custom forbids that a newcomer on these occasions should be slapped down.

Lacking the capacity to use the appropriate code, the newcomer can convey only elemental content, and this elemental content is expressed through a display of emotion. I do not, of course, mean that such a person weeps or screams: such behavior would not be tolerated, let alone rewarded, in those committees that I have in mind, and the offender would likely find himself eased out. I mean only that on these first occasions the newcomer is more likely to seal his position in the left column of Diagram 2 by a display of emotion than are the older members of the committee or than he is once he has found his feet. In short, an insufficient capacity to communicate means a capacity to communicate only elemental things that have the status of premises or axioms or basic values, that are held on faith and are exempted from doubt and debate, and that are coded in displays of emotion.

The newcomer to the established committee is a simple situation. The ground rules are already in existence, and they are known to everyone except the newcomer. Let us now speculate on what might happen in a more open situation. A new committee is set up and given a very general mandate. Entirely virgin soil is difficult to imagine. All committees have terms of reference, although they are sometimes very vague. Also, it is unlikely that even if this is a new committee, all the members are new to committee work. Even in that extreme case, there are still compilations such as *Robert's Rules* and a rich stock of manuals of procedure available for consultation. Inevitably, therefore, even the most open ground presents itself with some level of structure already upon it. But it is still not difficult to suggest a situation sufficiently indeterminate to augur likely chaos. Suppose a university to have been run by an entirely authoritarian principal, who made all the decisions himself. He retires and his successor establishes democratic institutions. Among these institutions is a Resource Committee, composed of the head of each department and charged with the distribution of resources of all kinds (space, money, faculty positions) among constituent departments. There has not been such a committee before, let us assume, and the members have had little chance to get to know one anothers' committee personae.

I think that such a committee would begin its career by exhibiting an oscillation between extremes analogous to that shown by the individual newcomer, but in one particular respect different. There can be no apology for not being familiar with how things are done, for as yet there are no set ways. Instead there is likely to be a periodical collective reaffirmation of the value of rational behavior, a kind of collective pretense that every problem they will face will permit logical consideration leading to *the* correct solution. I do not mean by this the search for the specific agreed premises from which to reason out the "correct" way of distributing resources: that comes soon enough. I mean rather the simple assertion, delivered with the appropriate display of emotion and commitment, that one must have faith in reason's capacity to solve all problems.

These ritual affirmations are antithetical to and likely to be provoked by two forms of behavior that indicate very clearly that in the situation we have postulated reason is unlikely ever to be king. First, as soon as the ritual affirmation ceases and the members begin the search for the actual premises on which they can all agree, they are likely to find themselves beset by differences in principle (like the familiar one of the priority of teaching versus the priority of research). These differences in principle are sometimes just that; on other occasions they serve as fronts for less principled divergences over sharing out the spoils.

At this stage the prevailing mode of exchange is likely to be assertion and counterassertion. There is no dialogue between persons, only a set of discourses addressed to an audience at large. It is not truly an exchange, not even a debate, certainly not a discussion: it more resembles a game of golf, where each person beats his ball along the course with only half an eye on what the other is doing, rather than a game of tennis in which each stroke has to be a considered response to the opponent's action. Each person is little concerned with understanding, still less sympathizing with, what his opponents stand for, and very concerned with making his own position so clear and so insistent that the rest cannot help but be persuaded. Positions may be sealed with displays of anger, defended with manifested grief or offered with ecstatic fervor. Moral selves (sometimes even divine selves) are much in evidence, counterbalanced from time to time by the civic selves proclaiming the possibility of reasoned solutions to problems. The time is not yet ready for joking and the silly self. Nor, for good reason, is the tactical self appropriate. The tactical self cannot be effectively used except when the capacity for communication is better than that postulated at the opening stage. Second, the person who does not join in the emotive posturing is likely to remain unknown and unnoticed, a creature of no consequence, an individual without a persona.

This stage can, conceivably, be terminal, the members never offering each other anything but assertion and counterassertion, and therefore never being able to make a collective decision. In the situation that I postulated—that of a committee charged with the distribution of resources—such conduct would clearly be intolerable, and either the committee would have to change its behavior and grow up, in the ways described in the next section, or else some other institutional device for distributing resources would have to be invented.

But there are committees that live this kind of life and are nevertheless useful. I know of one, as it happens composed of heads of departments, but having no charge other than to discuss with the principal matters of mutual concern, generally at a fairly high level of policy. The principal can find out what they think of the ministry's directive allowing students access to personnel files, and they can comment on his proposals on how to implement the directive to the letter but not in spirit. In the particular case I have in mind the principal serves sherry, which in some individuals encourages the uninhibited display of extreme attachment to principles. In the metaphor I have been using, such behavior is "immature"; nevertheless, it is clear that these committees are not without their uses. People can let off steam. The principal also might learn something. No harm is done by failing to reach decisions, for the committee is not required to do anything.

This is not the case for our imaginary committee charged with distributing resources. The members know that if this job is not somehow done, everyone will be the loser. Certainly there are individuals who will sacrifice their own interests—even sometimes their lives—at the behest of a principle, but committee members, especially those concerned with resources, generally manifest a more pragmatic outlook on the world and sacrifice the principles rather than themselves and their interests. In short, the members learn how to compromise their principles and how to communicate offers of compromise to one another. How should we describe what is happening?

The committee in its opening stage uses what we shall call simple coding. That is, only simple messages can be transmitted and these are typically about first principles, or premises, or where one stands, all in the category of "self-evident" or "brook no argument," and conveyed as assertions. The mature stage is marked by sophisticated coding. The characteristic defect of the stage of senility is overcoding. What, then, is happening when a committee's capacity to code becomes sophisticated?

First, the committee should become better able to perform the tasks that are its responsibility. This is partly because the sophisticated code is more suited to a discourse about problems, about matters of substance and content, about the world outside the committee: its capacity is not, as in the case of a simple code, confined to the expression of attitude.

Second, whereas the simple code is elemental in the sense that it conveys unanalyzed wholes, the sophisticated code is analytical not merely because it makes finer discriminations (distaste, dislike, contempt, hatred, fear rather than the simple snarl), but also because it contains rules for making discriminations. It is, as Umberto Eco (following Lotman) says (1967:173), like a grammar rather than like a text. In short, the sophisticated code is suitable for debate and discussion, for thought and argument, not merely for simple assertion. Why is this so?

The idea of codification combines two activities that common sense keeps separate: one is making an analysis and the other is conveying messages to someone else. The notion of sophisticated coding also has these two elements. On the one hand it means that the members possessing such a code can better communicate to one another detailed and complicated information. It also means that with experience the committee increasingly is able to codify its activities, and to do so it must make more and more detailed classifications and analyses of the world with which it has to deal. Thus it is better equipped to penetrate facades than is a simple code.

The use of a sophisticated code is itself a claim that one is presenting the world in an "objective" fashion, as a universe that has its own imperatives, uninfluenced by the attitudes and feelings of those who have to deal with that universe. It is a world in which matters of principle yield to the demands of practice: the discourse is about means, and ends are taken for granted. (Alternatively one might argue that the one great end of making *some* decision provides the value premise from which reasoning toward action may start.)

But this is not to say that a sophisticated code provides an ideal Cartesian world where every problem has a correct solution. In the debate between research and teaching, for example, it does not provide the master premise that permits one to work out which shall have priority. But such a code does enable the protagonists to communicate their way toward a compromise, or even to trick or bluff one another (or deceive themselves) into believing that the solution arrived at is in fact a reasoned one, rather than a bargain and a compromise.

What persuasive aspects are to be found when a sophisticated code is in operation? First, as has just been said, one of the requirements for the successful use of such a code is that people should not stand too often and too openly and too insistently on principle. They should not be allowed to go out on the limb of some eternal verity and hold up proceedings by trying to blackmail everyone else into accepting the same eternal verity. In other words, there must be unsealing devices of the kind to be described in a later chapter. One of these devices, play, has already been discussed. Play—not being serious and persuading the other person that he was not being serious either—serves to bring the discourse back to the level where compromises can be made and decisions reached. Play is not an element *in* a sophisticated code: it belongs with assertive rhetoric and is therefore like a simple code (see Chapter 6). It is an exterior device that makes the use of such a sophisticated code possible, in the same sense that oil is not part of an engine, but an external substance without which the engine cannot be run.

Indeed, play has more affinities with a simple code, for both

in its untriggeréd form at the opening and closing of meetings
and in its use as oil on the rough seas of contentiousness it is
an affirmation of solidarity made in a simple elemental way.
Nevertheless play is a sign that a sophisticated code is probably available.

To summarize. If a committee passes from the opening
stage to that of maturity, a simple code is augmented (not replaced) by a sophisticated code. A new element is added to the
simple code in the form of play, which serves both to symbolize mutual trust and to counteract displays of emotion that signal intransigent adherence to a principle or a position. Then
the periodic ritual reaffirmation of the effectiveness of reason
tends (realistically) to fall into disuse.

That is one kind of maturity. It is characteristic of the arena
committee. It will be remembered that our imaginary new
committee, the career of which we are following, was composed of heads of departments, each one the representative of
his department and presumably out to get the best possible
deal for his people. Now let us imagine a set of events that
changes this state of affairs.

First, assume that these are not elected heads of departments, but rather the "god professor" of the the type made
immortal in *Lucky Jim* (Amis, 1954), each certainly in competition with other professors to get more for his department but
also enough of an autocrat not to be answerable to the members of his department. Next assume one of those "revolu-
tions" that have taken place in many universities, which set
out to render mortal the god professor either by taking away
his power altogether or by setting controls upon it. Last, let us
assume that this revolution has neither yet failed nor succeeded: it is under way and the outcome is uncertain. What effect
will this have on the working of our imaginary committee of
department heads?

There may be one or two renegades among them who
would enjoy watching or even presiding over their own
dismemberment, but the most likely response is a closing of
ranks. They see themselves as under siege and in those conditions consider that they cannot afford internal dissension. In

short, there is likely to arise an augmented sense of mutual trust among the members, a relationship which is intrinsically valued, and which replaces that minimal level of trust which existed before as a means to allow decisions to be reached. In this way what once was an arena committee is on its way to becoming an elite committee.

It is not suggested that one needs the threat of a revolution from below before an elite committee can come into existence. The elite definition may be part of the charter from the beginning. Even when it is not, and even when there is unambiguously an arena committee, then in certain circumstances—for example, a slow turnover of membership—elite characteristics may emerge, the members beginning to put themselves and their collective work ahead of the interests of their constituents. In other words, there is a tendency to adopt the posture of being under siege even when there is no one outside the walls.

The metaphor of siege suggests that we ask what is being defended or, to put it less dramatically, what is it that provides the emerging elite committee with a growing sense of its own identity and importance. Surely this must be the code itself. It is strange that a tool that seems designed to deal with means should become an end in itself. That a collection of precedents for dealing with problems, of routines and procedures for communicating and persuading, of knowledge that divides and subdivides in ever more detail, ever likely to slide into pettifoggery, should become an article of faith, a commanding symbol that comes to transcend all other allegiances, is indeed a paradox. For it is not, as I have written hitherto, that the members of an elite committee come to value one another as persons: rather they are valued as those persons whose distinction is a capacity to use the code.

Of course they do not use that term. If they need to refer to the code (as distinct from using it) they probably will invoke such notions as a paternalistic responsibility for people who are deemed not to be qualified to make their own decisions. These lesser people are not qualified because they do not know how to use the code, and can make their feelings known only through the primitive expressions of a simple code. If the nonelite have the temerity to suggest solutions, they are told, "But the matter is more complicated that that," which is nothing more than the equivalent of "You do not know the code."

The code in fact is likely to become a private language restricted to the chosen, and inaccessible to the nonchosen both by reason of its complexity and in other, more direct ways. The complexity begins because the code is designed to handle complex matters; but the sophistication is likely to be carried beyond necessity to the point where it becomes both a source of aesthetic pleasure to those who can handle it and a device for ensuring that the many—the irresponsible, the inexperienced, and the unwashed—are kept on the outside. It is, in short, the familiar circle of the privileged: sophisticated codes are restricted to those who have wisdom, the possession of which is indicated solely by the ability to use the sophisticated code.

The sophisticated code, then, left unchecked may assume the mana of a religion. Its practitioners take their faith seriously. They also take each other seriously, and one of the expressive features of an elite committee, as we noticed earlier, is the absence of mutual teasing and joking. This sobriety is not simply the result of the members' being, so to speak, aldermen and beyond the age for horseplay. Rather the joking falls away because it is no longer needed to paper over the cracks of internal dissension, for there no longer is serious *internal* dissension: ranks have been closed in the face of outsiders, whether they are enemies or subjects.

To summarize. I have suggested a "career" for our imaginary committee, which begins with the contentious displays of emotion characteristic of a simple code, learns to control the displays and therefore the contentions by means of play and meanwhile starts to develop a sophisticated code, and finally may come to a stage where the sophisticated code itself becomes the focus for members' allegiance, for it is a symbol of their own importance and of the grave responsibilities they see themselves as bearing.

The metaphor of the committee career taken from human life has some unwanted connotations. The passage of time, in the case of committees, does not automatically and inevitably lead to senility. Indeed, as I shall explain shortly, it is quite possible to imagine a committee that is senile at the moment of its inception. Mostly I want the adjective to suggest "no longer competent to do a job," which is, although offensive to the elderly, a common connotation of "senile." What does "not competent to do a job" mean in the case of committees?

I do not mean those committees that I described earlier, places for sounding off and exchanging attitudes, stuck in the simple codes of the opening phase. They have a function—letting off steam, perhaps—but they do not have a "job." By that term I intend to suggest a performance that is designed to modify in some way the world outside the committee itself—to acquire resources, to distribute resources, to maintain high standards of teaching, to enforce discipline, and so forth. The incompetent committees are those charged with one or other of such tasks, but unable to carry them out.

There are two reasons why such failures occur (assuming always that the task would be feasible for a committee without one or another of these defects). The committee, although charged with a task, may never get out of the opening stage of the simple code and its emotional posturing. (You can set this up by appointing members who are long on heart and short on head, who feel deeply but think shallowly, who, through defects of either temperament or intelligence or both, cannot learn to operate a sophisticated code.)

The other reason for failure is the one here called "senility." Those developments that bring about an elite committee also produce an increasing fascination for and preoccupation with the minutiae of the sophisticated code itself. They can proceed to the point at which the code ceases to be a set of instructions for getting things done, constantly amended and adjusted in the light of experience, and becomes instead a sacred text, a scripture open perhaps for exegesis but not to any test of practicality. The committee meetings become ritual performances;

no new kinds of information are accepted because the received wisdom comprises all that is needed; and the committee is incapable of doing anything that it has not done before. But the world outside does not stand still; new events require novel responses, but the senile committee cannot perceive what is new and so cannot respond. In this way the sophisticated code loses its defining capacity—to renew and adapt itself—and comes in this respect to resemble the monolithic simple codes, which likewise remain impervious to feedback from the world outside them.

The two defects show themselves in different ways. Arrest at the opening stage—undercoding or simple coding—is shown in frequent displays of raw emotion—anger, grief, ecstatic celebration of one's own position, fear or contempt when faced by opposing creeds. Descent into senility—overcoding—is marked by the loftier emotion of love for the divinity (that is, for the code) and is without internal contention. Nevertheless, although differently manifested, both defects are of the same kind: expressive activity so fills the time that none is left for the job.

I have described four stages, at any of which a particular committee may settle. Whichever stage it is—arrested, arena, elite, or senile—the committee is unlikely in practice to perform exclusively in that mode. Thus a committee that normally exhibits arena characteristics may, given the appropriate context, for a time perform as an elite committee, or may lapse into senility, or may even revert to the arrested stage. What factors determine the characteristic mode of activity, or bring about shifts from one style to another?

Committees are artificial things. Certainly there are autonomous and inescapable tendencies in their growth, like the opening phase of emotive posturing and like the drift toward an elite style as the members get more and more familiar with one another and evolve a sophisticated code. But the pattern that in the end emerges is the product not of these tendencies alone, but also of the design established by those who have power to create the committees. Let us look at some imaginary examples.

A committee may be deliberately set up as a safety valve, to give people a chance to let off steam. It will probably not be described in that unvarnished fashion; it will be called "advisory" or a "users' committee." Such a committee will not in fact be given a job, as that word was defined earlier: its only decisions will be about what advice to give those who make the real decisions. Sometimes this situation may come about within a committee, as when an autocratic chairman makes all the decisions, the members remaining passive and acquiescent. On other occasions a committee is set up so that those who wield the power can avoid or postpone a decision that they are not ready to make by saying, "A committee is looking into the matter." If the committee members themselves accept this cynical view of their own creation, they have no incentive to work beyond a simple code. Their concern and their dealings are likely to remain with each other, for they have been forbidden contact with real problems. A variant of this situation is that which in one university I visited is called the "elephants' graveyard." Here the senile of all ages are put together and given such tasks as determining a policy for the award of honorary degrees during the next quinquennium. Such bodies are created ostensibly as elite committees and their work is defined as important. If the members accept both these official definitions of themselves and their work, they may well be at the senile stage from the moment of their inception, elaborating a scheme that will never have any connection with the world of action.

The arena committee and the elite committee are of importance in the conduct of affairs. One or the other may be created as a deliberate act of policy, depending on whether the prevailing ethos in that institution is democratic or authoritarian. If it happens to be democratic, then there are several linked devices that preserve the representative principle. One is to ensure that through elections the members remain accountable to their constituents, and if they do not, they can be removed. Even more effective is to mandate a rapid turnover of membership, no one having time to be "corrupted" into elitist attitudes. Another device, where there are a number of committees, is to insist on diversity of membership and to prevent that not uncommon situation in which the Planning Committee and the Budget Committee and the Personnel Committee and the Professorial Board all consist of the vice-chancellor and the registrar and a selection from the same ten senior professors, thus setting up a system of "interlocking directorships."

To bring about an elite committee, simply reverse the instructions. Appoint without election people who are powerful in their own right and appoint them for life; this was, and in some places still is, the normal way to create a professorial board.

The degree to which the members have the opportunity to become familiar with one another and to evolve a sophisticated code to the point where it becomes a private language—an argot—is one independent variable determining where on the continuum from arena to senile a particular committee comes to rest. The other variable is responsibility: the imperative nature of the job that they are expected to do. The imperative of the task lifts a committee out of the opening stage and brings about the perhaps reluctant compromises of an arena committee. One trades off principles with opponents so as to make some decision, knowing that otherwise everyone will be worse off. The more the task is seen as urgent, the greater the incentive to develop a sophisticated code and to move away from concern with representation. The "imperative nature of the task," however, is not an objective thing so much as a matter of judgment; the degree of success with which the task is being performed is also a matter of judgment. Both types of assessment may be made by an authority superior to the committee. This authority may set up a committee that in fact has a trivial task, as in the case of the committee that "is looking into the matter." Conversely, the authorities may set up committees with a real job, and then dismiss them for failing to carry it out.

Although committees by definition are subordinate things, they can in fact achieve a high degree of autonomy. Sometimes this power may be recognized by styling them "board" or "council"—the Professorial Board, the Academic Council, and so on. A degree of autonomy, whether formally recognized or not, leaves the task of assessment of how important the job is and how effectively it is being done in the hands of the committee itself. It is in these conditions, other things being equal, that one can best observe the tendency to drift from sophisticated coding to oversophistication and to replace a concern for the job with a concern for the niceties of the code itself.

To summarize. A committee's existence and the stage at which it comes to rest will be partly determined by the authority that established both it and the conditions in which it must work. First, if these conditions include a task, then this will tend to move the members out of the immature phase and encourage them to evolve—or make use of—a sophisticated code. Second, if the conditions permit the members to monitor their own performance and to judge its importance, then in the absence of a relatively rapid turnover of membership and of such devices as elections, which make the members accountable to outsiders, they will center their interests on themselves and their activities, tending to take on the role of guardians. Perhaps they will then become senile.

Finally let us look at how this framework, built on the three expressive styles of undercoding, sophisticated coding, and overcoding, can be used. The simplest application is to identify committees that come near to one or the other stereotype and show little variation. A similar exercise, also relatively easy, is to follow the career of a committee through the various stages until it reaches one or another point of stabilization.

But there is another type of investigation, of more interest in the study of strategies of persuasion. Committees, as we noticed, even those that are relatively stabilized in one or the other position—arrested, arena, or elite—are in varying degrees responsive to changes in their immediate context and may take on different styles. I recall, for example, a final examinations committee, which is a nonexpressive rational committee objectively applying absolute standards. But in fact this group worked like an arena committee (each representative determined that more justice—or at least no less justice—should be done to candidates in his school than to other people's candidates). Suddenly one day it became entirely elite and paternalistic when dealing with the case of a candidate who missed an exam because the police picked him up for peddling drugs. The case was discussed entirely on the premise that the least possible harm must be done to the good name of the institution.

I have used the word "response." This term suggests an outside agency, which, having set up the committee, monitors and regulates its performance. I have also suggested that there are tendencies brought about by such "objective" impersonal forces as the structural constraints that differentiate elite from arena committees. But changes do not occur unless someone intervenes. When a committee shifts temporarily or permanently from an arena to an elite mode, someone on the committee has taken an initiative to push it in that direction or to get others to acknowledge the change of position. Equally, when there is a movement from the opening stage to an arena committee and then to an elite committee, a number of initiatives has brought about these changes in gross style. It would be a wasted opportunity to treat these initiatives simply as random occurrences, like mutations in evolution. Rather they suggest two lines of inquiry: one into the distribution of power within the committee (which answers the "Why?" question) and the other about codes (which deals with "How?").

Where a committee settles on the line between immaturity and senility and how soon it gets there depend in part on the distribution of power among members of the committee (which may itself have been determined by an outside authority). The general rule is this: the more unevenly power is distributed, the swifter should be the movement out of imma-

turity. The extreme case is that of the successfully autocratic chairman who castrates his committee members by allowing them no effective part in the production of his
decisions. "At Cabinet Mr. Attlee's great objective was to stop
talk. There is evidence that two ministers simply talked themselves out of the Cabinet. Discussion was limited by the Prime
Minister's habit of putting questions in the negative" (Mackintosh, 1962:432). The more evenly power is distributed, then
ceteris paribus, the harder will it be to introduce the habit of
compromise needed in an arena committee, and the more
likely is a prolonged period of bickering immaturity.

The other set of questions is about the codes used. The three
codes fall into a pattern that resembles that of earlier chapters.
I have presented them genetically, so to speak: as stages in the
growth of committees. It might also seem that there is a case
for arguing that the criterion is one of expanding elaboration,
voyaging further and further into detail. But that would be
misleading, for it conceals the qualitative differences between,
on the one hand, the opening and terminal stages taken together and, on the other hand, the intermediate stage. At the
lower level simple coding and overcoding are opposed to each
other as crude to cultivated, rough to polished: the criterion is
stylistic and aesthetic. They unite and are together opposed to
sophisticated coding in a way that can be caught in several
phrases: the world of feeling to the world of action; displays of
emotion to restraint on emotion; expressive to instrumental;
intrinsic to extrinsic; and so forth.

We have left two related issues hanging and perhaps partly
camouflaged in the description of committee behavior. These
issues have arisen before and they will be taken up in later
chapters, but it will be convenient to mark them again here.

The first is that, willy-nilly, some of my sentences have
come out with a resonance of tacit approval for sophisticated
codes and contempt for the other two. The very words "simple," "crude," "*over*coded," "senile," "grunts," "snarls," and
so forth convey that suggestion quite clearly. But—this is the

second issue—the value judgment is not mine. It belongs in that "culture of persuasion" which I am describing and which I think is characteristic of formal organizations.

An important distinction in this culture is that between expressive and instrumental action. The simple meanings of these two terms are that the first vents emotions and feelings—lets off steam—and is to be comprehended initially in the context of the psychophysiological organism, while the second is designed to get things accomplished in the real world. Notice that the "real world" in this instance includes other people. Taking off from this fact, "expressive" in the culture of persuasion has to be set not only in a context of ideas about what is going on in the psychophysiological organism when emotion is displayed, but also in a context of how other people interpret and respond to such displays. In other words, expressive activity also has an instrumental significance: that of manipulating other people.

This makes even more inappropriate the implied disparagement of expressive activity in the comparisons made with instrumental action. We appear to have a problem between this and what was said at the end of an earlier chapter: play is not work. But play is not wasted. To be sure, there is an opportunity cost in the deployment of expression as against certain rational task-oriented activities. We have had examples and it is firmly part of the culture we are describing. But it is sometimes a necessary cost.

It is therefore appropriate that in the next two chapters we turn to a discussion of those persuasive devices that exist for getting people into the right frame of mind to do what you intend them to do. In the course of this discussion we also move from committees to a wider and more public arena.

CHAPTER 6

The Rhetoric of Assertion

We have already considered various manifestations of the human incapacity (or unwillingness) to use reason: postures used for sealing a position; the moral and divine versions of the self; the simple codes that characterize the childhood of committees and the oversophisticated codes that mark their senility. All, even the last, contain displays of emotion.

Emotion, however, is not displayed only in its raw form of bodily manifestations. Obviously it may also be conveyed— alone or in conjunction with actions—through words. That one has sealed oneself in a position, that the moral or the divine self is in operation, is a message delivered by means of what in Chapter 5 we called simple codes. If the wrong code is used, the message will not be understood. The nature of these codes requires further discussion; so does the meaning of "wrong." The latter problem will be considered in a later chapter.

We are looking in this chapter for those devices that allow one to make assertions, to close off questioning and doubt, and to exclude other people's assertions. This can, of course, be done in a practical way by force, or by manipulation, or by intimidation outside the arena of debate. John Byng, an admiral in the British navy, failed in 1756 to relieve a garrison beleaguered on the island of Minorca by the French. He was brought home, tried by court-martial, condemned to death, and shot on March 14, 1757, at Portsmouth. The victim had no choice but to "comply," and his compliance was not conditional on the prior acceptance of any message. (There is a message, of course, for others. As Voltaire remarked in *Candide*, "In this country it is thought well to kill an admiral from time to time to encourage the others.")

But we remain inside the arena of debate and our focus is on *rhetorical* devices that are directed to ensuring that only one side of the question gets a hearing. In the first part of the chapter, by means of examples, we show more fully what is meant by "assertion." This gives rise to a discussion of "fact" and "value"; then to a consideration of moral boundaries; and finally we describe various other devices—"ethos," the invocation of authority, the uses of fright, the focus on personalities, the significance of the vivid example, and lastly certain rhetorical tricks and figures of speech. All these allow the persuader to be assertive.

Let us begin with some examples, and search in them for the features of assertive rhetoric.

> Dreyfus is innocent. I swear it! I stake my life on it—my honour! At this solemn moment, in the presence of this tribunal, which is the representative of human justice: before you, gentlemen, who are the very incarnation of the country, before the whole of France, before the whole world, I swear that Dreyfus is innocent. By my forty years of work, by the authority that this toil may have given me, I swear that Dreyfus is innocent. By the name I have made for myself, by my works that have helped for the expansion of French literature, I swear that Dreyfus is innocent. May all that melt away, may my works perish, if Dreyfus be not innocent! He is innocent!   [Fox-Davies, 1913: vol. 2, p. 151]

That is Emile Zola speaking in 1898. Here is another man, Robert Emmet, executed in 1803 in Dublin:

> If the spirits of the illustrious dead participate in the concerns and cares of those who were dear to them in this transitory life, O, ever dear and venerated shade of my departed father! Look down with scrutiny upon the conduct of your suffering son, and

see if I have, even for a moment, deviated from those principles of morality and patriotism which it was your care to instil into my youthful mind, and for which I am now about to offer up my life. My lords, you are impatient for the sacrifice. The blood which you seek is not congealed by the artificial terrors which surround your victim—it circulates warmly and unruffled through the channels which God created for noble purposes, but which you are now bent to destroy for purposes so grievous that they cry to heaven. Be yet patient! I have but a few more words to say—I am going to my cold and silent grave—my lamp of life is nearly extinguished—my race is run—the grave opens to receive me and I sink into its bosom.   [Fox-Davies, 1913: vol. 2, p. 261]

Addressing the closing session of the National Council of the United National Independence Party in 1972, Dr. Kaunda said this:

Comrades, in that cold winter of 1961 we committed ourselves to the toal eradication of imperialism and colonialism from the Motherland. Because of that commitment, the revolution was successful. The call today is equally loud and clear. We need men and women who will commit themselves to this second stage of the revolution—the revolution of implementing Humanism in Zambia as this is the cause of the common man.

The hour calls for patriots; discipline; dedication and selflessness. Before this conference is over, as Captain of this ship I want to see how many true soldiers of the revolution I have. This is a serious challenge but given the right leaders and followers alike, victory is assured.

May God bless you all.

Zola, Emmet, and Kaunda *demand* assent. They are peremptory; they assert truths that they present as inescapable, defying argument, so essentially true that they are beyond the need for corroborating evidence. They are examples of assertive rhetoric, that flowering grafted like a rose on the briar root of emotion.

The same style can also be found in less dramatic situations. A committee new to its task will, as was suggested in Chapter

5, spend some time while the members cast around setting individual identities for themselves and establishing a collective
identity for the committee. This stage of committee history
does not find its way into the records, and I can find no published material suitable for quotation, but it is simple to invent
an example that is true to experience. Suppose a university
where a search committee has been set up to make the first and
senior appointment in a new subject—let us say, communications. That discipline runs the range from the hardest of hard
science at one corner to a technical but (so it seems to some)
rather subuniversity level at another corner (how to operate a
movie camera) to a most untechnical and anything but hard
corner where people write incoherent books about incoherent
pop stars. I can image speeches like the following being made
by the members while the committee is still finding its feet.

> *Chairman:* We have a difficult task but not an impossible one.
> The subject takes many different forms and we must decide be-
> tween them in making this first and crucial appointment. I think
> we should first look at the different branches in order to see how
> well they might fit in with existing areas of strength in the uni-
> versity. Then we should look for the best person in that field.

> *Member A:* By far the most important matter in this appoint-
> ment is academic integrity. I happen to know that the chancellor
> has rather fixed ideas on this subject, and unless we show our-
> selves to be strong and resolute, our advice will count for noth-
> ing. We must not allow ourselves to be dictated to by the
> administration.

> *Member B:* The priority, without a doubt, is to appoint someone
> who has a concern for teaching, and who can attract students. It
> would be a cardinal error to appoint someone whose first con-
> cern is with research, for in these days of falling enrollments
> nothing is more important than keeping up student numbers.

> *Member C:* There are some very good Marxist scholars in this
> field, and in that branch of scholarship this campus is rather
> weak. This is our chance to restore the balance that has been
> lacking for almost two decades.

One could invent other points of view, but these are enough to set the style. *There is no dialogue.* Each speaker asserts his priority in language emphatic enough to demand attention, but pays no attention to what others have said, neither looking for allies nor squaring off against opponents. The difference of principle between the chairman (support existing strength) and Member *C* (fill a gap) is not remarked upon by the latter, nor does anyone attempt to court Member *A,* who, being as yet without an expressed preference, is everyone's potential ally. Discussion, which would take account of varied points of view, is absent, and the members deal only in simple assertions of what each offers as *the* basic value from which to begin reasoning. They are not saying, "Take it or leave it!" but something even more emphatic: "Take it because it is inconceivable that you will not take it!"

The same peremptory quality is to be found in manifestos, as in this preamble to the A. F. of L. constitution, issued in 1886 (Fried, 1974:153):

> Whereas, a struggle is going on in all the nations of the civilized world, between the oppressors and the oppressed of all countries, a struggle between the capitalist and the laborer, which grows in intensity from year to year, and will work disastrous results for the toiling millions, if they are not combined for mutual protection and benefit.
>
> It therefore behooves the representatives of the Trades and Labor Unions of America, in Convention assembled, to adopt such measures and disseminate such principles among the mechanics and laborers of our country as will permanently unite them, to secure recognition of the rights to which they are justly entitled.
>
> We therefore declare ourselves in favor of the formation of a thorough Federation, embracing every Trade and Labor Organization in America.

This is the polished language of a formal document, the bulk of it contained in one grand sentence. In this way it differs from the more spontaneous utterances that we imagined for the members of the search committee. But it is also simple, in the same way that they are. It briefly defines the way the relevant universe is: ". . . a struggle is going on in all the nations of the civilized world . . . " (compare "I happen to know that the chancellor . . ." or ". . . in these days of falling enrollments . . ."); assumes that this context will be accepted as the relevant one; and then goes on to say what action should be taken. Once again there is no overt anticipation of dialogue, for those who are not at once convinced are outside the pale: the message is not for them, so much as for the true believers.

When there is an attack on the citadel of true belief, the same kind of oratory is provoked. Samuel Gompers, the first president of the American Federation of Labor (elected at the same meeting in 1886), although socialist in outlook, believed that the trade-union movement could only lose by allying and subordinating itself to a political party or a political ideology. Here he is, beating back an attack (Fried, 1974:172–173):

> . . . I want to tell you, Socialists, that I have studied your philosophy; read your works upon economics, and not the meanest of them; studied your standard works, both in English and German—have not only read, but studied them. I have heard your orators and watched the work of your movement the world over. I have kept close watch upon your doctrines for thirty years; have been closely associated with many of you, and know how you think and what you propose. I know, too, what you have up your sleeve. And I want to say that I am entirely at variance with your philosophy. I declare to you, I am not only at variance with your doctrines, but with your philosophy. Economically, you are unsound; socially, you are wrong; industrially, you are an impossibility.

Here, in addition to the argument from authority to which we will come later, there is the same basic assertion that rests on nothing but itself: you are wrong because you are wrong.

Here is another example, delivered in defense of the open shop by Alfred P. Sloan, president of General Motors, during a sit-down strike in 1937 (Fried, 1974:240):

You are being told you had better join a union. You are being told that to bargain collectively you must be a member of a labor organization. You are being told that the great automotive industry is to be run as a closed shop. You are being told that if you do not join now it will be impossible for you to work in any automobile plant when the union wins, unless you pay. In other words, you will be without a job, therefore you must sign up, pay dues; or else.

I want to say to you most frankly, that this is positively not so. Do not be misled. Have no fear that any union or any labor dictator will dominate the plants of General Motors Corporation. No General Motors worker need join any organization to get a job or keep a job. . . .

In these two examples, Gompers and Sloan, the style is different (in ways to be discussed later) from that of the A. F. of L. preamble, but no less grandiloquent. Nevertheless it remains simple in the sense that each speaker conveys a single imperative value, peremptorily delivered as a truth that validates itself.

What I have said so far is simple enough: the language proper for marking a value as authoritative—as demanding accord—is that of assertive rhetoric. This rhetoric is therefore used when no such value has as yet been established, as in the case of a committee new to its task; when such a value is being asserted as a guide for action and deliberation, our example being a manifesto; and when the speaker feels compelled to defend what he claims to be an established imperative value that has nevertheless been brought into question.

In all the examples the speakers (in Sloan's case the medium was a letter sent to all the employees of General Motors) assert that there can be no question about where truth lies; but they do so in different ways. Each imaginary member of the newly formed committee states his own point of view, without reference to what others have said or may say, although they cannot help being aware that other members may not agree with them. When Kaunda speaks of the revolution of humanism to follow the revolution that eradicated colonialism and imperialism, he calls for sacrifice and therefore implies difficulties and hints that not everyone will be found worthy on the occasion:

"Before this conference is over, as Captain of this ship I want to see how many true soldiers of the revolution I have." But he does not leave room for the opinion that humanism may not be the right course, still less for the idea that imperialism and colonialism may not yet have been eradicated. Elsewhere in the speech he has dealt with the opposition, the members of which it seems were distressed not so much with the doctrine of humanism but because it went along with the establishment of a "One Party Democracy" and their own political demise: "Government will take tough measures against troublemakers. . . . This is a statement of fact and not imagination. . . . If you are underground you are being warned, whatever you are, that you will be crushed immediately you rear your ugly head in an attempt to use violence. . . ." That and similar things having been said, by the time he came to his peroration Dr. Kaunda was able to push opposing views out of sight and speak as if his views commanded universal assent.

In two other cases, the speeches by Zola and Robert Emmet, opposing views clearly have a presence (indeed, they were dominant, since both Dreyfus and Emmet were already convicted) but a presence only in the form of their negation; and the denial is total and unqualified. Truth, it seems, is to be found all on one side: there is another point of view, but it is wrong.

The later examples show a similar pattern. The "Whereas" clause of the constitution of the American Federation of Labor—"Whereas a struggle is going on in all the nations of the civilized world, between the oppressors and the oppressed of all countries . . ."—is not phrased so as to invite discussion and it does not recognize the possibility of other opinions. Gompers blasting away at the Socialists—"Economically, you are unsound; socially, you are wrong; industrially, you are an impossibility"—and Alfred Sloan categorically denying the possibility of a closed shop at General Motors—"I want to say to you most frankly, that this is positively not so"—are compelled by events to recognize that others hold contrary opinions, just as were Zola and Emmet, but they assert that these opinions are totally wrong.

Thus we have a scale with three points marked upon it. At one end is the orator (to be considered in Chapter 7) who not only admits that there is more than one legitimate point of view but even that his own may not turn out to be the correct one. At the center of the scale are those who acknowledge divergence of opinion, but dismiss out of hand all opinions except their own. At the other extreme are those who, like Kaunda in his peroration or like the writer of the A. F. of L. constitution, although knowing that other points of view must exist, speak as if they do not and as if there is one universal truth that everyone must instantly recognize. The range between this end of the scale and the center marks hortatory or assertive rhetoric, by the use of which the speaker intends to eliminate all opinions that diverge from his own. He is not promoting a discussion and in that way searching for truth: the "truth" is known already and the orator's task is to see that it should command assent.

This task can be described in two ways: first, by a distinction between fact and value; second, by a distinction between ranges of audience. These distinctions will turn out to be two ways of looking at the one set of activities.

A "fact" is supposed to be an assertion that no sensible person wants to deny (Perelman and Olbrechts-Tyteca, 1971: 65–70). If someone does deny a fact, then either he has not understood or he is not a sensible person, out of his mind, and therefore excluded from consideration and therefore not in a position to assail the fact. A "fact" is supposed to be "objective" in the sense either that every experience confirms it ("What I say to you is a fact no less true than the fact that water always flows downhill") or that its denial makes nonsense ("If you doubt this, then you must doubt that two and two make four"). Here is an example, Joseph Chamberlain speaking in 1897 on the subject of patriotism:

> . . . *can any impartial mind retain a doubt* that the pressure of the European and civilized races on the more backward inhabitants of other continents has on the whole made for peace and civili-

zation and the happiness of the world? But for this the vast territories of the United States and Canada might have been left to a
few hundred thousand of Indian braves, inhuman in their cus-
toms, stagnant in civilization, and constantly engaged in inter-
tribal warfare. India would have remained the sport of contending factions, the prey to anarchy, and the constant scene of
cruelty and of tyranny; while Africa, depopulated by unspeakable barbarities and surrendered to the worst forms of slavery
and fetishism, would have pined in vain for a deliverer. *It is no
exaggeration to say* that in one single year of such conditions more
lives would have been taken and more cruelties enacted than in
all the wars that have ever been undertaken by civilized nations
in furthering their work of development and colonization.
[Fox-Davies, 1913: vol. 1, p. 250; italics added]

One kind of fact ("Two and two make four") is entirely a
matter of convention and its certainty rests on an agreement to
use words in such a way that they are given a precise meaning.
It is only within the confines of such artificial languages that
conclusive demonstration of truth is possible. Moreover, the
"facts" of an empirical nature (that water does not flow uphill)
also rest on similar conventions not only about language but
also about the conditions under which a proper experiment
may be conducted. The man who uses a pump to make water
flow uphill or points to rising damp in the walls of his house
has gone outside the paradigms that permit those truths to be
valid. He leaves them intact because he is not displaying that
"impartial mind" of which Chamberlain speaks.

These observations on the nature of "fact" and "truth," although now part of a popular philosophy, seem to leave unas-
sailed the rhetorical status of the word "fact." In rhetoric, to
proclaim something a fact is to tell the audience that they have
no alternative other than to give their assent, on pain of being
excluded as crazy people. It is something of a paradox that in
the very arena where the scientific certainty suggested by the
word "fact" is least appropriate (because the argument is about
values or about the paradigms that themselves permit the creation of facts), that word should have the status of a trump
card, stilling all further discussion. Here is Harold Cox, talking in 1909:

Take, for example, a sewing machine. Would that property be appropriated? It is a means of production, and the State is to control all means of production. Is a man to be allowed to have a spade for his garden? . . . Is he, indeed to be allowed to have a private garden at all? . . . You cannot follow out the Socialist creed *without arriving at this fact;* that under Socialism, according to the doctrines laid down, the State will become owner of everything. [Fox-Davies, 1913: vol. 1, p. 219; italics added]

The popular word complementing "fact" is "opinion," that which some people may but not everyone must hold. Values have the same standing. Whereas facts are held to be there like rocks in the shifting seas of experience, immutable and inescapable, values and opinions may change in the light of changing circumstances. Values are discarded when no longer of use or when one finds a better value, which means that values are held in an order of preference and can be traded off against one another. While a fact or a truth is supposed to be the same for everyone, for every normal person or "impartial mind," values and opinions command no such universal allegiance. We grudgingly recognize this, when faced with a particularly bizarre notion, by saying, "You are entitled to your opinion!" or "I suppose you have the right to your own opinion!"

Assertive rhetoric is intended—one of its tasks—to confer on values the status of facts. This does not necessarily mean that they will be presented as facts, although this is an extremely common rhetorical device—"By the very nature of things . . ." frames as if it were a fact the opinion that is about to be uttered.

Values may also be presented as moral or divine imperatives. Here is the peroration of Lincoln's 1865 inaugural address: "With malice towards none, with charity for all, with firmness in the right as God gives us to see the right . . ." (Fox-Davies, 1913: vol. 3, p. 257). Such moral imperatives have the same status as facts (without being presented as if they were facts) to the extent that the speaker either has located or can by his rhetoric implant supporting values that *to that audience* seem beyond doubt and questioning to be self-evident truths. That is the import of "God" in Lincoln's address. Here is Walter Reuther speaking in 1957 on the subject of racketeers in trade unions:

> I think we can all agree that the overwhelming majority of the leadership of the American movement is composed of decent, honest, dedicated people who have made a great contribution involving great personal sacrifice, helping to build a decent American labor movement. . . . We happen to believe that leadership in the American movement is a sacred trust. We happen to believe that this is no place for people who want to use the labor movement to make a fast buck. . . .   [Fried, 1974:291]

The repeated phrase "We happen to believe . . ." frames what is to follow as a self-evident undeniable value, beyond doubt and beyond questioning. It does so partly through the mild irony of the word "happen," which means "Some of you will no doubt be astonished to hear . . ."

What follows in Reuther's address is asserted as intrinsically valued, self-evident, and beyond contradiction, but it is not offered as if it were a fact to the truth of which everyone must agree. Indeed, something quite different is being done. The "we" does not mean "everyone"; on the contrary, it means "*we*" contrasted with those who are nonbelievers. Assertive rhetoric seems to require the presence, whether openly or implicitly, of the infidel: the person to hate or despise or ridicule, the person who, if not hated, is at least on the outside, the person whose difference from us makes clear the nature of our identity, who we are and for what we stand. It is rhetoric on the level of the moral self. Let us pursue this idea by looking again at Walter Reuther's words.

The racketeers themselves are clearly excluded from the congregation of believers embraced in Reuther's use of "we"; and there may be others at the lunatic margins of free enterprise whose existence Reuther himself fleetingly notices in this sentence: "If you want to make a fast buck, that may be your business, but you better make it outside of the American labor movement . . ." (Fried, 1974:291). In other words, whether or not people should live in the way that is implied by the phrase "make a fast buck" is not something about which the speaker wants to lay down a moral imperative that is good for all time and all people and in all places: it is sufficient that they stay away from the labor movement. This is not simply that man-of-the-world indifference to certain kinds of wrongdoing which, especially in America, masquerades as tough-minded realism; it is also a boundary-drawing device that separates believers from nonbelievers, and that most emphatically states that the value proclaimed and asserted is not honesty in general but the American labor movement itself

In this localization or compartmentalization of the moral world into true believers and those outside, we have a characteristic of assertive rhetoric which complements its insistence that truth is all on one side. Here is something that is supposed to be absent from the common-sense image of the world of science: an insistence that the listeners or readers make their choice (although it is "the only possible choice") and then stand up to be counted as the congregation of true believers, for only by their doing so is the "truth" validated. "Truth" is not a property of any objective "real world" but turns out to be "what right-thinking people believe." Assertive rhetoric is a moral rhetoric. It is a rhetoric of belonging, of including in the congregation those who choose to believe and excluding the rest either by ignoring them, ridiculing them, or making them the objects of anger and contempt. Divergent opinions are eliminated in this form of rhetoric not through discussion but by a simple elimination of the nonbelievers: an insistence that any belief that departs from the orthodox need not be taken into account.

In short, assertive rhetoric inescapably must proceed by begging the question: by simple assertion of the correctness of one answer to the question at issue. There is no other way of arguing about intrinsic values, for these are ends in themselves. The speaker asserts a truth by identifying the true believers who "happen" to be those who believe that truth. Accordingly, it is inappropriate to ask whether an argument advanced in this form of rhetoric is valid or invalid, and to test it by the rules of logic. The proper question to ask about as-

sertive rhetoric concerns effectiveness. It is intended to provoke attitudes of approval or disapproval, to compel assent, to
bring people over to one's own side. For doing so what rhetorical devices are thought to be effective?

One is, as might be expected, a presentation of the moral
self. In 1909 David Lloyd George, then chancellor of the exchequer, went to Limehouse and delivered a speech justifying
his budget. If one can judge from the frequency of the reported [cheers] and [laughter] and [loud and long-continued
cheering], the speech was well received by the 4,000 members
of the audience.

Toward the close of this oration, Lloyd George said:

> Why should I put burdens on the people? I am one of the chil-
> dren of the people. [Loud and prolonged cheering, and a voice,
> "Bravo David! stand by the people and they will stand by
> you."] I was brought up amongst them. I know their trials; and
> God forbid that I should add one grain of trouble to the anxiety
> which they bear with such patience and fortitude.   [Fox-Da-
> vies, 1913: vol. 2, p. 49]

Such a performance was called by Aristotle "ethos," and in
it the speaker establishes his good name, his ties with the audience, so that his own qualities will lend authority to what he
has to say. If Lloyd George is born of the people, he can be expected to sympathize with them and understand them.

A second characteristic of assertive rhetoric is the invocation
of authority in the form of a cause or a doctrine, or one's own
knowledge and wisdom. This is the speaker as divine self,
"His" mouthpiece, so to speak.

The month following Lloyd George's Limehouse speech,
the Marquess of Lansdowne had this to say:

> The Chairman referred to the speech delivered a few days ago
> by the Chancellor of the Exchequer at Limehouse. [Hisses.]
> What was the burden of that speech, and of other speeches de-
> livered by members of His Majesty's government? It is this:
> "We recommend this Budget to you because it is a poor man's

Budget." [Oh! oh!] May I venture to advise you to look with a certain amount of suspicion upon proposals which are based upon these appeals to class prejudice? [Cheers] [Fox–Davies, 1913: vol. 3, p. 138]

and later:

With regard to the tone of Mr. Lloyd George's Limehouse speech, I would like to be allowed to say that I wonder, if the ghosts of our great Chancellors of the Exchequer are able to follow what is said and done by their successor, I wonder what Mr. Gladstone or Sir Robert Peel would say, if they were with us now, to the kind of speech to which the Limehouse audience listened? [Fox–Davies, 1913: vol. 3, p. 140]

The Marquess of Lansdowne neutralizes the "man of the people" theme by calling it an "appeal to class prejudice" (the negative side of the moral self and a denial of the civic self) and counters by invoking authorities on his side: in this case the conjectured condemnatory ghosts of Gladstone and Peel.

We have other examples. Look back at Samuel Gompers describing how well qualified he is to have an opinion on socialism, having "not only read, but studied" the standard works, and kept a watch over the Socialists for thirty years and even knowing "what you have up your sleeve." If Gompers has studied a doctrine for thirty years, the listener is invited to assume, he must have something wise to say about it.

Another example, that of Zola, is somewhat wilder:

By my forty years of work, by the authority that this toil may have given me, I swear that Dreyfus is innocent. By the name I have made for myself, by my works that have helped for the expansion of French literature, I swear that Dreyfus is innocent. May all that melt away, may my works perish, if Dreyfus be not innocent. [Fox–Davies, 1913: vol. 2, p. 151]

One might fairly ask what literary skill and reputation have to do with the weight of a man's word on the innocence of Dreyfus, and it seems as if Zola himself senses this difficulty, for he

neatly turns the figure from one of authority to one of sacrifice: "May all that melt away, may my work perish . . ."
Dreyfus must be innocent, we are invited to think, if Zola
would stake his great reputation on it. It is, so to speak, the argument *in personam* used positively: one buttresses a value and
recommends it by recommending the people who hold that
value.

On other occasions the values—the orator hopes—are already accepted and he presents himself in association or even
identification with those values. There is a negative example
on the occasion when Lansdowne invokes class prejudice. The
values invoked may be those of class, of religion, of family
life, of free enterprise, and a thousand others. Patriotism, at
some times and in some places, seems likely to do the trick.
Here is Enoch Powell, speaking in Parliament to a proposal
(among other measures) to drop the word "British" from the
"British Commonwealth of Nations." He wound up his
speech with this: "It is because I believe that, in a sense, for a
brief moment, I represent and speak for an indispensable element in the British Constitution and in British life that I have
spoken. And, I pray, not entirely in vain" (Smithies and Fiddick, 1969:132). The same device is apparent, I think, in that
much-publicized rhetorical sleight of hand performed by President Kennedy in Berlin: "I take pride in the word: Ich bin ein
Berliner!"

A third characteristic of assertive rhetoric is the invocation
of danger. Here is a straightforward example, from the closing
section of a speech made by the same Enoch Powell in Birmingham in 1968.

> As I look ahead, I am filled with foreboding. Like the Roman, I
> seem to see "the River Tiber foaming with much blood". That
> tragic and intractable phenomenon, which we watch with hor-
> ror on the other side of the Atlantic but which there is inter-
> woven with the history and existence of the States itself, is
> coming upon us here by our own volition and our own neglect.
> [Smithies and Fiddick, 1969:43]

To disregard the warning is to invite calamity. Any doubt, any division, can only be a comfort and encouragement to a common enemy and will enable that enemy to prevail.

Very often in assertive rhetoric, as in the Birmingham speech and throughout that phase of Powell's career when he campaigned to keep colored immigrants out of Britain, there is a scapegoat, a person or a category of persons against whom emotions can be aroused. Hitler used the Jews in the same way.

Notice that ridicule will not serve the same end: it diminishes the threat. Nor must the invocation of danger be so vivid and so strong that it "Sadsacks" the listeners and brings about a loss of nerve.

From the above one might anticipate a fourth characteristic of assertive rhetoric. It tends to focus on persons rather than just on deeds. Assertive rhetoric is judgmental: a moral rhetoric in this second sense of morality. Acts and deeds are morally neutral; praise or condemnation attaches to the actor and his intentions inflect the praise or blame no less than what he has done. Or, to put it another way, his acts have no meaning until they are placed in a wider context, including the context of his intentions. Here is another section of Robert Emmet's speech:

> I appeal to the immaculate God—I swear by the throne of Heaven, before which I must shortly appear—by the blood of the murdered patriots who have gone before me—that my conduct has been, through all this peril, and through all my purposes, governed only by the conviction which I have uttered, and by no other view than that of the emancipation of my country from the super-inhuman oppression under which she has so long and too patiently travailed; and I confidently hope that, wild and chimerical as it may appear, there is still union and strength in Ireland to accomplish this noblest of enterprises. [Fox-Davies, 1913: vol. 2, p. 256]

Sometimes—for reasons that we will come to in a moment—a speech will contain a long recital of things that have been done, but this serves only to encourage the audience to make a judgment on the character of those who did the deeds. The Limehouse speech is full of anecdotes about rapacious landlords. ("What makes matters worse," said Lord Lansdowne, "is that not only the taste of the speech was questionable, but that apparently the facts were more questionable still.") Nevertheless, Lloyd George was not content to allow his facts to speak for themselves.

> Who is the landlord? The landlord is a gentlemen—I have not a word to say about him in his personal capacity—who does not earn his wealth. He does not even take the trouble to receive his wealth. [Laughter] He has a host of agents and clerks that receive for him. He does not even take the trouble to spend his wealth. He has a host of people around him to do the actual spending for him. He never sees it until he comes to enjoy it. His sole function, his chief pride is stately consumption of wealth produced by others. [Fox-Davies, 1913: vol. 2, pp. 43–44]

A fifth characteristic of assertive rhetoric is its use of *models* (that is, vivid examples) to lend immediacy to the discourse: they make it concrete and easy to comprehend. Here is an example—one of many—from the Limehouse speech:

> I know districts in Wales where a little bit of barren rock where you could not feed a goat, where the landlord could not get a shilling an acre of agricultural rent, is let to quarrymen for the purpose of building houses, where 30 shillings or 2 pounds a house is charged for ground-rent. The quarryman builds his house. He goes to a building society to borrow money. He pays out his hard-earned weekly wage to the building society for ten, twenty, or thirty years. By the time he becomes an old man he has cleared off the mortgage, and more than half the value of the house has passed into the pockets of the landlord. [Fox-Davies, 1913: vol. 2, pp. 44–45]

You may recall Chamberlain's argument for the benefits of empire: "But for this the vast territories of the United States and Canada might have been left to a few hundred thousand of

Indian braves . . . India would have been left the sport of contending factions, . . . while Africa, depopulated by unspeakable barbarities . . ." These are not to be thought of as examples offered in the spirit of "Let us see how far my generalizations hold up." They are in no sense a test, despite the appearance of offering corroboration; rather they function like symbols, making vivid, immediate, comprehensible, and appealing what otherwise would remain a dry, distant, and unemphatic generalization.

The presentation of a moral self, invocation of authority and of imminent peril, the attribution of praise or blame by focusing on persons and the use of models are some devices by which the orator may inhibit questioning and discussion and stimulate faith in and emotional attachment to his favored values and opinions.

At another level of analysis an immense array of rhetorical figures serve as conventional indicators of heightened (or lowered) emotion in the speaker and are intended to fire (or dampen) the passions of the audience.

They do so in a complex way. In some instances the connections seem plausible enough. Such a device as apostrophe (turning aside to address an absent person " . . . O, ever dear and venerated shade of my departed father!") seems certainly directed at arousing emotion. So too is alliteration. So also is hyperbole. Likewise persiflage, bathos, and meiosis point the other way; they are cooling devices looking for the laugh that will lighten the gravity of fear or anger. Others—metaphor, simile, and the like—seem to be neutral, available for use in either direction. But in practice I think that most of these devices are neutral, depending on the frame that is set around them. By themselves, they may make assertions, make the hearers into true believers, and banish doubt; but frame them in irony and dispositions are loosened from the bonds of true belief.

I do not have the skills or the space to discuss one very large feature: sentence construction. (Still less can this be the place to consider the structure and sequencing of whole speeches.) But the examples do invite the following observations.

Of all the speeches quoted, the most extravagant seem to me to be those of Zola and of Robert Emmet. Reduction to print, of course, removes the ambience that might serve to make these orations seem more natural, less contrived. We must also allow for translation in the literal sense in the case of Zola and in a wider sense that the passage of more than a century and a half requires in Robert Emmet's case. Let us examine the last speech more closely to see what it will indicate about assertive rhetoric.

The feature that to me seems to separate this speech from all the rest (let us leave out of account the formula-bound preamble to the A. F. of L. constitution) is that it has the air of being polished. So does the excerpt from Chamberlain's speech, which has four quite long, intricately constructed sentences, which most successfully carry the reader along, and presumably also carried along the audience. But in Chamberlain's case one does not get the sense—at least to modern ears—that the form in some way betrays the content; this is the impression that Emmet's speech gives me. The form betrays the content—and of all the speakers Emmet was closest to a most emotively powerful theme, his own death—because we feel that no man who was sincerely moved could have spoken with such artifice. Of course they all speak with artifice, but, at the present day, the artifices that Emmet uses suggest *acting* emotion rather than *feeling* it.

What is this artifice? It is not the apostrophe—the turning away to address the shade of his father—or the melodrama of the phrasing, or the slightly unfortunate juxtaposition of not very compatible metaphors in the closing sentences (lamps, running races, cold graves into the bosom of which he is about to sink). It is the complex hypotaxis that gives shape to the whole excerpt, with the exception of those staccato closing phrases. It is the intricate arrangement of balanced subordinate clauses that serve well enough for the quasi-expository style of Chamberlain, who, after all, is purporting to be narrating facts rather than expressing feelings. Emmet's content requires a form that suggests emotion, an arrangement of coordinate rather than subordinate clauses and sentences. This arrangement is clearly illustrated in Zola's passionate outcry and in the contemptuous anger of Gompers, and in the excited indignation of the Sloan letter: "You are being told . . . You are being told . . . You are being told . . . I want to say to you most frankly, that this is positively not so."

But, it might be said, when it comes to a situation that calls for emotion, a sit-down strike is not the same as being hanged for treason. What do they have in common? What the speakers have in common—and this applies to any use of assertive rhetoric—is the requirement to appear to have sincerity. Rhetoric has the peculiar capacity to destroy itself as soon as it is detected as rhetoric. That is why skilled orators apologize for their inability to speak well, and maliciously pay tribute to the eloquence of their rivals. "I am no orator, as Brutus is . . ." A sentence construction that suggests spontaneity, even mild incoherence, an absence of calculation of the effect of one's words, also suggests that the words come from the heart; they are not "just rhetoric." In assertive rhetoric thought must be seen to take second place to feeling.

> I am no orator, as Brutus is,
> But (as you know me all) a plain blunt man
> That love my friends . . .
> For I have neither wit, nor words, nor worth,
> Action, nor utterance, nor the power of speech
> To stir men's blood. I only speak right on.
> I tell you that which you yourselves do know,
> Show you sweet Caesar's wounds, poor poor dumb mouths,
> And bid them speak for me. But were I Brutus,
> And Brutus Antony, there were an Antony
> Would ruffle up your spirits, and put a tongue
> In every wound of Caesar that should move
> The stones of Rome to rise and mutiny.

CHAPTER 7

The Rhetoric of Compromise

One kind of assertive rhetoric centers on an adversary but does not address him. Typically, this is likely to be a message to the faithful, rousing their anger, boosting their courage, or, through ridicule of the adversary, stilling their fears. Here is Patrick A. Collins, speaking in 1899 at a banquet of the Charitable Irish Society in Boston:

> Seven hundred years after St. Patrick went into Ireland to do God's enduring work, an English King sent missionaries there to do another kind of work—and that work is not yet done. It never will be done; it simply never can be done while England is England and Ireland stands.
>
> For these last 700 years the ghastly story runs of England's attempt to force her rule, and for more than two centuries to force her newly-acquired creed, upon a people who loved their religion with all the fervour taught by their own apostle, and who loved liberty with a passion never yet comprehended by a tyrant. The eye sweeps the island in those dreadful times, and sees nothing but flame and blood, desolation, ruin and misery. It rests upon the statute book, and reads nothing but infamy. [Fox-Davies, 1913: vol. 1, 212]

These remarks anticipate applause, not a rejoinder. Indeed, at such a gathering, there would have be no one present to make a negative reply.

The position Patrick Collins takes is a sealed one; he displays a moral self, if not a divine self; the code is simple, and the rhetoric is that of assertion.

Now look at something different. Here is Mr. Justice Grantham delivering the peroration of a speech to the grand jury at Liverpool in 1911, replying to allegations that he had been politically partisan:

> Gentlemen, I have spoken to you not as a body of men of all political principles, but as to men of honour, whatever your principles may be, and I am sure none of you, however strongly you may differ from the views I used to advocate, will begrudge me this opportunity of clearing my character from these false charges. I have been amongst you off and on twenty-five years, doing my judicial work to the best of the ability that God has given me, and I was anxious to make this statement before those who would know something, at any rate, of what my judicial work has been.   [Fox-Davies, 1913: vol. 2, p. 274]

The speech is not without eloquence, nor does Grantham disdain a familiar device in assertive rhetoric: commending himself to his audience by complimenting them—"men of honour." But the ambience is quite different from that in which Collins spoke, and so, therefore, is the purport of the address. It is asking for an open mind. It anticipates deliberation, the weighing of evidence, and a reasoned outcome to the debate. The grand jury, having listened to the charges, now will hear Grantham's defense. The prosecutor and Grantham, the defender, stand as adversaries, and the occasion is so structured that, if justice is done, two sides of the question will be heard.

Grantham's implicit appeal for open minds and his anxiety to speak in front of those who are familiar with his judicial record suggest that the prosecutor had in some way occluded the merits of this record and, second, that his address had been designed to close off doubts in the minds of the jurors and to seal them in a position hostile to Grantham (position 1 on Diagram 1 in Chapter 3). The "men of honour" phrase indicates that fair-minded jurors avoid premature commitment. They also make up their minds on the evidence and are not biased by whatever political principles they hold outside the courtroom. In short, one can look at any judicial process—at least in one of its phases—as an attempt by the advocates to unseal whatever position their opponents have urged and substitute for it their own.

This process, of course, need not always take place before an arbiter or a judge. It may go on directly between two adversaries, each one taking a sealed position and endeavoring to undo the other's sealed position. This chapter examines some of the rhetorical devices available for doing that and looks for indicators in the code used that both sides are being loosened from their sealed positions and are preparing to bargain away their principles in return for the chance to further some transcendent interest. They come to recognize that if both hold out, both will lose.

This chapter is divided into three main sections. The first describes the ways in which one may attempt to establish guiding principles in situations of disagreement. The methods range from pure assertion of one's own position in an attempt to intimidate those who disagree, through the invocation of a powerful philosophy, the evocation of fear or compassion, appeals to solidarity, appeals for an "open mind," to emotive devices for evoking a civil self and institutional loyalties or a tactical self that has regard for its own interests. The costs of compromise are discussed and ambiguity is shown to be useful.

The second part addresses the question of what can be done, once some accord on general principles has been reached, to maneuver the other party into agreeing on the *specific* premises from which to reason in this particular case. The devices used are mainly pseudo-cerebral: the pretended but not the actual use of reason. We ask why these forms are preferred, when possible, to the use of assertion, and we isolate the essential task of such "reasoning," which is to make the appropriate connection between a course of action and either antecedent circumstances or likely consequences or both.

The third section is an extended description and analysis of an episode in the debates over a draft constitution which took place in the Indian Constituent Assembly in the years immediately following that country's independence. The episode concerns a compromise that was reached in a controversy about the part to be played by India's villages in the task of government. It shows how the legislators went about the task of finding a compromise and why they did so.

We turn now to considering tactics available for maneuvering agreement over general principles.

The first device is a frontal attack on the other person's premises or values. In our discussion of the rhetoric of assertion we have generally looked at those speeches that directly and positively advocate a point of view. Occasionally the negative tone dominates, as when Gompers berates the Socialists. There are, in fact, costs involved in doing this: to attack a person or a point of view is to expend resources, to give him or it prominence, and to recognize him as an adversary strong enough to be worthy of attack.

But if one has attempted to make one's own views prevail by parading their virtues, and has failed to shift the other person into favoring them, then the next step could be to shift him out of the citadel of his own values by administering some kind of psychological shock.

This is still the rhetoric of assertion, but it is directed toward conversion. It is addressed to an unbeliever. The victim is, so to speak, to be driven out onto the open ground and made to run for cover in your citadel. There is no appeal to the faculty of reason, simply a gross attempt—usually through arousing fear—to change his attitude. Enoch Powell's "River Tiber flowing with much blood" is an example. Here is part of a famous speech by John Bright, delivered in the House of Commons in 1855, during the Crimean War:

> The Angel of Death has been abroad throughout the land; you may almost hear the beating of his wings. There is no-one to sprinkle with blood the lintel and the sideposts of our doors, that he may spare and pass on; but he calls at the castle of the noble, the mansion of the wealthy, equally as at the cottage of the humble, and it is on behalf of all these classes that I make this solemn appeal.   [Fox-Davies, 1913: vol. 5, p. 58]

The appeal may play upon fear or shame or pity and compassion and is always raw in emotional display. But it does contain one small shred of reckoning: pointing to the values or goals or policies of the opponent, it says, "If you hold such values and put them into practice, these will be the consequences! Can you bear that?"

The shock appeals attempt conversion: as they stand, without further arguments, they are intended to shake the victim out of his own values, and implicitly there is nowhere for him to go but to your side. Another way is to point the discourse away from the clash of values toward a sentiment that—it is hoped—both parties can accept, and that can also be shown to transcend the erstwhile apparently dominant values.

Since we are beginning our discussion of ways to loosen sealed positions at the emotive rather than the cerebral end of the range of devices, it is important to realize that this hoped-for common and dominant value is unlikely to be established by rational argument alone, because there is a tendency for the transcending values to be no less available to one side than to the other. I may buttress my argument that the money should go to my department to recruit the newest young genius who has emerged in my subject on the grounds that the well-being of the institution is the supreme interest and that this is served by the presence of young persons of talent. If my opponent agrees that the good of the institution is *summum bonum,* then he surely must accept my claim and give up his demand to use the funds for his research institute. The riposte is obvious: to agree wholeheartedly that the institution comes before all else, and immediately deduce that nothing could benefit it more than enhanced research facilities. In such circumstances God is on the side of both battalions, for in the weaponry of argument, neither is bigger than the other.

Such appeals can be made—we shall come to them later—but the common interest that we have in mind at this point is one likely to be expressed at a noncerebral level. We have already had examples: joking and play call for amity. Overt signaling of the moral self—a hand extended or arms held wide for an embrace and many other much more subtle bodily movements—make offerings of peace when individuals have been quarreling and may open the way to an appreciation of common interests. Ritual or ceremony may do the same in a more peremptory fashion. A piece of homely wisdom said to have been passed around among publicans in wartime Britain laid it down that a fight in the bar among servicemen could be broken up by putting on a record of "God Save the King!"

Other devices take on the appearance of intellectuality. One set—the appeal to an authoritative philosophy—resembles the shock tactic in that its goal is to eject the victim from the security of his present beliefs. It differs in that the appeal is, ostensibly at least, to the intelligence rather than to raw feeling. In fact, since the detonators are usually exploded as single words or short declarative *ex cathedra* sentences—Marxism, Islam, capitalism, human nature, monetarism, Gandhi, or whatever—the invocation is pseudo-cerebral rather than genuinely an appeal to use one's mind, and the name is intended to work like a magic spell or evocation of the divinity when one takes an oath. If the persuader is unwary enough to get drawn into a detailed argument about just which aspect of Marxism is relevant to the present case and finds himself cornered into trying to demonstrate why his beliefs are more Marxist than his opponent's, then he is lost; or at least, this tactic of appeal to authority has failed and he must look for other devices. He is in an even worse position if it turns out that he has picked an inappropriate detonator word and is met with the riposte: "That's all right if you are mad enough to believe that stuff, but most people here have other ideas!"

Another argument that makes use of the invocation of an authority brings us closer to the field of action. Whenever people find themselves either looking for the common ground or trying to make the other person cross the floor to join them, it is generally because the persuader needs the other person's acquiescence to get something done. If he can assume that the opponent feels the same way, and accepts the necessity for coming to a decision and taking action, then he has the chance to make the argument from inevitability (or impossibility, depending on where you stand). This argument generally softens things first by acknowledging that there are some desirable features in what the other side is advocating, but the policy is impractical: perhaps for technical reasons, sometimes because (it is asserted) superior authorities will not permit it. Conversely one can argue—as do some of the authoritative philosophies—that one's own policy merely recognizes the inevitable, and no sensible person tries to avoid the inevitable.

There is an obvious logical slippage in all this: the question is begged by asserting in the first premise what is really at issue. Nevertheless, these devices move us away from the overtly emotion-laden invocations of the shock tactic or the solidarity tactic. The next device comes as close as one can get—in this effort to reach agreement on fundamental principles—to the use of reason.

This is the direct appeal to the value of an open mind. When India gained its independence, a constituent assembly was convoked, charged with bringing into existence a constitution for the new India. Its members were to consider a document that had been, of course, drafted by jurists. Much of the credit for the work went to Dr. B. R. Ambedkar, a man who had risen, despite his origin as an Untouchable, to high rank in government. The draft came before the Assembly for comment and approval. One general complaint was that the spirit of what was proposed was the spirit not of India but of Britain. In particular it contained features that would have offended Gandhi, the father of the nation (by that time assassinated), and specifically it focused on the individual rather than on the community. Ambedkar, one of the few in that assembly who both came from the lowest level of Indian society and at the same time had the weight and authority to speak his mind, did exactly that. Speaking of village communities (the virtues of which lay at the foundations of Gandhian philosophy), he said: "I hold that these village republics have been the ruination of India. What is the village but a sink of localism, a den of ignorance, narrow-mindedness and communalism? I am glad that the Draft Constitution has discarded the village and adopted the individual as its unit" (Avard, 1962:24–25). That is good, effective assertive rhetoric, and it had its effect. Outraged members leaped to the defense of the sacred Gandhian ideals, using all kinds of rhetorical device, including the *argumentum ad hominem* (for example, that Ambedkar had been so much involved in becoming a learned man that he had no time to take part in the fight for India's freedom) and stopping short—so far as the evidence available to me shows—only of touching on Ambedkar's Untouchable status. That status and that experience, together with Ambedkar's firm contempt for Gandhi, whom he regarded as a hypocrite, was, one would assume, what lent emotional fuel to his intervention in the debate.

Other matters of contention surfaced, and from time to time there were appeals to let reason prevail. The whole affair of the "sink of localism" was subtly handled to take the fire out of it (I will discuss it later). As an example of the direct appeal, I quote the prime minister and leader of the nation, Jawaharlal Nehru:

> This House cannot bind down the next generation, or the people who duly succeed in this task. Therefore, let us not trouble ourselves too much about the petty details of what we do, those details will not survive for long, if they are achieved in conflict. What we achieve in unanimity, what we achieve in cooperation is likely to survive. What we gain here and there by conflict and by overbearing manners and by threats will not survive long. . . . [Avard, 1962:22]

That is perhaps an appeal to be reasonable, rather than to use reason. Here is a more direct example. It is Richard Cobden, speaking in the House of Commons in 1845 on free trade.

> There is a widely-spread suspicion that you have been tampering with the feelings of your tenantry—you may read it in the organ of your party—this is the time to show the people that such a suspicion is groundless. I ask you to go into this Committee—I will give you a majority of county members—and you shall have a majority of members of the Central Agricultural

Protection Association in the Committee; and on these terms I ask you to inquire into the causes of the distress of our agricultural population. I trust that none of those gentlemen who have given notice of amendments will attempt to interfere with me, for I have embraced the substance of their amendments in my motion. I am ready to give those honourable gentlemen the widest range they please for their inquiries. I only ask that this subject may be fairly investigated. Whether I establish my principle, or you establish yours, good must result from the inquiry; and I do beg and entreat of the honourable, independent country gentlemen in this House, that they will not refuse on this occasion to sanction a fair, full and impartial inquiry.   [Fox-Davies, 1913: vol. 3, p. 219]

The speech implies that out there beyond the debating chamber, where people use the device of amendments or of packed committees, there is an "objective" world on the nature of which anyone who is "fair" and "impartial" and thorough will have to agree. It is an explicit appeal to the authority of fact and a plea for the use of scientific procedures to observe and to draw the right conclusions from what is observed.

But it is more than that. Notice that even as we move away from the emotive end of the spectrum of rhetorical devices, those devices, albeit weakened, are still present. Like Justice Grantham complimenting his jurors, Cobden woos his fellow members (and with the same term)—"the honourable, independent country gentlemen in this house." The address also carries tones that recall the "enclosing" devices in Walter Reuther's remarks: those that separate the worthy from the unworthy, impartial seekers after truth set apart from those moved only by partisan contentiousness.

Cobden presents reasoned impartiality as an end in itself: "I only ask that this subject may be fairly investigated." It is inconceivable that anyone could then get up in the House and ask: "Why should we bother about a fair investigation?" When reason is offered in this way as a fundamental value, it cannot itself be justified as a means to some other end. Like any other ultimate value or premise, if it is to be defended, then the only devices available are those of assertive rhetoric. Indeed, the use of reason never can free itself from assertion. Behind each act of reasoning lies an axiom or fundamental value that will be reached sooner or later if one asks often enough "Why?"

The appeal to use reason is an appeal to the civic self ("This is your duty") or sometimes to the tactical self ("This is the smart thing to do").

This does not, of course, imply that the civic self is devoid of commitment. A person who accepts as appropriate and good a set of rights and duties thereby displays his sentiment of respect for the institution in which those rights and duties are framed. He is required to renounce those sentiments and feelings that will not serve the ends of the institution. The ultimate value is given, and room is therefore made for the exercise of reason.

Institutions, envisaged as sets of rights and duties, are cold analytical things without much appeal. Therefore, insofar as an appeal to the civic self is an effective rhetorical device for unsealing someone from a sealed position, it must meet two criteria. First, as we noticed in the case of direct verbal appeals for solidarity and in the case of appeals to the authority of omnibus philosophies (covering all topics) such as Marxism, it is open to the "me too" or "holier than thou" riposte. There has to be some way of convincing the opponent (or the umpire, if there is one) that what the opponent proposes is not in the line of his institutional duty. Second, the cold impersonality of the institution, analytically and factorially broken down into right-and-duty sets, must be warmed and made whole by symbols and by rituals, through metaphor and through poetry.

Here, by way of example, are three excerpts from addresses by a vice-chancellor to the faculty members of his university. The first gives an unvarnished statement of what he sees to be a major problem.

And yet this University needs much more from its staff than mere teaching and the pursuit of individual research interests.

There is a need for continuity and stability as well as for the enduring commitment to the institution and to its development.
. . . These characteristics do not easily fit into the quite under-
standable individualistic preoccupations of many. The importance of painting on the larger canvas requires a rather different
perspective and perhaps comes a little easier to those who are
more secure and to those who have already arrived, so to speak,
at a clearly defined level of professional achievement rather than
to those who are still, as it were, "on the make".   [University
of the South Pacific, 1976:15]

That is eloquent, certainly, and with a neat and somewhat
malicious twist in the final phrase which connotes not only
ambition, but also dishonesty. But it is on the whole plainly
stated. At the end of this speech, to convey the same message,
the vice-chancellor borrowed the grave cadences of Gibbon's
prose:

In the end more than freedom, they wanted security. They
wanted a comfortable life. And they lost it all—security, comfort and freedom. When the Athenians finally wanted not to
give to society, but society always to give to them; when the
freedom they wished for most was freedom from responsibility—then Athens ceased to be free.

That—annihilation—is the fate that awaits those who will
not sink their private interests and will not, to serve the institution, go "the extra mile."

A speech by the same man in 1975 ended with this (loosely
quoted from Josiah Gilbert Holland, "The Day's Demand"):

> God, give us men,
> Men whom the lust of office does not kill
> Men whom the spoils of office cannot buy
> Tall men, suncrowned,
> Who live above the fog
> In public duty, and in private thinking.
> For while the rabble with their thumb worn creeds,
> Their large professions and their little deeds,
> Mingle in selfish strife,

Lo! Freedom weeps, Progress stands still
And sleeping Justice waits.

Is that not the perfect invocation of the civic self? Neither
ambitious nor corrupt, doing their duty in the light of cool
reason, untainted by the emptiness of rhetoric ("large profes-
sions") and unimpeded by "selfish strife," such men, "committed to the institution and to its development," serve the
cause of freedom, progress, and justice.

Finally there is the appeal to the tactical self—the invitation
to be smart and to look after one's own interest. This element
is present in the appeal to inevitability, for to fight against
what must be is to waste time and energy, if not to court disaster. It can also be part of the appeal to use reason, as when
Nehru argued that the most enduring measures would be
those reached by compromise and in agreement.

This kind of appeal comes into its own when there is a reminder of past obligations, a promise to undertake future obligations, or a direct invitation to work toward a deal. Here is
the conclusion to a speech in the House of Assembly, Cape-
town, delivered in 1913 by J. X. Merriman:

> I dare say I may have said a great many things which may be
> distasteful to my honorable friends, but I do claim their atten-
> tion, because at a time when they were not in such a dominant
> position, as they are now, I pleaded for right and justice, tolera-
> tion, moderation, and delay in this matter. . . . I think we
> should read the Bill a second time and then send it to a Select
> Committee, where we shall be able to hear the views of people
> interested in both sides.   [Fox-Davies, 1913: vol. 5, p. 259]

The last sentence is an appeal for open minds, less eloquent
and less vehement, but of the same kind as that made by Cobden. The opening sentence, "I dare say I have said a great
many things which may be distasteful . . . ," serves to unseal
Merriman from whatever position he had until then taken in
the debate. The center of the extract, reminding his opponents

of past obligations, is an explicit and clear claim that there has been and is a continuing relationship, and that favors done call for favors reciprocated, if the relationship is to continue.

The appeal to the tactical self is, as I have said, cued into several of the forms already discussed. Essentially it says: "Think out these consequences and realize that they will be bad [or good] for you." But I have in mind something a little more complex—those addresses in which, like that of Merriman and even more clearly Cobden, the speaker signals that his own tactical self is standing ready to enter into discussions. It is not the stance: "Follow my line, because the alternative is disastrous for you." Rather it is: "You have your line and I have mine. I am willing to deviate, provided you will do so too."

To abandon a position into which one has hitherto sealed oneself may be expensive psychologically (interpreted to oneself as a loss of nerve or a sign that things are falling apart). If it must be done in public, then it is also likely to be expensive politically, for—other than in particularly sophisticated enclaves such as the law courts or the legendary smoke-filled rooms—compromise is looked upon by those who do not have to bear the responsibility for the consequences of refusing it as a traitorous act. It shakes the foundations of whatever ideology was serving to make the world a secure and comprehensible place. It makes a bad impression to be caught without principles:

. . . just Bread-and-Butter politicians, looking at matters on their intrinsic merits just as they affect *them*, and not bothering their heads about what are called First Principles. Theories are thrown to the winds, and practical politics take their place. Like the historical Socialist, they may be in favor of a general dividing up of all property, except pigs—because he *had* two pigs. Bread-and-Butter politics! [Fox-Davies, 1913: vol. 2, p. 165]

Second, to offer a deal is also to confess a degree of weakness, a message that can go both to the opponent and to the bystanders. If the offer is unambiguously and publicly re-

jected, one has—other things being equal—lost face, and perhaps support.

For both these reasons—the risk of being seen to be either
weak or lacking in principle—it pays to be ambiguous. The
deal lurks behind a facade of concern for the common interest
and it is likely to be so wrapped up in imprecision that, if need
be, afterward one can deny that there was ever any suggestion
of a deal. Alternatively, the bargaining goes on completely behind the scenes.

In 1959 the Orissa Congress government was having a hard
time. A narrow majority had been lessened by desertions to
the level of one: 69 to 68.

> Several times, while speaking in the House, the Chief Minis-
> ter had appealed to the Opposition parties to "put the execution
> of the plan above party interests". He had also held discussions
> with the leader of the Opposition after the "snap" defeat in Feb-
> ruary. He made a final appeal when replying to the debate on
> the Appropriation Bill. The *Amrita Bazar Patrika* wrote "The
> leader of the Opposition was not taken aback by the appeal. He
> made a suitable reply".And about this time there began to ap-
> pear other newspaper reports of negotiations for a coalition be-
> tween the two main parties.
>
> Six weeks later, on May 15th, the Congress Ministry re-
> signed. On May 22 a Coalition Ministry, consisting of the
> former Congress Chief Minister, the former leader of the Op-
> position and one Congressman from the previous cabinet, took
> office.   [Bailey, 1963:7]

The left-wing parties, which remained to form the Opposition, regarded the whole business as nothing more than a trick
to stay in power.

I have placed this form of appeal last because it comes nearest to the world of calculation and reckoning and seemingly
furthest from the vibrant emotions of, for example, Emmet's
address. But even in this case, reasoning and calculation can
begin only after the two contestants have sealed themselves in
agreement. This sealing is done at two levels. One is public
and will be accompanied by whatever level of emotive asser-

tion (about "first principles" or "theories" or "the execution of the plan") is thought necessary to build the facade. The other is private, possibly never spoken, but certainly known: "We are both out for our own advantage. Neither of us can defeat the other. Therefore let us agree upon the joint maximization point of our separate utilities."

We have looked at six ways in which those who recognize that there is no choice but to seek deliberately to shift their opponents from a sealed position and at the same time to signal that they are themselves ready to "listen to reason" may do so. It is a move, so to speak, toward the central column of both diagrams, the exit route into rationality. That column was headed "Indifferent" in Diagram 1, and the word signifies *both* the anticipation of the interaction that is not marked by emotion *and* a diminished attachment to any principle other than that of an open mind.

These six ways were: the psychological shock; the unspoken invocation of solidarity through play or similar actions; the parading of an authoritarian philosophy as the master value; direct appeal to the value of an open mind; a call to duty; and the suggestion that a deal may be made.

Insofar as these devices are effective, they serve to establish agreement on the principles that will guide the discussion that follows. They are therefore likely to influence the nature of that discussion: those who come through play and joking not only to recognize the possibility of amity between them but also to feel it are likely to conduct themselves differently from those who reluctantly acknowledge a necessity to collude. Those who admit to themselves that they have been unnecessarily contentious and unnecessarily emotional and accept the value of reason—that is, they agree that there is probably an objectively correct solution to the problem—will not be waiting, as do those in the "strange bedfellow" situation, for the other person to trick them. Furthermore, compromises are not always fifty/fifty; the greater the power, the less that has to be conceded, as in *Tom Brown's Schooldays:* "He never wants anything but what's right and fair; only when you come to settle what's right and fair, it's everything that he wants and nothing that you want. And that's his idea of a compromise."

Nor are the devices exclusive. We saw in the quotation from Merriman how he combined in adjacent sentences a reminder of mutual obligation, an overture of frienship ("I dare say I may have said a great many things that may be distasteful to my honourable friends . . ."), and an appeal for open minds. The psychological shock tactic is likely to be a loosener and make way perhaps for an appeal to reason or for the offer of a deal. If it turns out not to be a loosener, but a successful assertion prising the opponent entirely loose from his sealed anchorage, then we are not dealing with the rhetoric of compromise.

In fact it is overly simple to pose the situation as I have so far done: that the overture is rhetoric to loosen conviction and establish agreement, while the rest of the piece is a reasoned argument toward the best solution. Rather the process will resemble that which I described earlier when discussing the movement in and out of rational argument in the course of a committee meeting. There will be episodes of unsealing and resealing and further unsealing, with no necessity for the same rhetorical devices to be employed on each occasion of unsealing. The best that can be said is that the device used in each unsealing episode is likely to frame the nature of the discussion that follows it.

These devices, as I have said, serve to establish the *general* principles by means of which a reasoned discussion can be conducted. But they are general, not specific. The deliberations that I have in mind are not those that look for truth in the abstract—whether sin is original or whether our will is free or, for that matter, what is the proper function of a university—but rather they are exercises in practical reasoning, engaged with the intention of reaching a decision and taking action. All may come to agree that justice for all equally must be the guiding principle and everything should be done "right and fair," but then you must "come to settle what's right and fair."

So we come to a second round of assertion, by means of

which the *specific* principles that concern the task in hand are settled.

The devices that will be considered in this section are called "pseudo-cerebral." They have the appearance of using reason, but do not do so. They seem to invite the listener to calculate the consequences of what is proposed or to deduce the motivations behind the policy or in some other way to exercise his logical capacities, but in fact they serve to mask the absence of agreement on a premise on which to base the argument. That is, pseudo-cerebral devices have the effect of an assertion, but not its form.

On many occasions the use of these devices is a conscious and deliberate subterfuge—part of that arsenal of tricks and traps which gives rhetoric a bad name. In other cases one would be reluctant to say even that the device was inappropriate, let alone wicked and deceitful. These devices, like the emotion-rousing tactics of assertive rhetoric, are an inevitable part of a discourse carried on in a natural language. They are also necessary, as we notice elsewhere, when decisions have to be made and when there is no agreed premise from which to begin the exercise of reasoning toward a conclusion or when the variables are too numerous or too complex or too inaccessible to allow for computation. Detecting fallacies is an exercise as enjoyable as any other kind of puzzle solving, and inevitably there will be an air of self-congratulation in my sentences when the examples are paraded. But such smugness is misplaced and mildly despicable. We all conduct our discourses in this way; and we need to do so.

These devices are more common than those found in emotion-laden discourses such as Emmet and Zola produced. At least I think that this must be the case, although I have no idea how one would set about counting in order to validate such a sweeping generalization. But it should be the case, for the following reasons.

First, they are more durable than devices that rest on the arousal of strong emotions. It is as if we have a limited capacity for such excitement, and frequent use of anger or grief or joy soon blunts the sharp edge, so that beyond a certain point more and more resources must be used to gain the same level of emotional affect. This is not so in the case of reason and consequently the use of reason is also cheaper.

Second, arousing emotion is like using a sledgehammer. There is no way of exerting gradual force and there is control over only a very limited range of force. The delicate probing that will allow one to desist, if that seems a good idea, is not a possibility.

Third—and this follows from the second characteristic—those whose emotions are thoroughly aroused are sealed. To maneuver them in another direction is difficult. Furthermore, following the clichés of our own culture, those who are excited are that much the less able to think for themselves. That, of course, is the intention of assertive rhetoric: but overexcitement is an inappropriate condition for those who are supposed to implement plans and carry out orders. That, as we have seen, is one reason why the civic self is stripped of "passionate intensity" and such men should live "above the fog" and "in private thinking."

Fourth, as we focus not on one set of people but on the entire situation, emotion met with emotion leads to impasse and escalation of the conflict if the emotions are negative. Ambedkar's "sink of localism" description of village communities looked likely to turn a debate with the Gandhians into a fight.

There are two other conditions that should make pseudo-cerebral devices more common in use than emotion-raising devices. The first is the high value set, in some cultures and in some cultural settings (bureaucracies, and especially universities), on the use of reason. The overemotional committee member is likely to find himself relieved of committee service. The second—and this should follow from all that has so far been said—is that councils and committees, at least those that have a task to perform, will very likely have set behind them the stage of establishing the basis of their cooperation, and a resort to displays of emotion to make an assertion will be seen as a deplorable regression into immaturity. It happens, of course, as we saw in the discussion of play; and for this reason we should expect those devices that were listed for the establishment of general principles to occur also in those discourses that are directed to setting up premises for specific problems. But, as I have said, they are expensive and dangerous, and, once the general principles have been set, there should be a reluctance to go in for "hyping" and a preference for pseudo-cerebral modes of persuasion.

There lies the difficulty. The speaker must spare the emotion. He must appear to use reason to establish agreement on values, principles, goals, or premises that cannot be established by reason. The solution is the use of pseudo-cerebral devices, that verbal sleight-of-hand which imposes, without appearing to do so, an assertion.

What are these devices and how are they employed? Let us begin by setting out a scenario of the simplest kind. Later we shall consider examples, but examples are drawn from life and are therefore rich and complex and sometimes also confusing. So here first is a sketch map of the country in which pseudo-cerebral devices are to be found.

Suppose a committee or a council or an assembly charged with reaching a decision. The personnel are first the protagonist, second the antagonist, and (sometimes) the judge or umpire as third person. In fact we need take account only of the protagonist and the antagonist during the present discussion, since, other than is supposed to be the case in law courts, the third party often turns out to be only the two antagonists combining in a decision. Audiences, of course, both those with formal power to adjudicate and others with little power, do have an effect on the course of an argument, but that is not our present topic. Rather we focus on the structure of arguments.

They take this form. First there is a proposed course of action (A); second there is an antecdent state of affairs (B) which is the occasion for advocating that course of action; third there is a set of consequences (C) which will follow if the action is taken—the rectifiction of whatever it is in B that has prompted A.

Now suppose that, for whatever reason, you are not in favor of *A*. What is to be done? In essence the task is to break or change the linkages that bind *A* with *B* or *C*.

This can be done by showing that *B* is not what it has been said to be. The Russian invasion of Afghanistan may be presented as a part of a carefully laid strategy to gain control over the oil countries of the Middle East (*B*), and therefore immediate military counteraction (*A*) is required. Recall the consequences of allowing Hitler to go unpunished for his incursion into the Rhineland. Recall also that this was one of Eden's arguments for the attack on Egypt over the Suez affair: stop Nasser before he becomes another Hitler. Stop them before they get too strong. If, for whatever reason (practicality, conscience, or a different reading of *B*), you are opposed to military action, you may argue that the Russian invasion is an ad hoc affair, not part of a long strategy, and was undertaken to secure the boundaries, out of much the same kinds of fears that cause the United States to keep a hand on the regimes that rule Latin American countries. If your reading of the situation is accepted, then you have broken the connection between *B* and *A*.

But you may have difficulty in doing so. You may not have that information required to make your case. You may have the information but it may be so technical and complicated that your audience could not possibly understand it. Conversely, if you are putting forward an *A* of your own, and suspect that either *B* or *C* or both would be too incomprehensible or too unpalatable to be accepted by those who have to be convinced, then you must so structure the situation that the connection between *A* and *B* and *C* is not made.

B and *C* are the premises, and *A* is the conclusion. Arguments take this form:

The future of the government depends on contributors to the party who expect favors in return (*B*).

The Magnificent Motor Corporation is a substantial contributor (*B*).

Therefore outlaw strikes in their plants (*A*).

It seems unlikely that even the brashest right-winger would

go on the platform with that argument. Instead *A* will be kept but attention diverted from the welfare of the M. M. Corporation by speaking of the public good or the "British disease" or by producing reams of statistics to show how strikes fail to benefit the strikers; or any one of a variety of such devices.

In short, the central act in pseudo-cerebral persuasion is that of breaking or obscuring or changing a link (thought undesirable) between a course of action on the one hand and the occasion for it or the consequences of taking it on the other hand. Now let us look at an example.

When Dr. Ambedkar made his fierce attack on those who deplored the lack in the draft constitution (in which Ambedkar, as law minister, had a large hand) of attention to village communities and its fastening on the individual as the carrier of rights and duties, he relied on a value that was, at that time, beyond reproach. This was *freedom,* the condition of not being dominated by others, the condition that India had, only the year before, attained through its "freedom fight" against the British. The issue, as in the case of Tom Brown and compromise, was to find what the word would mean in practice. Here is one of Gandhi's interpretations:

> The centre of power is not in New Delhi, or in Calcutta, and Bombay, in big cities. I would have it distributed among the seven hundred thousand villages of India. . . . Then there will be voluntary cooperation between these seven hundred thousand units. . . . Voluntary cooperation will produce real freedom and a new order.   [Avard, 1962:21]

Here are the same ideas set out by Vinoba Bhave:

> We want an order of society which will be free not only from exploitation but also from every government authority. The power of Government will be decentralized and distributed among the villages. Every village will be the State in itself: the centre will have only nominal authority over them. In this way, gradually we will reach the stage when authority in every form will have become unnecessary and will, therefore, fade away giving rise to a perfectly free society.   [Misra, 1956:56]

Ambedkar thought otherwise and said so loudly and trenchantly:

> They do not want any Central or Provincial Governments.
> They just want India to contain so many village Governments.
> The love of the intellectual Indian for the village community is
> of course infinite, if not pathetic. . . . I am therefore surprised
> that those who condemn provincialism and communalism
> should come forward as champions of the village.   [Avard,
> 1962:24–25]

Ambedkar knew and his opponents could have been no less
aware that in most villages the people are divided into ranked
groups that do not intermarry. Custom inflicts progressive
stigmata as one moves down the scale: in short, there is a caste
system. Ambedkar, as we mentioned, came from the bottom
and had spent much of his life championing the rights of his
fellow Untouchables. So the village offered no freedom, and
to make it the cornerstone of self-government would be to
perpetuate and intensify the present discontents of the lowly.

Those who wished to see the draft constitution changed and
founded on corporate village communities were for the most
part not those in power. Pandit Nehru, the dominating figure
at the time, looked for freedom and prosperity in a socialist
form of society, adequately industralized and governed
through the modern agency of a democratic but also certainly
a centralized state. The times were not conducive to experi-
ments that would weaken the central government, and Nehru
said as much. From the beginning the village-firsters must
have known that they would lose the battle (not that anyone
properly imbued with the spirit of Gandhi would be deterred
by that prospect).

The proposed action (A) in this case, coming from Ambedkar and those who drafted the constitution, is the recognition
of the individual as the prime bearer of rights and duties. The
amenders want more recognition given to corporate village
bodies: that is their A. Let us see what versions of B and C the
amenders produced to put down Ambedkar's policy and to
promote their own. If their arguments are better illustrated

than the replies, that is because the only version of the debate to hand is a polemical booklet published by a group (Avard) strongly sympathetic to the idea of a village-based society. But such a bias does not impede our arguments, since our concern is to look for ways of structuring persuasive devices rather than to write history.

The argument to be met (leaving aside the question of modernization and economic development) was that, given their present structure, village communities inhibited freedom, and therefore should not be made important units in government. In the record available to me, no one questioned the main premise (freedom is desirable), although there was of course much talk about responsibility and stability too. But neither did the amenders (at least in the Avard report) address in detail and directly the minor premise (village life inhibits freedom). One Muslim lady spoke up in agreement with what Dr. Ambedkar had said about villages. Two other members did so during the third reading (see below). The great majority of the amenders went off in other directions.

They did have much to say about village life, and—whether consciously or not—the speeches worked toward separating the tie that Ambedkar had made between the village and "iniquity" and "commualism" (that word is used in India to refer to bigoted strife between religious groups or caste groups). Here is an example, referring to Mysore:

> A great deal of public expenditure has been incurred on this account. All officers concerned from the Dewan to the Tahsildar have, according to their lights, given personal attention to the condition of the villages. . . . The results are, in my opinion, encouraging and in some cases, quite gratifying. . . . about 30% could be classed as good; that is to say they had held regular meetings, collected panchayat taxes, undertaken some optional duties and carried out works of public utility and weekly cleaning by voluntary labour contributed by the villagers and taken steps to ensure the vaccination of children and so on.   [Avard, 1962:42–43]

A kind of tactical metonymy is going on in this speech: the speaker is taking a part of the whole and focusing on it (the level of efficiency found in local government institutions), and so directing attention away from the other question about equality, freedom, and justice. Indeed, there is a perfectly acceptable way of introducing such a move and the speaker used it: he said that he, just like Dr. Ambedkar, spoke from his own experience.

Other kinds of metonymy provide diversions into detail (a standard way of avoiding confrontations with principle, although in the example following one encounters less the smart debater than a somewhat ingenuous antiquarian).

> Mr. Madhava Rau said that the ballot box and ballot paper were not known to our ancestors. I would like to point out to him, that the ballot box and the ballot papers were described in the inscription on the walls of a temple in the village of Uttaramerur. . . . The election took place not only for that village but for the whole of India. That was just a thousand years ago. It is not known to my honourable friend and that is why he made such a wrong statement—a grievously wrong statement and I want to correct it. [Avard, 1962:45]

Another speech (Avard, 1962:46–48)—unfortunately too long to quote in detail—deserves paraphrase. The speaker had been reproached by a friend, he said, for his interest in preserving village communities: "The bullock cart days have gone: they will never come back." Ponderously sidestepping the symbolism, he replied that bullock carts would be used to serve the villagers instead of just taking firewood to the city. His next sentence took him to the front in Kashmir, where "those friends in the battlefield" asked him to see that the price of food at home was reduced. Therefore, he concluded, village republics will be "of service to the military people." Village republics will put an end to food shortage, cloth shortage, the black market, and inflation. Also communism (". . . we are seeing what is going on in China, we saw what was done in Czechoslovakia, and we know what the position is in Burma") would, if village republics were established, "be checked immediately."

This is not metonymy; rather it goes in the direction of hyperbole. Village republics are not simply an issue in the organization of local government: think of a problem, and they are the solution. The technique is that of the debater who, unable to make his opinions prevail within the existing context of relevance, inflates that context. A common way of doing this is to convert an apparently routine decision into "a matter of principle," thus setting aside an agreed set of premises for something more general and probably more a matter of contention.

The various extracts that I have quoted abound with logical fallacies, outstanding being *ignoratio elenchi*—refuting an argument that has not been offered. There are frequent confusions between sequences and consequences, setting items next to one another and insinuating that they are causally linked. Vinoba Bhave leads the mind down from the state through the term "decentralization" (dispersal of power) to the villages and concludes that "authority in every form will have become unnecessary and will, therefore, fade away giving rise to a perfectly free society." The assumption behind this argument is that decentralization is like an avalanche, unstoppable once begun. That premise is suppressed. So is the obvious riposte that ten small tyrants are not necessarily an improvement on one big tyrant: decentralized power is still power.

The amenders, fresh to the subject in comparison with Ambedkar and those who had long been engaged in composing the draft constitution, lacked the resources to make valid logical arguments against the proposal. Consequently they resorted for the most part to the rhetoric of assertion rather than to the rhetoric of compromise. They used arguments from authority of various kinds. "The ideal of our great leader, Mahatma Gandhi was the "Rural Swaraj"—that every village should be self-sufficient and self-supporting. I am sorry to say that part has not been fulfilled in this Constitution" (Avard, 1962:57). The premise—and it required no enunciation—was: "What Gandhi wanted for India is an imperative for us."

Indian traditions were used in the same way. This is the *argumentum ad verecundiam,* the appeal to traditional values.

Ours is an ancient, a very ancient country and the village has always had an important position here . . . in our country the village occupied such an important position that even in the legends contained in the most ancient books—the Upanishads—if there are descriptions of the forest retreats, of the Sages, there are also descriptions of villages.   [Avard, 1962:41]

Or:

The one thing—and it appears to me very objectionable—which I wish to reply is Dr. Ambedkar's remark that the Indian soil is not suited to democracy. I do not know how my friend has read the history of India. I am myself a student of history and also of politics and I can say with definiteness that democracy flourished in India much before Greece or any other country in the world.   [Avard, 1962:41]

The premise in both these extracts—again unspoken and not needing to be spoken—was: "India's traditional values should give shape to the new constitution." Why this should be so does not enter into the discussion: the argument is simply offered as a value (and a moral boundary) to which every real Indian must subscribe. It could have been defended, of course, starting from the premise: "Newly independent countries need a strong sense of their own identity and distinctiveness."

There were also many arguments *ad hominem* against Dr. Ambedkar. We saw one: "I do not know how my friend has read the history of India." Here is another example:

With all deference to Dr. Ambedkar, I differ from him in this regard. His attitude yesterday was typical of the urban highbrow; and if that is going to be our attitude towards village folk, I can only say, "God save us." . . . Perhaps the fault lies with the composition of the Drafting Committee, among the members of which no one, with the sole exception of Sriyut Munshi, has taken any active part in the struggle for the country's freedom.   [Avard, 1962:27]

The premise is: "Those who did not take an active part in the Freedom Fight should not be allowed a part in shaping India's future." Even aside from the problem of what "active" should mean, the spirit of that proposal is so much out of line with the Gandhian ethic of infinite forgivenesses (and what Nehru practiced) that it could hardly have been put forward openly.

So much for the amenders. As we have seen, their rhetoric was mostly that of assertion. Now let us look at the strategy of those who defended the draft constitution, with the expectation that in their remarks will be found a rhetoric of compromise.

They compromised. An amendment was accepted: "Sir, I beg to move. That after Article 31, the following new article be added: 31-A. The State shall take steps to organize village panchayats and endow them with such powers and authority as may be necessary to enable them to function as units of self-government" (Avard, 1962:44).

When invited to comment, Dr. Ambedkar said no more than: "Sir, I accept the amendment."

The secretary of Avard, in his introductory remarks, made this comment on the amendment and its reception. (It subsequently became Article 40).

> This is how the present Article 40 which forms part of the Directive Principles of State Policy was incorporated into free India's Constitution.
>
> That this much only was possible under those circumstances was realized and sorrowfully agreed. How much sorrow, disappointment and unhappiness yet remained could still be felt at the third reading of the Constitution between November 17–26, 1949. Not that all agreed. The views of some members were more or less akin to those of Dr. Ambedkar. But the overwhelming opinion of the House was for recognizing the village and giving it a place in Indian polity.   [Avard, 1962:18]

The disappointment came from the placing of Article 40. It was in that part of the Constitution which in effect made recommendations to the state governments. It—or, preferably, some measure of the same intent but more general—was not placed in the fundamental principles. Instead, some of the amenders grieved to perceive, there stood in Article 326: "The elections to the House of the People and to the Legislative Assembly of every State shall be on the basis of adult suffrage." Direct adult suffrage and therefore "the dignity of the individual" left little room for the corporate village community. It turned out to be a constitution where "the people will be in power, where the individual will occupy the centre of the stage and the development of the individual personality will be the aim of our social good" (Avard, 1962:21). So the compromise, on the part of the drafters, must have seemed to their opponents to be a Tom Brown compromise: the drafters gave a little to gain a lot. How did they "sell" it?

During the third reading there were some who remained unrepentant. An outraged amender said:

> Let alone giving a dominant position to the villages in the Constitution, they have been given no place whatsoever. No doubt, I have seen that in a small article mention has been made of village panchayats. But it is nothing more than a reference. Our Constitution is silent about the shape that our villages will assume and the place they will occupy in the future.   [Avard, 1962:74]

On the other side there are the two reports in Avard (other than the one sentence from the Muslim lady) that firmly support Dr. Ambedkar.

> I disagree with most of my friends, particularly the Hindu friends who expatiate on the existence of the republic system of government i.e. republics in our old Hindu polity. I disagree with them. My contention is that our lower classes, the lower castes of our society, whom we call Harijans, have all along been kept in a depressed condition. Consequently there was no democracy. If there was a democracy, if there was a republic, it was among the higher classes, what we call the higher castes. If you look at the Constitution from that point of view, I think the removal of untouchability and the introduction of adult franchise are two of the very best elements that have been introduced in this Constitution.   [Avard, 1962:78]

And:

> There is another criticism that the village as a political unit has
> not been recognized. I fear that behind the back of this criticism
> is a distrust of adult franchise. What was conceived under the
> village unit system was that the village voters would be called
> upon to elect the Panchayats and only the members of the Pan-
> chayats were to take part in the elections to the various assem-
> blies, Provincial and Central. But now, it is the village voter
> himself who will be called upon to weigh the issues before the
> country and elect his representative, and so he will directly par-
> ticipate in the elections. I claim this to be a more progressive
> arrangement than having village units elect the electorate indi-
> rectly. It has been said that the genius of the country does not
> find expression in this Constitution. I do not understand what
> is concretely meant by this charge.   [Avard, 1962:76]

There were also a few who spoke up against the principle of
decentralization.

> The great Mahatma was an advocate of decentralization. . . . As
> long as there are warring nations we cannot think in terms of
> decentralization. As long as there is economic inequality, the
> goal of decentralization will elude our grasp. It is only with the
> end of the state that we can usher a decentralized society. As
> long as there is militarism it is not possible to decentralize power
> to any extent whatsoever.   [Avard, 1962:75]

And:

> A strong Central Government is the need of the hour; and I
> prophesy that the future will tell you that this centralization was
> a blessing. All along the ages and our history bears ample testi-
> mony to this fact, the overmastering problem before India has
> been one of integration, and consolidation and unification. A
> unitary and centralized form of Government is suited to the
> needs of this country. However, in future if our experience
> shows that in certain matters some more power should be given
> to the units, I feel there would be no difficulty in getting the
> change effected by the amendment of the Constitution as pro-
> vided for in Section 368.   [Avard, 1962:77]

So there were on both sides some who held hard to the line they had taken before the compromise was offered. But from others came a note of conciliation and compromise.

First there was a good deal of parliamentary politeness directed at Dr. Ambedkar, sometimes slightly grudging:

> Mr. Vice-President, Sir, I feel happy that the Government have with grace accepted this amendment and agreed to introduce it in the Constitution. We should have tried to introduce this at the very beginning of the framing of the Constitution. [Avard, 1962:45]

Or, more generously:

> . . . if there was a mistake, the mistake was on our part in not having been vigilant enough and brought this before the House in proper time. When this was coming so late as that, I did not expect Dr. Ambedkar as Chairman of the Drafting Committee to be good enough to accept this. [Avard, 1962:46]

And, less kindly:

> During the course of the speech he made while presenting this Draft to the House, Dr. Ambedkar made some remarks about villages which caused me and, I believe, a great majority of the members of this House, great pain. It is a matter of deep pleasure to me that he has at last accepted the amendment. . . . We need not complain if one comes to the right course, though belatedly. [Avard, 1962:49]

Second, there were a number of conciliatory speeches saying, in effect: "You have got what you wanted," and at the same time picking up some of the rhetorical themes used by the amenders.

> There are provisions in the Constitution which show that we have whole-heartedly followed the Gandhian philosophy. The Constitution contains the seeds of all that Gandhiji had taught us and those seeds would flower if the Constitution is worked properly. [Avard, 1962:66]

Others were more specific:

> Then there is the charge that Gandhian principles have been sac-
> rificed. I already submitted that we have embodied provisions
> for the removal of untouchability, for national language, for
> communal harmony and for goodwill and guarantees to minori-
> ties, encouragement of gram panchayats and village industries
> and for protection of milch cattle. These are the planks on which
> Gandhism flourished in this country. If these principles have
> been embodied in the Constitution, I want to ask how Gand-
> hism has been sacrificed in this Constitution. I submit that
> enough provision has been made for carrying out of the pro-
> gramme that was enunciated by the Father of the Nation. This
> Constitution is a harmonious blending of the best Indian tra-
> ditions—the political and constitutional experience of other
> countries and the Gandhian ideals.   [Avard, 1962:67]

Third, there was a conciliatory theme: "We would have
liked to do what you suggest, but you did not give us the
time." The consitutional adviser wrote:

> Even if the panchayat plan is to be adopted, its details will have
> to be carefully worked out for each province and for each In-
> dian State with suitable modification for towns. Apart from
> other difficulties, this will take time and rather than delay the
> passing of the Constitution further, it would seem better to rele-
> gate these details to auxiliary legislation to be enacted after the
> Constitution has been passed.   [Avard, 1962:17]

In the same document, he reminded the legislators of the
work already done:

> It may not be easy to work the panchayat idea into the draft
> Constitution at the present stage. Articles 67(5) and 149(1),
> which, I believe, embody decisions already taken by the Constit-
> uent Assembly provide for direct election to the Lower House,
> both at the Centre and in the units. These decisions will first
> have to be reversed if elections are to be indirect, as required by
> the panchayat plan. Whether this will be practicable, I do not
> know.   [Avard, 1962:79]

If the Constitution were to contain detailed provisions down to the level of the village, then it would "be of inordinate length and even more rigid than it is at present." This is the voice of the expert, not, I think, "blinding with science" but just stating the cost.

The final note of conciliation was sounded over the theme of rigidity. Nehru had already told the legislators, in the course of the opening debate, that "this House cannot bind down the next generation." One of the speeches quoted above ended with "I feel there would be no difficulty in getting the change affected by the amendment of the Constitution as provided for in Section 368." Finally Dr. Ambedkar reminded his audience that the Constitution was no more than a beginning: it is "futile to pass any judgment on the Constitution without reference to the part which the people and their parties are likely to play" and "however good a constitution may be, it is sure to turn out bad if those who are called upon to work it happen to be a bad lot" (Morris-Jones, 1957:89).

In this example we have seen frequent recourse to assertive rhetoric. But for the most part the debate took place under an umbrella of agreement about certain fundamental values.

Some of these values are explicit and inviolable—such as freedom. But they are also vague, and as in the case of wanting to do always "what's right and good" it remains to be decided just what is right and good, so also there is no clear principle, before the debate begins, as to how freedom should be translated into the articles of a constitution.

Another such value is the necessity for working in harmony. "What we achieve in unanimity, what we achieve in cooperation is likely to survive," said Nehru. This value does get itself translated into action, in the form of a consensus (at least among the members of the Constituent Assembly) about the fundamentals of parliamentary structure and parliamentary procedure, in particular the legitimacy of an opposition and its duty to oppose. Both sides must conduct themselves in conflict so that the other survives to continue in other debates.

Other values come openly to the surface only occasionally in the Avard selection. The need for a strong central government is one example, and perhaps it appears only rarely because the subject distressed those who compiled the book and who wanted power decentralized. But at the time there could not have been a man in the Constituent Assembly who was not aware of the perils of internal factionalism, the menace of foreign enemies, and the brink of chaos along which they walked. To rock the boat too much—which meant to undermine Nehur's power to govern—would be to invite disaster on everyone.

Finally there was, I suspect, an entirely unspoken consensus about where real power lay. It lay with Nehru and the government and its law minister, Dr. Ambedkar. They were at one and the same time holding the ring and fighting the bout. It may be that the occasionally extravagant language of the amenders came out only because they knew that Nehru would not allow the lid to be blown off. From the other side, the government, knowing that it controlled the resources and would not lose the debate, could afford to be indulgent and conciliatory.

Given the different levels of overarching consensus, it is not surprising that the drafters, with the exception of Dr. Ambedkar, ignored the challenge of assertive rhetoric and cooled the affair by manufacturing a specific (and contrived) consensus to permit agreement over the question at issue. Nor, in view of the same general consensus (especially perhaps the hidden item of who in fact held the power), is it surprising that the amenders in the end accepted the contrived specific consensus and submitted through their vote (although not all of them in their words) to a weak (for them) compromise.

In pseudo-cerebral persuasion there are many forms of logical slippage and sleight-of-hand (fallacies, in other words) besides those I have described—for example, from today's newspaper a vigorous advocacy of public funds in support of "private" schools, when the intended beneficiary is in fact parochial schools. Bentham's book provides an entertaining catalogue (Larrabee, 1952). My purpose has not been to review them all—an impossible task—but to point out what they have in common. (1) They detach a policy or course of action from the ambience or consequences that have been offered to recommend it (or to condemn it). (2) They do so by means of a link that violates the rules of logical reasoning. Indeed, if pseudo-cerebral devices are to succeed, they must inhibit a rigorous use of the categorical syllogism.

Pseudo-cerebral devices differ from straightforward emotive assertion in that they purport to address the head rather than the heart. But since the occasion for their use arises only through conflicting premises, they cannot employ logical reasoning. Instead they deceive those addressed, making them feel (mistakenly) that the course of action recommended must follow from a premise or value that they accept. The pseudo-cerebral persuasion is a form of *covert* assertion. It is manipulation.

I have also suggested, following other apologists for rhetoric, that for reasons of complexity or because of an unshiftable conflict of values, persuasion through rhetorical (that is, nonlogical) "reasoning" may be the only way in which a decision can be reached (Bailey, 1981).

That theme takes us into the next chapter, which is about the use of reason in reaching decisions.

CHAPTER 8

Sophisticated Codes

Through the idea of pseudo-cerebral rhetoric, we have introduced a shred of intellectuality into the notion of persuasion. In this chapter our investigations lie squarely in the central column of the diagrams, where rational purposive debate leads to decisions of an overtly instrumental nature, and where the concern is not to get people into the right relationship with the persuader but to get things done in the "real" world. We shall give rational purposive interaction a full run, so to speak, and we shall find out, through examples, whether it can outdistance the competition provided by displays of emotion and by rhetorical devices.

Our subject is sophisticated codes. A sophisticated code is the handmaiden of orderly debate and rational decision. The chapter begins with a description of the characteristics of such a code. We then ask how the code is framed: that is, methods for making plain to other people that you think this is an occasion for *its* use rather than the use of some other code. We then consider three cases illustrating progressively greater difficulties in staying within the bounds of rational discourse. The actors slide into rhetoric, usually the rhetoric of assertion. Last, we ask why a sophisticated code sometimes fails to perform one of its main functions—monitoring the "real" world—and what is likely to happen when it does fail. The sophisticated code, in short, seems to be perpetually at risk: risk, in one direction, of sliding into the ritual senilities of oversophistication, and in the other direction of regress to the infantilism of assertion through displays of passion.

First, what is a code? It is a set of rules and conventions that advise what modes should be used for communicating with (and, in our particular concern, for persuading) other people. Part of such a code must be descriptions of contexts and of how to recognize them, together with rules for connecting types of context with types of communication. Thus, to recapitulate briefly some of the features described in earlier chapters: a code of assertive rhetoric is to be used when there is total disagreement about values (or when one wishes to enhance such disagreement by anathematizing an enemy); it should be addressed to the heart; certain figures of speech are appropriate and others are not; it should be so constructed as to occlude any riposte; and so forth. Pseudo-cerebral rhetoric is for use when one wishes to disguise disagreement on values; it should appear to be addressed to the head; it should anticipate a discussion and leave the door open for a rejoinder; and so on. Assertive rhetoric uses a simple code; pseudo-cerebral persuasion purports to use a more sophisticated code. There remain two kinds of code—the sophisticated and the oversophisticated—to which we have not yet applied the term "rhetoric." Whether or not it is appropriate to do so can be decided after we explore more fully the difference between "simple" and "sophisticated."

Communication is one aspect of a relationship. Certain relations—those I have called moral—have no other purpose than the relationship itself: people in love should not count the cost, and the joy of the relationship is its own reward. The teleological question does not arise. Other relationships are directed toward achieving a goal that is apart from the relationship; for example, what goes on between teacher and pupil. This is rational purposive activity. The purpose of their interaction is the transfer of knowledge or the furtherance of research. Of course the interactions are not devoid of affect, and are likely to be less fruitful if they do lack the proper sentiments. Between teacher and pupil there should be mutual respect and mutual consideration. But if those feelings go beyond the "proper" limit and turn into love (or hatred), then the instrumental side of the relationship is likely to be damaged. Of course these matters are very subtle, and too many variables are involved to let us apply to any particular case a simple "arm of the scale" model, suggesting that when the intrinsic value put on a relationship rises, then inevitably and by the same amount its instrumental effectiveness must fall. Nevertheless, when we are setting out a framework for thinking about such things, it seems reasonable to pose questions about the degree to which a particular form of communication inclines one way or the other: toward an intrinsic relationship or toward achieving a purpose that is outside the relationship.

A communication through the rhetoric either of assertion, or of compromise is directed mainly toward relationships. In both cases the purpose is to make a friend, or to distance someone as an enemy, to make the other person trust you or fear you or believe you or whatever else. Even when the attempt is mainly directed toward arousing one or the other of these feelings about a third party or about a state of affairs, the persuader cannot succeed without first gaining the trust of the person addressed. Trust is a kind of small loving and is an intrinsic relationship: to the extent that you have trust, you are not constantly making a reckoning and balancing what you put in against what you get in return. This does *not* mean that, in this world of committees and politics and rhetoric, people do not create or destroy relationships for a purpose that is extrinsic; of course they do. But it does mean that the code both of assertive and of pseudo-cerebral rhetoric focuses attention on the relationship itself, and pushes into the background the instrumental aspects. You make an alliance because it is to your advantage; but the idiom through which the ally is courted and the alliance maintained is a moral one. The code enjoins that amity should appear to come first: advantage should be seen to be no more than incidental. Even when the union is transparently one of convenience, both those codes insist that the partners should collude in a pretense that this is not so, and the codes provide the idiom for saying it is not so.

The sophisticated code reverses these positions. The main focus is on the task to be performed. It may be necessary to cooperate with other persons (it is so, by definition—that is why we can talk of a code of communication) but the relationship so formed is secondary and purely instrumental: it is supposed to be free from affect or to contain only that degree of affect which is instrumentally useful. People are met to solve problems and perform tasks in the world outside their meeting. If they are required to get along with one another, that requirement is incidental. Getting along is not the purpose of the meeting. That is the first rule in a sophisticated code.

Such a code purports to deal with reality. It is directed toward taking action and getting things done, or with assessing the success of what has been done. If we think of a range of discourse from that which is concerned with pure knowledge to that which is applied, the sophisticated code directs the latter kind of discourse: not "What are the goals of university life?" but "How should we cope with the present shortage of classrooms?" To talk of "reality" or of "problems in the real world" or of "practical reasoning" is to go down to the lowest level of abstraction; in other words, to hold equal as few variables as possible. A code that is to be used for communication about affairs at that level must itself tend toward specification and away from generalization. The engine repair manual that tells you that it is essential to have a healthily large spark across the points of the plugs is not of much use unless it goes on to specify the various actions that must be taken to ensure a large spark. Codes of committee procedure, or judicial procedure, can afford in their preamble to talk of rationality or justice, but in their particulars must come down to who may speak, to whom, sometimes for how long, and about what. In short, sophisticated codes have a tendency to slide toward detailed specification.

They also and for the same reason, tend to deal with positions on a continuum, dividing it by many marks along the line, rather than dealing just with the two ends. Because the sophisticated code is the vehicle for practical reasoning, it cannot have the intellectual luxury of simple binary judgments. In some cases, of course, that is possible; for example, a verdict of guilty or not guilty. But even then, when it comes to pun-

ishment, the court in many cases cannot start with the committing of a crime and stop there but must go on to ask how
heinous was the crime. When Lloyd George is making fun of
the landlords, he can present them at one end of the line: bad.
But if he proposes to take action against them (as he claimed
to have done in his budget), then he (that is, his servants in the
Treasury and his colleagues in the Cabinet) should have been
involved in complex calculations about how much landlords
could afford, how to cope with different types of landlord,
how strong would be the resistance, and so on—all calculations of "How much?" rather than of "Either this or that."
Not black and white, but everything is a shade of gray, and
what must be ascertained is the degree of grayness. So sophisticated codes are detailed and specified, not only because they
take into account many variables, but also because they must
see those variables as a series of points along a continuum and
cannot simplify by dealing only with one or the other end of
the continuum.

Because such a code is designed to deal with reality, it must
contain, for those who work with it, the means to monitor
their performance and to change their policies, plans, or procedures (including the code itself) in order to cope with changed
circumstances. That is, one of the defining rules of a sophisticated code (without which it is not sophisticated) is that the
code itself is not sacred, that its efficacy must constantly be
questioned, and that in the end no procedure can ever be so
firmly established that it cannot be changed.

The code, therefore, must give those who operate it the capacity to judge success and failure. On some occasions success
or failure is so transparent that the verdict is "objective"—
which only means, as I argue elsewhere, that anyone who
reaches a different verdict is deemed to be out of his mind.
The Germans lost World War II, and the capitulation, the
Nuremberg trials, the reparations, and the occupation forces
all serve as "objective" indicators that they did. But thirty
years later, looking at the thriving German economy and the
far from thriving state of affairs in Britain, one could make a
plausible case that it was Britain that "really" lost the war. That

kind of judgment is not objective in the same way: it is patently a matter of opinion, and can be argued several ways, depending on what indicators of success and failure are selected. So there are many other occasions on which the decision about whether a plan has failed or has been successfully implemented cannot easily be made. But if that decision is not made, then the process of feedback and adjustment is halted. We should therefore expect to find in sophisticated codes a recognition of such difficulties and we should expect procedures built into them for finding "objectivity." But objectivity, I have argued, in the context of persuasion means only a measure of agreement on the judgment of success or failure. We therefore find these agreements conventionalized as voting procedures, in the role of a judge or arbiter (one whose decision may not be questioned), or in oracles and the like (drawing lots, consulting astrologers, seeking guidance through prayer)—devices that put the decision out of the hands of the people concerned and into those of a divinity. Perhaps it seems strange to count such "superstitions" within the apparatus of a sophisticated code, but the fact remains that they are ways of breaking an impasse and contriving a form of objectivity.

The users of a sophisticated code assume that there is an objective world outside those who are debating and making decisions about what to do, a world that sets immediate and clear and inescapable imperatives; indeed, that is the fundamental assumption, the premise on which everything else is built. But this does not mean that all those who take part in a discourse guided by a sophisticated code are objective in the sense that they are free from values and attitudes. Instead it means that there is a large measure of agreement about goals and purposes and procedures. To some extent this is likely to be a tacit understanding that differences should not be aired and should be treated as irrelevant to the task in hand. But one can also infer from the way in which communication often operates through nuances (a topic to which we shall come in a moment) that there is also a great deal of common and shared understanding. To be able to operate a sophisticated code, those engaged in the discourse must be largely beyond the need to sell one another on rapport. They are debating about means: the ends are given. Of course, that is the good bureaucrat's dream world; the reality of their experience is different. We shall come later to consider the fragility of sophisticated codes.

The term "code" has several senses that are relevant to our discussion. Both in my definition and in the subsequent argument I have used it to mean a set of regulations, like a code of law, or a housing code, or a code of honor. But it can also mean a system of signals, like semaphore or Morse. It can also mean secret writing. All three senses share, in different degrees the ideas of restriction. Law codes apply to particular categories of person and not to others. A code of honor sets a boundary around a class (as in the case of "gentlemen") or around those belonging to an institution (the code of the regiment, or Boy Scout "honor"). Systems of signaling are restricted to those who know how to operate the code. Restriction is precisely the intention in the case of ciphers.

Those who can work within a code, in any of its senses, are to some extent experts. Experts have a set of common understandings, which enable them to communicate with one another with brevity. They do not have to spell things out in detail. In other words, and paradoxically, while the sophisticated code (in the sense of a set of regulations) tends to grow in bulk because it must deal in specifics (I argued that point earlier), its mode of communication (code as a signaling system) moves in the other direction. In Britain, at the time when the "Establishment" was the journalists' topic of the day, I heard a radio interview with a man of affairs. He was making the point that those within the circle (it was the world of banking and finance and business corporations) did not need to waste words in communicating with one another. "A week or two back a friend telephoned. He is a banker and he had in mind to bring someone I knew onto his staff. He asked my opinion. "A worthy chap," I said. "Thanks," he said. "That's good to know. I'll look elsewhere."

Those are the features of the ideal sophisticated code. To summarize: it is a vehicle for debate; it puts the solution of problems in the "real" world ahead of relationships between those engaged in the debate; it is designed to make those who use it responsive to feedback; it includes devices for judging performance and contrivances for making that judgment "objective"; it handles specifics rather than generalities and therefore tends to be filled with detail, but at the same time opinions and ideas and points of view tend to be communicated in hints and allusions; and built into it is the assumption that it is an instrument to be changed and modified and even discarded if it fails to let people do the job properly.

Now let us look at the way such a code is framed.

A code supposes at least two people between whom messages pass. Before that can be done they have to agree on the code: a suggestion as to how they should communicate has to be made and accepted. This does not, of course, mean that every committee meeting (or any other task-oriented assembly) has to open with a formal agreement on the conventions that will guide their discourse, although such a statement from the chairman is not uncommon, especially in the case of an ad hoc group, the members of which have not met before: "Gentlemen, my practice on such occasions as this is to assume that everyone has read the documents and understands the question at issue, and then to ask each member in turn to give us his thoughts. We will then have a general discussion, which I will summarize from time to time, and in that way we will, I hope, come to the right decision. It should not take more than an hour." He may also remind them of the regulations that govern their conduct and their deliberations; for example, of the requirement that both the documents and the deliberations must be kept in confidence; or that, since they are an advisory committee, they should not attempt to compromise a disagreement, because a plain and clear statement of difference in principle will be of more service to those required to make the decision than would a confused compromise.

Coded into that last statement on compromise is a claim that the debate should be carried on under the conventions of a sophisticated code. An agreement on principles is assumed: the committee's task is to apply those principles to the present case and deduce the correct solution. It is implied that if they cannot agree upon that solution, then their reasoning is at fault, possibly because they have allowed other principles or interests to get in the way. Even if they themselves fail to achieve the Cartesian ideal of matching each problem with its correct solution, that ideal must be preserved.

In the case of committees that meet regularly, there may be no need for an initial framing, because the code to be used has been established in previous meetings. Nevertheless, as we noticed when discussing play and joking, deliberations are likely to be punctuated from time to time by words or actions that remind those taking part of the values and premises that should govern the debate. These reminders are themselves not part of the sophisticated code: they are assertions (sometimes, as I have demonstrated, in an oblique manner) that the sophisticated code is the appropriate one. They may also be phrased in terms of "responsibility," of "work to be done," or of terse reprimands to members who allow their civic selves to be overcome by emotional displays indicating a moral self or a divine self or a disruptive silly self: "That kind of behavior will get us nowhere!"

These are examples of explicit claims that a particular communicative procedure should be in use. Is there a distinction to be made between claims and signs? Signs are those features by which we recognize a particular form of communication. Thus a sophisticated code is engaged with a "real" world, it is apt to be specific and detailed, and so forth; assertive rhetoric is concerned with feelings and attitudes and relationships, tends to invoke authority, to separate "us" from "them," to make judgments about persons rather than systems, and so forth. But signs also can function as claims. Can we therefore make a distinction between the kind of framing that says, "Please let us use this code!" and another kind that simply launches into the code, implicitly inviting a reply in the same mode? In Losa, in the province of Cuneo, in northern Italy, some of the inhabitants had three languages at their disposal: the village dialect, Piedmontese, and Italian. To begin an exchange in one of these languages invites the person addressed to respond in the same language. The choice of one or other language carries various messages about relationships and status, but that is not our present concern. Rather it is this: the code itself, so to speak, is its own frame. The speaker cannot, on pain of being thought odd, open with an appeal to converse in a particular language other than in that language. He can, of course, reject an offer, but he is likely to do so by using one of the other languages. The claim, in other words, can be made only through signs; it is not made explicitly.

The same is true of the framing of assertive rhetoric. To open such an address with the statement "Now I am going to arouse your emotions, for it is the appropriate thing to do" would be to frame the message in a denial. Rhetoric (in any form), once perceived and labeled as rhetoric, is thereby canceled. It is said (Rhodes James, 1969:122) that Winston Churchill, having delivered during the war a moving speech in the House of Commons (his audience was moved and he too, as was his wont, gave every sign of being impassioned), came out of the chamber, encountered a friend, and, with an "impish grin," said, "That got the sods, didn't it!" Imagine the effect of such a statement to the "sods" themselves, before or after the speech.

The case of sophisticated codes (and of pseudo-cerebral rhetoric) is different. There is a choice. One may launch straight into the address and thus cajole the hearer into accepting the code. Alternatively, one may frame the address with direct claims or appeals that it is apposite. The same choice is open in the case of pseudo-cerebral rhetoric, inasmuch as that form of address masquerades as task-oriented discourse.

Such explicit framing is, as I have said, itself a form of assertive rhetoric, and the conditions that make for the use of assertive rhetoric also apply to it. If the speaker feels that the premise of task priority has been accepted, he may slide straight into the sophisticated code. If that is in doubt, then he is likely to spend time and energy asserting (in the case of pseudo-rhetoric "demonstrating") that the task must have priority.

In the course of making these general observations about the features and indicators of a sophisticated code, relatively few examples have been offered. In fact, they are hard to find because in *natural* discourse (as distinct from an artificial language) the absolute standard of objectivity and impersonality never remains free from contamination by other forms of exchange. Once again, having set the ideal types at each end of the line, when we come face to face with the world of action, we cannot ask whether this is in one category or the other, but rather how much of each category has gone into making the mixture that constitutes the event. I have also several times remarked that a sophisticated code is a fragile thing and that there is a tendency for debates to slip easily into one or another form of rhetoric. Indeed, a main argument is that on many occasions there is no means other than the use of rhetoric to reach a decision.

In this section we shall further examine this law of entropy (a phrase obviously more agreeable to those who would like to believe in a Cartesian scientific universe than to others reconciled to living in the middle ground of muddling through and settling for approximations). We shall do so by means of examples, beginning with one that comes nearest to that end of the continuum at which rational discourse is found and a sophisticated code is used. Then we shall descend by degrees toward rhetorical exchanges.

The first example (Morris-Jones, 1957:398) comes from the Provisional Parliament in India, in March 1952. The finance minister (Deshmukh) is replying to a debate on the Finance Bill.

Shri C. D. Deshmukh: Then there is the question which crops up again and again. I am informed that it is wrong to say that in U.P. and Madhya Pradesh the Election Commissioner's instructions were not observed. No ballot boxes used by any State were unapproved by the Election Commission. A ballot box which is not closed and sealed properly can of course be opened with a hair pin or any other pin. But merely because a ballot box is tamperable one need not necessarily draw the conclusion that in all cases over whole States the boxes were tampered with.

Shri Kamath: Nobody says that.

Shri Sondhi: That is not the allegation.

Pandit Kunzru: May I know whether the Election Commission has sent for the Presiding Officers and asked them how they sealed their boxes as soon as the voting was over?

Shri C. D. Deshmukh: I could not say what action the Election Commission has taken. This is the information that I have received from him.

Shri Kamath: In the States other than U.P. and Madhya Pradesh the ballot boxes were manufactured by Godrej or Allwyn. In these two States the boxes were manufactured locally.

Shri C. D. Deshmukh: I did not deny that, but that does not necessarily mean that they were tamperable.

Mr. Deputy Speaker: Were they not steel boxes? In Madras wooden boxes or plywood ones were used and no such thing happened. I was myself a candidate.

Shri Kamath: In Madhya Pradesh the boxes used were cottage industry products.

Shri C. D. Deshmukh: I am sorry I shall not be able to throw any more light.

The Minister of Works, Production and Supply (Shri Gadgil): Veritable Pandora's box!

Shri Kamath: Where is Pandora?

As Morris-Jones remarks, it is a lively debate without being hostile. It might not have been so, for Deshmukh was the only I.C.S. man (Indian Civil Service—a *corps d' elite* established by the British) in the government and on frequent occasions came into conflict with his Congress colleagues (Brecher, 1959:456). Why was the debate restrained and kept more or less within the bounds of a sophisticated code?

The members of the house are dealing with a practical and very specific matter—tampering with ballot boxes—and discussing, in a somewhat desultory fashion, whether anything had gone seriously wrong and what might be done about it in the future. It is not, judging from the tone of the debate, considered to be a matter of great moment; and no doubt that fact helps to keep the exchanges at the civilized level required in parliamentary procedures.

There are occasional slips. Deshmukh points to a piece of pseudo-cerebration—the hyperbole involved in assuming that if a hairpin can be used to open a badly sealed box, then all the boxes in that state had been rigged—and implicitly attributes it to his complainants. But he is promptly brought back to the standards of a sophisticated code: "Nobody says that" and "That is not the argument." A few moments later there is an example of the enthymeme. In the discussion of locally and cottage-industry-made boxes, the unspoken premise is that boxes made in the state are inferior to those made by Godrej or Allwyn; there is even the further premise, for those with resolutely cynical minds, that local boxes might be deliberately made to the specifications of local politicians to meet their standards of tamperability. But that premise, which might have given an excuse particularly for those enamoured of cottage industries (another Gandhian concern) to take offense, was never uttered. Instead it was countered, in a perfectly rational and low-key manner, by pointing out that wooden boxes (presumably locally made) had been used in Madras and there had been no complaints.

Another sign of the acceptance of a sophisticated code is that people were willing to take "That is all the information I have" or "I am sorry I shall not be able to throw any more light" as reasonable replies. It indicates that they have the matter in proportion; that they have their eyes on the problem and realize that no further progress will be made toward its solution by pressing for more information on that occasion; and that they are not intent on humiliating or harassing Deshmukh.

Notice finally the mild play at the end of the extract. One hopes that Shri Kamath was also at play, and has not gone down in history as the man who wondered whether Pandora was not that place near Bhandara.

The second example also has a mild humor about it. Unlike Shri Deshmukh and his colleagues who were discussing what had already taken place, and what lessons might be drawn from it, Austin and his colleagues are making a decision about what they should do. The material is taken from C. P. Snow's novel *The Search*. The occasion is a committee set up by the Royal Society to report on "the desirability of a National Institute for Biophysical Research." At their first meeting they debated where they should meet. The following is taken from Snow, 1960:220–223 (the book was first published in 1934). I have left out some of the author's comments.

"I take it," said Austin, "we shall meet at regular intervals until we have thrashed out a report. And I take it that London, either here in Burlington House or in my rooms at the College, is the obvious meeting place."

"I wonder," Desmond put in, his eyes darting around us, "whether we mightn't perhaps do better. London's a long way for some of us—particularly Professor Fane."

Fane smiled.

"Oh, perhaps Professor Fane will say he doesn't mind leaving Manchester," said Desmond cheerfully. "That's reasonable enough: but ought we to bring him quite as far? We could put you up at Oxford, you know. As often as you like to come. I could put two men up in B.N.C.—and the other Colleges"—he waved his hands, and seemed to indicate Colleges pressing hospitality on scientific committees.

"It would be inconvenient to many of us," said Austin, "to have meetings out of London. And it would upset the centre of gravity of the Committee."

"I should like to remind Sir George," said Pritt, in a high, harsh voice, "that we're not paid travelling expenses. If we have all the meetings in London, it will come unfair to those who live out of town. I should like to support Professor Desmond's suggestion that we have them in Oxford—and Cambridge. And in London in vacations." . . .

Fane said, "If we took a distribution of our geography, we

should reach a centre somewhere round Banbury. Would that satisfy Desmond and Pritt?"

Desmond at once responded to the satirical smile: "While we're about it," he said, "we might have a good time every weekend at the seaside. Go round the coast, starting at Eastbourne and going west. Like Labour Party Conferences."

"We're not as rich as Trade Union Leaders," said Pritt. The rest of us were beginning to smile. Constantine was working out something; he spoke for the first time:

"Our average income must actually be a good deal greater than the Trade Union Chairmen or Secretaries," he announced. "Even if none of us had any private means, which is improbable statistically and which I believe isn't true." With his born indifference to money, he might have expected the others to disclose their incomes: but, knowing that most of them would be shocked, I headed him off:

"Where do these Committees usually meet?" I asked. It was a relic from College meetings, the question of an irrelevant precedent. But it pleased Austin.

"The first I ever sat on," he said loudly, "was in old Kelvin's day. He died a year or two later, but, of course, he didn't expect us to go to Glasgow; he came to London himself, without any argument. I consider our friend Pritt has got this out of *proportion*."

"Perhaps," said Fane, "we could get out of this impasse by what might be called an equipollent compromise. If we met in rotation three times in London, once in Oxford, once in Cambridge and once in Manchester, that would represent us with equity enough to satisfy Desmond and Pritt: and, in addition, be quite remarkably inconvenient."

"Only twice in London," said Pritt. "Miles is co-opted. He can't count for this."

"As Chairman I should rule that Miles did count for this purpose," Austin enunciated, "if we adopted any such unworkable plan."

Desmond broke in, "Of course, we've got to have an arrangement which will work. It's easier if we meet at the same place. And at the same time. Like lectures. And bridge-parties. And any sort of whoopee."

"We're wasting time," said Pritt. . . .

"We're considering a suggestion from our Oxford and Cambridge colleagues," said Fane.

"The sense of the meeting is, I feel," said Austin, "that we meet in *London*."

Fane, as the reader will have gathered, held his appointment in Manchester, at that time about four hours' journey from London. Austin, Constantine, and the narrator (Miles) were based in London. Those who believe that charity begins at home (but should be pocketed discreetly) will be pleased to know that Desmond and Pritt held appointments in Oxford and Cambridge respectively, each about two hours' travel away from London.

The chairman begins with an assertion that is a statement of the task in front of them: they are required to "thrash out a report." Although an assertion, this is legitimate and acceptable to all the members of the committee, since they have already committed themselves to it by accepting the invitation to take part or to be co-opted. He draws the reasoned conclusion that they will have to meet at regular intervals in order to do so, and this statement too—a specification of part of what has to be done to fulfill the task—is beyond argument. (That is to say, the members make no argument; a generation later, one or another of them might have made a bid for a ten-day "workshop" at some agreeable conference center.)

One senses behind all this a quiet assumption that they live in a Cartesian universe: they have been set a problem and will use reason to find the correct solution. After all, every one of them (except Miles, who was co-opted) is a fellow of the Royal Society, the ultimate accolade of distinction in the British scientific world. Such men, cool, dispassionate, their creative thinking framed for the most part in the unambiguous symbols of the natural sciences, obviously need no reminder to make them value reason and eschew the tricks of rhetoric.

Then, in his second sentence, the chairman pulls just such a trick. London, he says, is the "obvious" meeting place. It is a monstrous enthymeme: neither major nor minor premise is offered and the conclusion alone is asserted. He might have made an appropriate argument, suggesting, for example, the inconvenience of transporting secretarial help and documents around the country, or in some other way making deductions from the nature of the task, which would have provided a legitimate and acceptable premise, to the place of meeting. But it is also a more than blatant piece of pseudo-cerebral persuasion. The word "obvious," especially in the context of "thinking" men, carries suggestions of inclusion and exclusion. It is an indirect moral statement that those who cannot accept this conclusion are not merely mistaken; they are also unworthy and should not be in such a gathering of distinguished intellects.

Clearly I am squeezing this a little to make a point. But the reaction of Desmond and Pritt is consistent with such an interpretation. It seems that they are sufficiently moved to make them emulate the chairman and stay away from rational arguments related to the task. Instead they fish out the unspoken premise: "Where we meet is to be decided on the basis of the members' convenience." Then they add, without speaking it, the further assumption that no man's convenience should weigh more than another's. In fact Desmond lightly covers that rough fact of clashing self-interests with hints about the delights of Oxford and the insalubrity of Manchester.

The chairman responds in two ways, neither of which fully conforms with the canons of a sophisticated code. To travel around would be "inconvenient to many of us." This is no more than to butt one assertion against another. But then he attempts to strengthen the case for the three London-based members against the three outsiders by talking of the "centre of gravity." The words are ambiguous. He may mean that the committee is the creation of the Royal Society and the Royal Society has its rooms in London. That is indisputable but possibly not very persuasive. But he talks of "the centre of gravity of the Committee," by which he can only mean the three London members, thus asserting—and offensively—that they are intrinsically more important than the members who come from Oxford, Cambridge, and Manchester. (Later this leads to an argument about the status of Miles. As a co-opted person, is he truly a full member of the committee?)

This produces two diversions. Pritt, using the same form as the argument about inconvenience, buttresses it with an argument about expense. Constantine, a wealthy man evidently, implies that the money involved is trivial and may therefore be ignored, and appears likely to use a sophisticated approach to demonstrate that what he says is correct by taking a means test. The narrator, Miles, prevents this, knowing that "most of them would be shocked." It is interesting to work out the significance of their being shocked. First, a means test would be a violation of that proper reserve which is supposed to shape the interactions of the English upper classes. If one has a heart, it is kept in the chest cavity and not worn on the sleeve; and that goes also for one's finances. Second, it might bring to the surface not only income but also class differences between the members. (Earlier Snow tells us that Pritt, who raises the question of money, has gone to "a Chair in Cambridge" after "a long tenure of a professorship in one of the Welsh Colleges." In case you do not know the relative status of Cambridge and "one of the Welsh Colleges," notice the capital letter; "Chair" and "professorship.") Third, and perhaps most significant for our purpose, the ambience in which a sophisticated code can be made to work is one in which the importance of the person is suppressed. It is also the bureaucratic ethos: whatever attributes a person has outside his office are of no account.

The second diversion is into play. Fane, nicely ironic, makes a pretense of using a sophisticated code to work out the geographical center (Banbury). Desmond, responding to the tone, leads them off to seaside junkets, thus indicating through the symbols that they were getting away from the serious task that lies before the committee. Desmond has been the first to raise objections to regular meetings in London; by now he evidently thinks that they have gone far enough and should get back to work.

The narrator must feel the same way, because he uses a device that he calls an "irrelevant precedent" to bring the discussion back to a serious level. But it misfires. Austin, the chairman, is delighted to recall that Kelvin "didn't expect us to go to Glasgow; he came to London himself, without any argument." The implication is that if the great (and then old) man could travel overnight to attend meetings in London, then the lesser people on Austin's committee can travel lesser distances and do the same. He then attacks Pritt, telling him he has "got this out of *proportion.*"

Fane once again resorts to ironic play, apportioning the meetings according to residence. " . . . that would represent us with equity enough to satisfy Desmond and Pritt: and [he adds with donnish waspishness] in addition, be quite remarkably inconvenient." But the irony is lost on Pritt, who attempts to elaborate and make more specific the arrangement (and suit the out-of-town members better) by questioning the status of Miles.

At this point one of the devices available in a sophisticated code for breaking an impasse is used—the chairman's authority. "As Chairman I should rule that Miles did count for this purpose," Austin says, adding, "if we adopted any such unworkable plan."

Then both Desmond and Pritt yield, but in different ways. Desmond sprinkles his agreement with play: regular meetings, like lectures and "any sort of whoopee," are best held in the same place. Pritt (after another exchange, which I have omitted) says, "We're wasting time." With these statements both of them acknowledge that they have a task in front of them. This enables the chairman to use his authority once again, masking it behind the ceremonial phrase of consensus "the sense of the meeting."

Turn now to a third example. It describes another Indian legislature: the Central Legislative Assembly in 1928. India was then ruled by the British, and the executive could not be removed from office (Morris-Jones, 1957:390–391). The occasion is the general discussion of the budget, and the finance member, the Honourable Sir Basil Blackett (hereafter BB), is fielding the comments. The particular exchange to be described took place after a statement by His Excellency the

Commander-in-Chief. Their antagonist is the member for the cities of the United Provinces, non-Muhammadan urban, Pandit Motilal Nehru (hereafter MN, and, incidentally, the father of Jawaharlal Nehru).

MN: His Excellency said that some of the Indian soldiers who were sent to China made large remittances home. That again was a very interesting piece of information to give. Where did these remittances come from? Was it the savings from their salaries, or was it loot which they were allowed to make from the poor Chinese? If it was . . .

BB: The savings from their salaries, Sir.

MN: What about their savings in India then? Why should they be able to save money in China, in a foreign country and not in India?

BB: I do not know why, but I can assure you that they did save.

MN: I am sure they did; but probably they were let loose upon the Chinese who . . . (Cries of: "Withdraw" from the Government Benches.) I am not going to withdraw. I repeat a thousand times that our soldiers were not used . . (Cries of "Order" and "Withdraw".) You may shout yourselves hoarse. I will not withdraw. I say our soldiers were not used for the honourable purposes for which a soldier should be used. (Cries of "Hear, hear" from the Congress Party benches.) They were used in order to humiliate the nationals of another country who wanted to assert their independence against . . .

Mr. G. M. Young (*Army Secretary*): You said they looted.

MN: You exacted from them a duty which, if they had been independent, they would have refused to perform.

BB: A lie.

MN: Am I to substantiate what is human nature to my learned friends over there? I say it is human nature and I repeat it a thousand times over in spite of all the noise that has been made on the other side.

BB: I say it is a foul slander.

MN: Then you are so full of animal nature that you have no idea of what human nature is or ought to be. It is nothing but animal nature which prompted the sending of these troops there in spite of the protest we made in India. . . .

By the end of this extract the facade of sophistication has clearly cracked: "foul slander" and "you are so full of animal nature" are hardly within the bounds of parliamentary decorum.

Let us first set the scene. MN replied to the address of the commander-in-chief by complaining that plans to "Indianize" the army—that is, appoint Indians as commissioned officers— were, like certain other proposals, "for the purpose of throwing dust in the eyes of the world." There was a want of sincerity: "The insatiable greed of the Government for domination would not contemplate even at a remote date the contingency of India's standing on her own feet." He detested the word "Indianization." "What do you mean by Indianizing India?" "The Army is ours; we have to officer our own Army; there is no question of Indianizing there. What we want is to get rid of the Europeanization of the Army."

But mixed in with this assertive rhetoric—which was, as we shall see, appropriate to the large context—was a continuing strand of sophisticated discourse. MN specified what he meant by the want of sincerity and indicated what might be done to reach the goal. There was money enough to found training academies in India. Moreover, men were sent to Sandhurst for officer training in England, and failed the course because they had not sufficient command of English. But they had been selected because they belonged to the "martial races" or had a family tradition of service in the army, whereas there were many other candidates who could have passed the course.

Just as the vituperation about looting was a token of the resentment felt about Indianization, so also was this question, as the extract makes clear, itself a token of the larger grievance: India's subordination to the British. From this springs the startling lack of civility apparent in the debate. Deshmukh and those who questioned him in 1952 nevertheless shared the commonalty of free India. Government and opposition each viewed the other as legitimate: they were working together, in rivalry but also in cooperation, for the good of the country. But this overarching premise of agreement was absent in 1928. The government, in Congress' eyes, was alien and autocratic. It had set up the forms of democracy but did not permit the reality of even a partial and limited democracy. The government, represented in this extract by the three Europeans, lacked legitimacy. From the government side the Congress opposition had forfeited any claim to legitimacy by its irresponsible behavior in hastening toward precipitate independence. Given so fundamental a difference in the definition both of reality and of goals, it is not to be wondered that the maintenance of a sophisticated code was difficult.

But the simulacrum of sophistication remained. In the opening part of his address, MN refers to an Indian whom he accused of colluding in the effort to throw "dust in the eyes of the world" as "my friend." The commander-in-chief is mentioned as "His Excellency." A committee on the subject, from which MN resigned, announcing that he was happy not to have to put his name to the recommendations, is mentioned as one on which MN "once had the honour to serve"; irony perhaps, but more likely just habit.

A sophisticated code also appears—intermittently—in the substance of the debate, even in that acrimonious section dealing with the question of looting in China. The complaint comes out in the form of reason: troops cannot save and send remittances home when they are in India. If they do so from China, then the transmitted funds must have been the proceeds of looting. The way could have been opened to factual argument: for example, that there are overseas allowances or few opportunities to spend money abroad. But this, route was not taken. Notice that BB replied as Deshmukh did: that he did not know the answer, but he was sure that the remittances came from savings. Deshmukh's questioneers were content to let him say, "I am sorry I shall not be able to throw any more light." MN was not. Instead he moved quickly from the lesser to the greater charge: Indian troops had been taken to China and had been made to perform tasks ("humiliating" the Chinese who were fighting for their independence, like the Indians) they would not have done if they had been free men. They were not used "for the honourable purposes for which a soldier should be used." That word "honourable" in the context of professional soldiers at the officer level has a very sharp edge.

There was then a swift—and seemingly ill-tempered—push back toward a sophisticated code: "You said they looted." That means: "You have made a charge and you should substantiate it with evidence, like a reasonable man." (The remark also, clearly, serves a rhetorical purpose in diverting—but only for a moment—attention from the topic of the dishonorable use of Indian troops by the government.)

From that point until the end of the extract the sophisticated code has vanished. MN begins that way by putting forward the premise of human nature (that is, all troops loot when they can) but swiftly attaches the innuendo that the government and the officers connived at this activity. Then the symbols take control, and Sir Basil Blackett is told that he is "full of animal nature."

At the end of his address, apparently calm enough to turn away from abuse directed at persons, MN produced this piece of pure assertive rhetoric: ". . . this is an age-long affair. There have been Empires before this which have done the same thing. They have ignored the lesson of history, and the British Empire is doing the same. I will not say more on this occasion but sit down after again repeating the warning that the day of reckoning is not very far" (Morris-Jones, 1957:392).

Notice the personal abuse and the interjections of "lie" and "foul slander" earlier. Even following Ambedkar's "sink of localism" speech, which gave great offense, the tone of the reprimands sounded "more in sorrow than in anger." But in the present instance the moral exclusion is made explicit: the critic and his antagonist are not of one kind, because the latter is "full of animal nature." MN's moral outrage recalls Churchill likening Mussolini to a jackal.

The forms and procedures for the use of a sophisticated code were there, for this was, after all, a legislative assembly. As we have seen, they were to some extent manifested. But the umbrella of agreement about fundamentals was absent and the antagonists turned away from the (lesser) question at issue—the Indianization of the officer corps—to indulge in mutual disparagement. One characteristic of a sophisticated code is its conditioning people into being receptive to feedback. In this case there was none. At least in this exchange, there was no "objective" discussion about feasible rates of training young Indians to be officers in the Indian Army, and such "objective" comments as those made about the process of selection at the opening of MN's address were left unanswered. No doubt a case could have been made, but the issue too soon was pushed up to the level of the fundamental divergence: an independent India.

So there are three examples of situations in which the use of a sophisticated code is formally required. In all three cases the people have a hard time in staying within that limit: some slight lapses in the case of Shri Deshmukh, greater difficulties (but surmounted) for the members of the Royal Society's committee, and by the end of Motilal Nehru's speech a more or less total regression into assertive rhetoric.

The debate over the ballot boxes is on the whole rational, rather dull and pedestrian, workmanlike, the eyes being focused on a task that is apparently not of commanding importance. No one involves himself with the other person in any direct way. (They do so indirectly by their very civility.) They stay with the subject.

After the very first statement by Austin in the debate over where the committee should meet, personal interests are involved. So are the personalities—this is, of course, partly the result of the novelist's artifice. We see the authoritarian character of Austin, learn of Constantine's quaintness, are told that Pritt has the values of a "peasant," and Desmond is presented as a jovial and skillful manipulator of other people. Here is Desmond, for example (Snow, 1960:222): "He was enjoying himself. His sentences finished a little breathlessly, I noticed, and he looked round for an answering smile. The supreme commercial traveller, I thought again: and I recalled a public house where I went as a youth, and the travellers gathered round the fire. They would have welcomed Desmond as a man and a brother." The analysis continues on the next page: "The danger was, I told myself, that one forgot how that flickering mirror, that immediate salesman-like response, went hand in hand with an intuitive cunning; that men of Desmond's sort sometimes had the unconscious craft of a coquette; and that Desmond, who had very little mental machinery, against Constantine, who had the best I knew, would always win in a worldly battle of wits." People are like that, in life as well as in novels, and they cannot leave their entire personality at the door when they curtain themselves off in committee. Such traits, like the personal interests, provide a rough journey for those who would like to travel by the map of a sophisticated code.

Motilal Nehru, in a long passage (not quoted here) near the beginning of this speech, addressing himself to the task (the Indianization of the army's officer corps), makes use of a sophisticated code. He offers rational arguments about increasing the number of military colleges in India, about ways of making a sensible selection of candidates, and so forth. Also the manner of the address retains some of the indicators of a sophisticated code found in the conventions of parliamentary exchanges. But, as the speech goes on and he is interrupted, the task vanishes and is replaced by a discourse on persons and to persons. He questions their good faith. They pretend to subscribe to a common value, but they are not sincere. They are not sincere because they are afraid that an Indian-officered army will hasten India's freedom. That is the real issue, and since he does not believe that the government accepts either the lesser goal (army officers) or (still less) the greater goal (independence for India), he regresses to the rhetoric of assertion, in this instance to accusations, abuse and threats—"the day of reckoning is not very far."

So a sophisticated code, being the vehicle of rationality, is a fragile thing. Even when there is agreement on the task and on its importance, the inevitable divergences that arise over means can readily be linked to values that are independent of the task—like the "convenience" of the members of Austin's committee. Sometimes they may even be not just independent of but superior to the task; the issue of "fairness" in that same committee has this potentiality. (It was trumped by upper-class English reserve and reticence about personal money matters.) Such issues can be inflated to the point where they shut out the task.

Now we turn in the other direction and consider what happens when a sophisticated code slides not toward the other two forms of rhetoric (pseudo-cerebral and assertive) but toward ossification and ritualization.

A sophisticated code contains devices that enable those who use it to decide whether what they do is succeeding or failing. There is first the main injunction to work at the task—to "thrash out a report," to "implement the plan," or whatever. There are reminders, when the discussion drifts away into something irrelevant: "We are wasting time." Then there are contrivances such as voting, calling for an outside opinion, producing periodically a progress report, or even the institutionalization of a loyal opposition. Lastly there is the overarching scientific assumption that methods and procedures are just that and no more. They are tools that should be sharpened when they lose their edge or discarded if better tools are found. To the extent that the code is truly sophisticated, everything but the goal itself (and sometimes that too is changed) ranks as an instrument to be valued only for its usefulness. The rule is: It is a sin to fall in love with your paradigms.

But, of course, people do get to feel affection for their paradigms and become emotionally involved with their parameters, wanting them to be constant, not just in the case considered, but in every case and for all time. The monitoring devices and the assessment procedures have exactly the purpose of countering this tendency. But they may fail, and a committee that once coped with a real world and could digest experience and gain new strength from that experience, even when negative, now becomes senile and the sophisticated code becomes oversophisticated. When that happens, the monitoring and assessing devices are likely to be preserved in their form (to some degree), but everyone colludes in seeing that the books are cooked and that any experience that might question the value of the code is filtered out.

This is not the natural history only of committees. The same process can be observed in research teams; in schools of inquiry (functionalist anthropology, symbolic anthropology, structuralism, etc.); in religious sects and religions generally, for that is what "religion" means—faith; and, indeed, it is the tragedy (or, perhaps from the point of view of inner peace, the saving) of every succeeding generation to live partly in the past and to close off the experience that might have come from the acquisition of present skills or the adoption of present values. It can also happen to governments:

> Nowhere was the consequence of the suppression of debate and the raising of alternative policies as dramatically obvious as in the area of security affairs. The security policy of Prime Minister Golda Meir and Defense Minister Moshe Dayan had boldly proclaimed that the retention of territories captured in the 1967 war gave Israel such strategic depth that the Arab countries could not possibly wage war against Israel. When a few isolated intellectuals attempted to question the major assumption on which this policy was based they were subjected to severe criticism which at times bordered on the questioning of their patriotism. No greater evidence of the perceived immutability of these assumptions exists than the fact that the army intelligence, when confronted with evidence of the buildup of the Egyptian and Syrian forces (prior to their attack), interpreted this as merely an exercise—so convinced were they of the premise that the Arabs would not attack Israel. So sure were the politicians of their oft-repeated policy that they delayed mobilizing the reserves when they were first presented evidence of the mobilization of the Arab armies.

> In a meeting with the Secretary-General of the Labor Party on October 17, 1973, local leaders reported "deep shock among the people" who "were asking questions which reach the sources of trust", and which indicated a growing "crisis of confidence in

the Government." Yadlin, representing the views of the top leadership replied, "The people will be wise. When the time comes for them to vote, they will vote correctly" (Aronoff, 1977:145). Such statements succinctly summarize the arrogance of power that had become characteristic of the leadership of the Labor Party as well as their insensitivity to public concerns. [Aranoff, 1980:20–21]

It can also happen with individuals. The following vignette, which will serve as an allegory for the senile committee, cannot describe an uncommon event. From time to time, in the various institutions in which I have worked, a term or even a year has been spent on a weekly seminar under the title of "Work in Progress." One's colleagues and outsiders are invited to talk about their current work. The experience of such seminars can be instructive and stimulating and may broaden the mind; one is also saved the agony of having to agree on a specific topic and the possible chore of having to work up a paper on a subject that is at the periphery of one's interests. It may happen on such occasions that one listens to a distinguished scholar setting out a research design that is embarrassingly flawed. Most designs have holes in them, and it is the legitimate purpose of the seminar to point them out and discuss what might be done. The speaker is expected to come to his own defense, to counter criticism or to accept it and build it into a new design, so far as he can on the spot. Most speakers accept this challenge and there should then ensue what is called a "constructive discussion."

Different critics display different degrees of aggression in making their points. It depends on their personality and on the custom of the institution, some places making sure that everyone has filed his teeth to a point before he comes into the seminar room, and others being more gentle and more indirect. The clarity of the comments also, of course, can vary. The instance that I have in mind revealed a young man who was habitually aggressive to the point of offensivenesss, but also remarkably clear-headed and articulate. Having listened to the great old man's design for research, he took it apart, piece by piece, demonstrating to his own satisfaction and that of everyone else in the room (except the great old man) that the research was likely to be sterile because one could forecast the results without ever looking at the empirical data: in short, it was banal. He stopped and everyone waited to see how the great old man would handle this, for he was, after all, a great old man and a renowned debater. "Thank you," he said, "that was most interesting. Now does anyone else have any comments?"

Let us go back to the committees. A sophisticated code, as we have defined it, can be in use only when the committee has a task that has to do with the "real" world outside the committee. Not all committees fall into this category. I described earlier groups that are sounding lines for the authorities or means of letting off steam, and they do not come within our definition because the only task concerns the members themselves and their well-being, not the world outside. Other committees have their task usurped or are set a task that cannot be performed. For the latter I have in mind a committee set up to plan for the acquisition and distribution of resources in a particular university over the next three years. Resources came from outside, from one particular authority, and there were few alternative sources, none of significance. The committee swiftly reached the conclusion that "they" were not giving us our fair share, and that something should be done about it. But when it came to deciding what should be done, they were at a loss, for they had neither the skills nor the information required to make concrete plans. Having met regularly and having come always to the same conclusion (that the university was not getting a fair deal), in effect they ceased to be task-oriented because they decided that the task given them was impossible.

That, in my definition, does not make them a senile committee, and did not drive them to the use of an oversophisticated code. They were, in fact, acutely sensitive to the world of experience (that is, to feedback) and had concluded that in the real world the goal set them was impossible of achievement. What happened to them I do not know. The most likely outcome, supposing they continued to meet, would be a marked rise in the frequency of play and ridicule, because they could not continue to take their work seriously.

So, as we see in this instance and the episode of the great old man and the letting-off-steam groups, there is a genus of committees that has no task in the world outside. Within this genus there is a particular species: the senile committee making use of an oversophisticated code. Its defining characteristic is that, despite available evidence to the contrary, the members continue to believe (or to behave as if they believed) that they are still performing an essential function.

Having defined institutional senility (or the senility of individuals or generations or whatever) as an incapacity to profit from experience, we now briefly recapitulate the conditions that bring about such a state.

We can be brief because these conditions have been discussed elsewhere. One of them is accountability: being answerable to someone outside the committee. The ideal case is the arena committee: that in which each member comes as the representative of some outside interest and is charged with fighting for that interest during the committee's deliberations. But, as I have argued, the members of such a committee get to know one another, and learn to make compromises, and perhaps learn to respect one another; they are then likely to learn to set a higher value on the general interest represented by the committee than on the particular interests that they severally are supposed to serve. This leads to the second condition, which is continuity. Frequent turnover, especially through elections in which the members become candidates and have to submit to the power of their constituents, will inhibit the development of elite sentiments. These sentiments crystallize in the notion of paternalism: that the committee has a collective wisdom superior to that found in those whose interests they are serving and whose lives they are directing.

For the ideal elite committee there are no constituents; there are only subjects. That, by and large, was the relationship between the Congress and the British executive when Motilal Nehru said his piece in the 1928 Central Legislative Assembly;

at least that is how Nehru and the Congress saw it. That also, until the upheavals of the 1960s, was the position of most students in most universities. Of course, an elite committee need not be without commentary on its performance; but the commentary does not come from below.

That commentary is supposed to come, in part, from within. The members of an elite committee are expected to have a highly developed sense of responsibility that requires no stimulation from the comments of those whom they rule (or "serve," as most of them prefer to say). The notion that they might be incipient sufferers from hypertrophy, obstinate, rigid, and stupid, is negated by concepts of "firmness" and "resoluteness" and "strength of character." Indeed, in the building of elite formations, as I have observed in new universities, much stress is laid on "character," and the spirit that governs the selection of such men has a tinge of the feudal—and more than a tinge of a witchcraft outlook on life. By that I mean the philosophy that places structural arrangements and bureaucratic regulations second to the genius of the individual. Find the good men, give them the job, and the structure will take care of itself: history, from this point of view, is the story of great men. When things go wrong, then the negative complement of the "great man" theory emerges in the form of witch hunting: get rid of him and find a better man—failures have nothing to do with faulty structures and there is no cause to change them. As we shall see, taken beyond a certain point this kind of thinking is characteristic of an oversophisticated code. But so long as the "right man" has been found for the job, he can be trusted to police himself and monitor his own performances. That is a part of wisdom, and—although the word is out of fashion and to use it about oneself would be to be thought, to say the least, somewhat smug—that quality best summarizes and encapsulates the nice balancing of firmness and flexibility with which the elite learn from observing themselves and their actions: they are wise men. Up to a point, it can work.

Many elite bodies also have outside sources for monitoring and assessment. They are not likely, other than in a token way, to permit their subjects to become constituents and voice their criticisms directly. Rather someone from outside the institution but within the "Establishment" is appointed as critic and commentator. Thus Oxford and Cambridge colleges have "visitors," bishops or other distinguished persons, who make ceremonial visits from time to time to see that all is up to scratch. (Perhaps that is a mildly unfair example, since the institution of "visitor" is something of a relic from past times. But notice in Snow's novel [1956:175] about a Cambridge college and the election of a new master—which is set in time between the two World Wars—that the statutes ordained that when the fellows could not divide so as to produce a clear majority for a candidate, the visitor had the right to step in and make his own appointment. That is, by the way, another impasse-breaking device of the type found in sophisticated codes.) The visitors and similar "inspectorates" are likely to be outside the institution but they are very much within the culture, having the same values as those whose work they are inspecting. There is, of course, an argument for this, if you subscribe to the fundamental assumption of wisdom and knowledge being restricted to the elite: that they alone are qualified to decide whether things have been well or badly done. That is the argument that allows most police forces in the world to do most of the inquiring into their own shortcomings.

In such circumstances there may well be scope for an honest and effective monitoring of what has been done; but there will be much less room for questioning the wisdom of fundamental goals and policies.

So much for the conditions that bring about the movement from an elite to a senile committee. We now ask about the code itself and the transformation from sophistication to over-sophistication. What processes are we likely to observe as the form is changed?

It all begins with attention to a good bureaucratic maxim: so far as is possible eliminate the human being as a maker of choices and decisions. Let everything be foreseen in the rules.

The policy of choosing "sound men" and leaving them to get on with the job unfettered and unhindered by regulation is an outlook profoundly antagonistic to bureaucratic values. As we remarked earlier, human beings have personalities that go beyond the bureaucratic persona and influence it, and these personalities cannot be checked in at the door, and so there enters uncertainty and other bad things such as favoritism and prejudice. Therefore personal choice must be eliminated and in its place must be put decision by regulation.

Why is there this horror of ambiguity? If there is choice because the rule is not clear, then there is a debate. If the regulations lay down how the debate shall take place, what constitutes victory, and so on, then not much is lost. In any case, even the fullest regulations cannot cover every eventuality; and even the stupidest drafter of bureaucratic regulations knows this. But a debate, as we have seen, may rise to the level of questioning general principles, may uncover inconsistencies, and thus may intensify the uncertainty. What was a debate becomes an altercation and then a fight. At that stage the sophisticated code has gone, the task has been lost from sight, and those who should be cooperating to get a job done are busily attending to each other's demise.

There are other potential disasters, too. The obvious solution when a gap is found in the regulations is to write a further regulation closing it; and so on. So begins a process of involution that produces such monstrously slow-moving machines as the colonial bureaucracies. A few years ago, purchasing a large-scale tourist map from a government department in India (costing a little more than $1), I spent two hours (passed in pleasant small talk with a number of officials) and signed my name no fewer than seven times on different documents. There were many other signatures on the papers too, as higher officials checked and certified the work of lower officials. But there is no need to elaborate the point: the potential for complexity in procedure and the consequent incomprehensibility is well known in every country, not India alone.

What is the outcome? One is the emergence of a species of tactical self, the person who can manipulate this very complexity to make it serve his own purpose. Here is a brief comment on Robert Moses, once park commissioner for New York:

> The key body whose approval was necessary—the Legislature that under the State Constitution alone had the power to create new authorities—had been fighting for years to keep Moses from gaining more power, from building his own empire within the state government. The Legislature would never approve the bills Moses was drafting if they understood them.
>
> So Moses would have to keep them—and all the other officials involved—from understanding. He would have to persuade Mayor, City Council, Legislature and Governor to approve his bills before they realized what was in them.
>
> In 1924, he had faced a similar problem—and had solved it successfully, persuadng the naive assemblymen to introduce, and hostile Republican legislative leaders to accept, bills that appeared innocuous but gave the Long Island State Park Commission vast new powers. This time, however, the job would be harder.   [Caro, 1974:624–25]

Caro spends the following six pages explaining in detail how it was accomplished; and it was done successfully. Moses was both skillful and cunning at drafting bills; and the bill, although very specific where it was to Moses' advantage, was to most other people incomprehensible until Moses chose to point out what powers it gave him.

Situations like that, together with the obvious inertia and inefficiency caused by excessively detailed regulation, may lead to reforms designed both to make the regulations more effective and less costly in time and effort to achieve their given purpose and designed to prevent abuses by cutting away the undergrowth in which villainy may flourish. That is, once the condition of oversophistication is diagnosed, there may be pressure to go back to first principles and redesign the code in order to restore its pristine sophistication. But this too, from the point of view of those who favor a sophisticated code and see its necessity, has its dangers. For the debate is not now about the details of implementation (how to make the ballot boxes tamperproof) but is apt to rise quickly to the level of first principles (freedom for British-dominated India) and thus to weaken the overarching consensus that is required for the use of a sophisticated code. The affair ceases to be administrative and becomes political: cooperation is lost and competition takes its place, and settlement can be achieved only by recourse to the nonrational devices of rhetoric.

The alternative outcome is a takeover by the code itself, so to speak. What are the signs in the code itself that this is happening?

There will very likely not be much retrenchment in the representational forms of debate: different points of view will be presented and most of the arguments will still be offered as if they were propositions capable of being proved true or false by the evidence. Oversophisticated codes preserve the forms of sophistication. The difference is that the propositions are not put rigorously to the test, for to do so would require careful attention to the information that was coming from the world outside the committee. Instead there is likely to be a resort to various pseudo-cerebral devices, which allow the members to rewrite negative feedback as positive, or to shut it out altogether. For example, there are a number of "quietist" devices. One is to "demonstrate" that the situation is by no means so serious as people have represented and there is no need at the moment to take action: left alone, the problem will solve itself. Another is to sketch out the kind of measures that might be taken, or to speculate about them, but to add that the time is not ripe and that to act now would be to act foolishly and invite disaster. That, broadly speaking, was the attitude of the British in Motilal Nehru's time about the Indianization of the officer corps and still more about Indian independence. A third possibility—and one that truly has the air of a sophisticated code—is to work out a long step-by-step program, showing logically that each advance is necessary before the next one can be taken: one thing at a time and learn to walk before you try to run. Alternatively one may simply praise the way things are, as in Mr. Macmillan's famous phrase "You never had it so good." If there is a difference in values, you can paper it over by claiming that all the facts are not available to those who do not agree with you, and once they learn those facts, then they can but accept your position. Whatever the devices, they all serve to demonstrate that what appears to be inaction is in fact prudence, and that what appears to be insensitivity to the wants of others is in fact a more true appreciation of their real needs than they have themselves. There is an ingenious secondary elaboration of beliefs to prove both to others and to the elite themselves that they are aware of what their duty is and that they are performing it.

Along with these devices goes the growth of a specialized vocabulary (Bailey, 1976). This is presented as the inevitable concomitant of specialized tasks, a form of necessary expertise, a striving for precision and logic and scientific reasoning. Sophisticated codes are pushed away from natural language and seek to avoid ambiguity in symbolic languages, such as those that characterize mathematics, logic, and the sciences. The language of the law, in particular that part which concerns itself with the writing of contracts, is an example; so are administrative regulations.

Such languages serve to make a further barrier between the elite body and the world beyond them. Those who live in that world do not know how to communicate in a language that the elite will accept as comprehensible: communications in natural speech violate the canons of the code and are likely to be judicially deemed meaningless, even when their meaning is perfectly plain. Nor is it only a matter of language in the strict sense. If, being on the outside, one does not know how to set in motion the correct procedures, then one fails to get the license, or the permit, or the passport, or whatever it is that one wants. More generally, if one does not have the right demeanor, the appropriate culture, the right kind of clothing, or various other acceptable ways of comporting oneself, then access is likely to be denied.

Along with specialized language goes a process that might be called "remoralizing" within the elite body itself, as it moves from the sophisticated to the oversophisticated code. When a sophisticated code is in use, the person counts for little and the task is all-important. Coming to oversophistication, the members begin to doff the civic self and to take on a moral self. They relate to one another as fellows privileged to work within the same code. The frequency of expressive communication within the group increases. They readopt the orator's devices for presenting themselves—ethos—to one another. They compliment themselves by denigrating outsiders as irresponsible, ignorant, shiftless, and incapable of looking after their own interests.

Finally they develop among themselves an indirect language connoting moral solidarity and trust. They do not hold each other accountable and do not ask for detailed evidence. "A worthy chap," the man says, and his colleague knows at once that in their code this means the chap tries hard but is incompetent. There is a not very nice story passed around among the British elite, employers of servants in India, most of whom could not read, of a letter of reference in which was written: "Bhagwat is a good plain cook. If you are thinking of giving him a berth, make it a wide one." That is not subtle, but it makes the same point. Not to know the language is to be on the outside. Here finally, is an anecdote from *The Search* (Snow, 1960:222) which demonstrates the point. Desmond had capitulated, agreeing that they should meet at the same place at the same time—"Like lectures. And bridge parties. And any sort of whoopee."

> Fane smiled. His eyes were cold grey.
> "I suppose you're thinking of Uncle Toby?"
> Desmond laughed as heartily as if he had understood. Constantine's face suddenly broke into wrinkles of laughter. Pritt looked at him with distaste.
> "We're wasting time," said Pritt.

For that instant Desmond was on the outside, but covered himself. Pritt, it seems, having held a professorship in one of the Welsh colleges and being irascible and peasant-minded to boot, was never likely to be on the inside.

At the beginning of this chapter we left open the question of whether or not a sophisticated code should be categorized as "rhetoric." We can now give an answer.

The sophisticated code is the only one that can be openly asserted. You cannot say directly (assertive rhetoric), "I am about to excite you. Get yourself in a suitable position to be aroused!" Nor yet (pseudo-cerebral rhetoric), "Stand by to be blinded with science!" But you can say, "I am going to use reason. Use your critical faculties both to follow and to improve upon my arguments." What is the significance of this fact? It is both an indication, in ways analogous to those noticed in an earlier chapter, of the weakness of the sophisticated code and an explanation for that weakness. The users are invited to test, to improve upon, and if necessary to reject the product. (So they are too, of course, in the case of pseudo-cerebral rhetoric. But in that mode one tries to present arguments in such a way that they will be proof against real criticism.) In the case of a genuine sophisticated code, it is made clear that this is a means to an end and not an end in itself.

The codes of rhetoric used for assertion or for compromise (with some exceptions in the case of the latter) are not like this. They are not presented openly as codes; they are not labeled. They are not requests or suggestions to adopt these rules or those rules to regulate communicative exchanges. They are direct action: it is the difference between "May I kiss you?" (which allows for "Yes" or "I have a cold" or "You have halitosis") and going straight into the performance (which allows no preliminary response at all).

One may conclude that a sophisticated code is not to be categorized as rhetoric. It is a form of communication certainly, and also a form of persuasion. Its users intend, as they do when they use the rhetorical codes of persuasion, to create in their hearers a frame of mind (in this case set of beliefs) that will eventuate in action—even if the action is no more than saying, "I think you are correct." But it is not rhetorical persuasion.

It is not rhetorical persuasion because it is quite open about the facade. The users of a sophisticated code are in effect saying this: (1) There is a real world out there and we must try to understand the constraints it puts upon us and the resources it offers. (2) But we can see it only, as it were, through the screen (facade) of one or another conceptual framework. (3) The conceptual framework is a tool and we should change it as soon as we judge the constraints from the real world are too much to bear or the resources coming in are too few.

By contrast, codes found in the rhetoric of assertion and in most parts of the rhetoric of compromise do not acknowledge a facade. They say only "This is the real world. There is no other."

Where does this place an oversophisticated code? The answer can be only that it lies within the domain of rhetoric, for the users of such a code have transformed the filtering and organizing device of a conceptual framework into something that is solidly opaque.

We concluded Chapter 5 with a discussion that, having separated expressive from task-oriented activity, argued that the former also has an instrumental aspect in that it can be used to manipulate other people. We then, in Chapters 6 and 7, examined rhetorical devices for getting people into the right frame of mind to accept the appropriate values and premises that would serve either directly as a stimulus for action (Chapter 6) or as a basis on which to make a purportedly reasoned argument (Chapter 7). In the present chapter we have considered ways of cultivating in others a frame of mind suitable for the use of reason.

Throughout this discussion, and throughout the book, beginning from that very word *quantilla* ("how small an amount") in Oxenstierna's statement, reason has been embattled, under constant attack, and, as often as not, seeming to lose ground. It is vulnerable for all the reasons given: its own dependence on a prior (nonrational) agreement about first principles; the fact that there are some situations so complex, so far beyond possible computation, that even if everyone wants to use reason, it cannot be used; and because it dispenses with the protective shield of a single "palatable and compre-hensible" definition of the world.

So the amount of reason is kept small, if Oxenstierna is cor-rect. But there must be some use for reason. There *is* a real world of people, things, and events. You may put it out of sight with the shields of rhetoric or of oversophisticated codes. But the world of constraints and resources is still there, and those who shut it out are likely to be hurt without knowing why they are being hurt. The only way of gaining protection from, and being able to use, the resources of the real world is to employ the rational discourse of a sophisticated code. This does not, of course, provide total access to the real world: it functions like those selectively perforated overlays used to score multiple-choice tests. But at least you are provided with windows that may look at least onto some areas of reality.

That, in the end, must be why reason does not vanish alto-gether. It is indispensable.

In the final part of the book we shall look in detail at two cases that show reason triumphant: the skilled manipulative use (more skilled in the second case than in the first) of over-heated hearts by cool heads.

Part III

THE TACTICS OF
PERSUASION

CHAPTER 9

The Principle of Abomination

Dans les affaires de ce monde, c'est un grand avantage que de pouvoir inspirer une grande colère passionée à son ennemi [In the affairs of this world, one gains a considerable advantage by provoking one's enemy into a rage].
—Benjamin Franklin

Other things being equal, that is true. But why is it true? I gave one answer when talking of the dozens, the game of competitive insults. The infuriated competitor, our culture insists, can no longer use his head and think up a suitable verbal rejoinder. But this tells us only what he does not do and leaves undescribed a wide range of actions, all of which cause him to forfeit the game. He may hang his head and say nothing; he may stammer and stumble through an incoherent reply; he can walk away; he can kick the cat; he can lash out with his fists and so on.

These responses are very different from one another by whatever criterion is chosen to measure them: dignity, violence, or whatever. But what do they have in common? They are "wrong" moves; they cause the game to be lost. Why are they wrong? They are wrong because they failed to fit the context. That is, the action and the context put together make a combination that is not rewarded.

Let us spread this "principle of abomination" more widely. By "abomination" is meant the mixing of items that should be kept apart, the product being (literally) ill omened, something to be deprecated (that is, one prays that it should not have come about). This has an obvious relevance to the culture of persuasion, for there are infinite ways of getting a mixture wrong and of producing some combination of selves, codes, content, and situation which the auditor finds incomprehensible, or bewildering, or unconvincing, or unpalatable, or shocking, or downright revolting. The persuader has then destroyed the "ethos," which is the basis of the auditor's trust and confidence in him.

But we are still left with the central question unanswered. What are the "wrong" combinations? Clearly they are those judged wrong in that culture: we are not in an objective world. They are combinations that fail to be persuasive. But why are they not persuasive? When we begin to look at instances, we find complications.

Consider this example, which comes from a novel by John le Carré (1977:217). The speaker is referring to the wife who has left him. (Italics in the original.)

> "Of course, *kisses* mean nothing with her," Peter Worthington explained, as a matter of information. "She kisses everybody, the pupils, her girl-friends— she'd kiss the dustman, anyone. She's *very* outgoing. Once again, she can't leave anyone alone. I mean *every* relationship has to be a conquest. With her child, the waiter at the restaurant . . . Then, when she's won them, they bore her. Naturally."

What is a "conquest"? It is a one-sided moral relationship, in which you exact a sincere offering (of love) but give in exchange only the simulacrum "kisses." You seal the other person in what is for him an intrinsic relationship while leaving yourself unsealed in a de facto (but *deniable*) position of exercising power. Politicians practice exactly this kind of sleight-of-hand on the multitude when they demand one-to-one devotion to themselves as leaders, a moral tie that they cannot possibly reciprocate.

One common-sense question immediately presents itself: Was Elizabeth Worthington sincere? I have said that her posture was deniable, and I have no doubt that, if confronted, the lady would manifest outrage at the idea that her kisses were nothing more than empty demonstrations. Indeed, nowhere in the book—not even in that statement by her husband—is it conclusively and clearly demonstrated that she consciously and calculatedly deployed her charms. It could, of course, be inferred from her behavior (kissing the dustman, for example) that the display of affection was nothing more than a display. But elsewhere in the book she is shown to have loyalty to those who have befriended her or have been her lovers. "Tell him I kept faith," she said. "It's what he cares about most. I stuck to the deal. If you see him, tell him, 'Liese stuck to the deal' " (le Carré, 1977:516).

But sincerity is not the heart of the matter, except insofar as we look at the response of the other people involved. To be insincere, so far as the culture of persuasion is concerned, is to be judged by another person not to be presenting a "true" self. That is the measure of sincerity, not some kind of objective truth about inner motivations, for—whether in novels or life—that kind of truth is unattainable, sometimes even for oneself.

The heart of the matter for our inquiry is the mingling of a moral self with a tactical self. What is the relationship between these two selves? At the root level (the level of basic meaning) they are antithetical and cannot both simultaneously characterize the same action. But at other levels we know that they coexist, as "percentages," so to speak, of a relationship between people, as in the case of ambivalence. But in the example of Elizabeth Worthington, the coexistence is more complicated. First, the tactical self (exercising power and making "conquests") could not be effective without the cover of the moral self (love). Second, it is a *cover*. For those who are persuaded to accept Elizabeth's testimonials of affection, there is *apparently* only one single uncomplicated self—the moral self exhibiting love. In short, the presentation of an "abomination" is prevented by concealing one part of the mixture.

To be recognized as sincere, whether in public or in private interactions, is of great importance. The tactical self, presented nakedly as itself and nothing more, can command respect or

admiration, like any other skill. But the hidden hand of a tactical self behind the offering of other selves (all of them—civic,
divine, moral, even the silly self), once suspected, gives a
new frame to the message and, in most cases, diminishes the
appeal. So we come back to a feature of rhetoric that is fasci-
nating just because it carries the seed of rhetoric's own
destruction: once it is detected as rhetoric (the conscious manipulation in a covert way of the feelings and sentiments of
others), its effects should be neutralized.

The necessary falsification is achieved by secrecy, a word
that recalls Simmel: "We simply cannot imagine any interaction or social relation or society which are *not* based on this
teleologically determined non-knowledge of one another"
(1969:312).

The teleology, however, can exist on both sides of a "deceptive" relationship. That Elizabeth Worthington sees the advantage of concealing a desire for conquest behind
demonstrations of affection, like any other courtesan, is easily
comprehended. It is not so immediately obvious—but I suspect is a fact of everyone's experience—that the "deceived"
party may collude in the deception, perhaps preferring the
simulacrum of love to no love at all, or perhaps just reluctant
to provoke a scene, wanting a quiet life. It is also possible that
the deceiver knows that the "deceived" is not in fact deceived;
and so on.

What emerges from this? We have come to the threshold of
a particular form of abomination that lies at the center of the
tactics of persuasion and that allows the cool head, as we said
earlier, to make use of the overheated heart. The abomination
consists of bringing out into the open what in that particular
culture may be known but is collusively deemed to be unmentionable. Those who violate this rule are punished by the failure of their efforts to persuade.

The task now is to discover what kinds of things lie below
the line in the category of "unmentionable."

Now let us make a second approach, this time through rhetoric. We made a distinction between assertive rhetoric and the

rhetoric of compromise, and separated both from a task-oriented discourse based on reason. One criterion for separating them is the goal: to convert or to reinforce faith, in the case of assertive rhetoric; to bring about a compromise, in the case of the rhetoric of compromise; and to find the best available solution to a problem, in the case of a discourse carried on through a sophisticated code. We have also attempted to find differences in form and style between the three different types of discourse. For example, grandiloquence diminishes as one passes from assertion to offers of compromise and diminishes to the point of vanishing in a reasoned discourse. The use of the syllogism in its proper form goes in the opposite direction: present in reasoned discourse, perverted into enthymemes through pseudo-cerebral devices in the rhetoric of compromise, and inappropriately used in the rhetoric of assertion.

Thus we have attempted to link form and style with the speaker's goals and with consequences. But this is clearly oversimplified. Just as the presentation of a moral self (kisses from Elizabeth Worthington) may cover a bid for power and control (the tactical self), so also one form of rhetoric may be used to disguise a goal that is "officially" attained through another form of rhetoric. The word "officially" recalls the necessity to conceal the rhetoric and the manipulation. At one level the rhetoric of assertion is for use in making assertions; the rhetoric of compromise indicates a desire to compromise; and a sophisticated code signals agreement about fundamental values and a wish to concentrate on finding the best means to solve present problems. If the form and style are convincing, then the onus of proving that the speaker is doing other than what he implicitly (or explicitly) claims to be doing lies on his opponent. To make such a challenge is to take a risk and to expose oneself to a variety of arguments *ad hominem* (mean in spirit, cynical, forever doubting and suspicious and therefore oneself suspect and unworthy of trust).

That is the "official" level. But at another level, form and style may be used for quite other than their "official" purposes. We have already had examples. Sometimes these may be counted as legitimate, and risk minimal shame if detected, as when counterassertive rhetoric is used to soften an opponent and make him more open to accepting compromise. Equally grandiloquence and a display of strong emotion in favor of the use of reason is entirely aboveboard and cannot invite recrimination.

But there are other ways of using one form of rhetoric to attain a hidden goal that are not defensible if brought out into the open. A sophisticated code is appropriately and "officially" used for solving problems, for deciding on the means to an end already agreed. But, as we have seen, in the case of oversophistication, it may be used as a device to exclude people who might otherwise take part in the discussion. It may also be used, as in the case of "blinding with science" or "snowing with statistics," as a form of assertive rhetoric—a type of argument from authority. Such a discourse has the force of assertion without having its form. The form says one thing; the purpose of what is said (or done) can be quite different.

There are other ways of offering the form without the substance. One may speak the language of compromise, and so present oneself as a reasonable person willing to yield in the interest of the general good, but at the same time so construct the substance of the compromise that one's opponent cannot accept it, because *he* will know (although the audience may not realize it) that to accept such an offer is to give away all. In the following example, Sir Charles Dilke, the recipient of an offer to compromise, saw matters in exactly that way. It comes from a book by Roy Jenkins. Dilke, with his then ally Joseph Chamberlain, had been attempting to find an office in Gladstone's government which carried with it a seat in the Cabinet. The Irish secretaryship fell vacant in 1882, when the previous incumbent was murdered in Dublin. The position was offered to Dilke, but it carried no seat in the Cabinet, and he declined. Jenkins writes (1968:155) that Dilke "feared that the public might believe he had been influenced by personal cowardice." Other pressures came from his colleagues, and while we need not assume that Gladstone had deliberately set him up in this way, these pressures make very clear that Dilke experienced the discomfort of being seen to be the one who refuses to be "reasonable." The first offer was carried by his friend Chamberlain. Dilke "declined without hesitation and with some anger."

> Mr. Gladstone and Lord Carlingford then sent back to say, personally from each of them, that I was to be present at the Cabinet at every discussion of Irish affairs; and I then asked: "Why, then, should I not be in the Cabinet?" Carlingford came back to the Foreign Office again and again, and cried over it to me; and Lord Granville came in twice, and threatened me with loss of prestige by my refusal, by which I certainly felt I had lost Mr. Gladstone's confidence. I was angry with Chamberlain at having placed me in this position. Had he acted on this occasion with the steadiness with which he acted on every other he would have told the Cabinet that the offer would be an insult; because he knew that this was my view. . . . Lord Granville came in finally, and said in his sweetest manner (which is a very disagreeable one) that he had vast experience and had "never known a man stand on his extreme rights and gain by it." This I felt to be a monstrous perversion of the case. . . . [Jenkins, 1968:153–154]

From his own point of view, Dilke had everything to lose:

> Acceptance would not only have been a personal mistake; it would have been a political blunder. Outside the Cabinet I should not have had the public confidence, and rightly so, because I could not have a strong hand. I should have inherited accumulated blunders, and I was under no kind of obligation to do so, for I have never touched the Irish question. Never have I spoken on it from first to last. Many of the measures rendered necessary by the situation are condemned by my whole past attitude; but they have really been made inevitable by blunders for which I had no responsibility, and which I should not have been allowed to condemn. [Jenkins, 1968:155]

That is an example in which the rhetoric of compromise, even if inadvertently, has the consequence of an assertive attack on the victim's good name. The lesson, moreover, is driven home by some straightforward assertive rhetoric (Lord

Carlingford's tears, for example, which one hopes were meta-phorical) and by threats of lost prestige.

The form did not match the purpose. In substance, Dilke decided, this was not a true offer. The implied amity, ex-pressed in the form of an invitation, was negated (in Dilke's opinion) by what was offered. The form was friendship. The substance of what was offered had the purpose of conveying a lack of trust and a lack of confidence.

When you are taught woodworking, you learn the "official" method of driving screws into wood. You are told that certain tools (that is, certain forms) are used for specific purposes. To drive a nail into wood, a hammer is used. For a screw, prepare hardwood by first drilling a hole, and softwood by making a hole with a gimlet or a bradawl, and then use a screwdriver. Later, outside school—and never under the eye of an instruc-tor—you will find that the quickest way to do the job in soft-wood is to hammer the screw down half its length and complete the job with a screwdriver.

So it is with persuasion. When all is aboveboard—above the line—and "official," the form and the function of the persua-sive device used are matched by convention and there is noth-ing underhand, nothing to be concealed. But there are other occasions when the most effective job is done below the line by cross-matching form and function (using a hammer to start a screw). This is likely to meet with the disapproval of ev-eryone (except other carpenters who are up to the same trick), because it is a sign of laziness and because it somewhat weak-ens the hold of the screw and because the screw may get bent; so it is best done unperceived, and only a chucklehead would boast about doing it. But this world of bending rules is not a random affair. Hammering screws into hardwood is courting disaster. In other words, there are likely to be rules about how to bend rules. This is the object of our inquiry.

We shall investigate the matter by looking at cases, using them not, as in earlier chapters, to give examples of generali-zations, but rather as "natural" situations that provide the raw material for analysis. Our general design will be to work first at the "official" level sketched out in earlier chapters, and then

to see what residue remains to be explained by a more Machiavellian approach.

The following case is taken from the *Los Angeles Times*
(September 14, 1980, pt. 2). It concerns one Melba Bishop,
newly elected to the Oceanside City Council, a lady distinguished for her "gusto and proclivity for disruption." The
two other persons mentioned, Casey and Burgess, are also
members of the council.

> "I'm an outsider," Bishop said. . . . "I'm not in with the regular
> City Hall crowd, and I think I'm a little threatening to some
> people."
>
> Describing herself as a grass-roots representative who still
> walks precincts to talk to voters, Bishop paints a political por-
> trait in black-and-white of "special interest" domination at City
> Hall.
>
> "It's easy to get isolated in this place," she said about working
> in City Hall. "You only run into special-interest groups, law-
> yers and developers. You can almost get into a cocoon."
>
> But her rankled colleagues say Bishop's portrayal of business
> and real estate interests unduly influencing city policy are over-
> blown and inaccurate.
>
> With such comments, Bishop lights the fire that heats the
> water she sometimes finds herself boiling in.
>
> Bishop admitted there probably are no "back-room deals"
> shaping Oceanside's future. Her reference to such deals are
> mostly rhetorical to underline a "philosophical point of view"
> among city officials that City Hall should dictate policy with lit-
> tle or no advice from citizens, she said.
>
> "What the ordinary citizen wants in this town is a chance to
> have some kind of control in his life," she said. "The council as
> a whole doesn't understand that."
>
> Her colleagues don't agree.
>
> "I'm trying to talk to Melba about making all these state-
> ments without any basis in fact," said Casey, who added that he
> has remained accessible to voters and is a critic of development.
>
> Casey said Bishop's statements reflect the fact that she is "new
> (on the council) and extremely naive in the real world."
>
> Burgess, a successful local real estate agent, was reluctant to

discuss Bishop's role on the council, saying the sometimes bitter exchanges in open session indicate serious disagreements.

But Burgress said Bishop seems more anxious to impress voters than discuss issues, and the differences are "more political than philosophical."

While those differences spawn animosity in open meetings, Bishop said it becomes even harsher during executive sessions closed to the public.

"They're rough on me," she said. "Sometimes they're really rough."

Notice that this case is not purely discourse: rather it consists of reports and commentaries intended to explain the way in which the various antagonists behave during argument. We therefore find several levels present, ranging from the direct reporting of remarks made in the council meetings to the startling self-exposure of Ms. Bishop when she admits, apparently readily enough, that her accusations about back-room deals were just "rhetoric": that is, they were not true.

Some things were going on in the back. Melba Bishop's opponents argued that "it was impractical to publicly negotiate every detail of a complicated, multi-million-dollar real estate transaction." This could be the familiar—and valid—argument that in order to carry out complicated tasks in the real world (where Ms. Bishop was "extremely naive"), one must use a sophisticated code, and such a code by definition allows access only to the few who have the knowledge to make proper use of it. Ms. Bishop in fact knew and acknowledged that development was a main concern: "I don't think," said the mayor of Oceanside, "that there is a lot of difference [among council members] on where Oceanside should be going" evidently including the "disruptive" lady in this category. Avis, a former councilman who resigned to represent a land development company, agreed that "Bishop has given fair hearings to developers bringing projects before the city. She has not rejected them out of hand, which often is a tendency of new council members."

There is apparently a foundation of shared purposes, and one might expect that differences over the means of achieving those goals might be resolved through the medium of a sophisticated task-oriented code. Why, then, do we encounter the following?

"We need to safeguard the public against deals being made in the back room," she said.

When Bishop uttered those buzz words, several of her council colleagues reached for their microphones.

It was impractical to publicly negotiate every detail of a complicated, multi-million-dollar real estate transaction, they argued.

They also read Bishop's idea as another publicity and political gimmick by the freshman councilwoman, and that irritated them even more.

"You're always bringing this up about deals being made in back rooms," said Councilman John Casey, his face flushing crimson and his voice rising.

"You're playing to the audience," he charged, adding that he had never heard of any "back-room deals."

Councilman Ray Burgess, bushy moustache twitching, curtly accused Bishop and Mayor Larry Bagley of having "made more deals than any of us in back rooms."

Bagley and Bishop objected.

"I will take personal umbrage at that remark," said Bagley, normally a soft-spoken, even-tempered mayor.

"Take it, be my guest," Burgess retorted.

Angrily, Bagley slammed down the gavel, cutting off discussion.

What "lights the fire that heats the water she sometimes finds herself boiling in" is evidently not a difference over whether land development should take place. Even the question of defining and safeguarding the public interest in the course of such development is not the main point at issue. The main point is "philosophical": the responsibility of a representative.

On the one side is paternalism. "Constitute government how you please," wrote Burke, "infinitely the greater part of it must depend upon the exercise of powers which are left at large to the prudence and uprightness of ministers of state" (quoted in Schaffer, 1973:54). It is technically impossible "to publicly negotiate every detail," and one must trust the elected representatives to be guided by prudence and uprightness. There is no way in which every detail can be made comprehensible to the ordinary person.

This is the philosophy of an elite and of Ms. Bishop's opponents. But it must remain somewhat covert. At the present day, in Oceanside and elsewhere in North America, such ideas are not acceptable, at least in appeals to the public. Its defense must be made not in terms of the intrinsic merit of the rulers, but rather on the grounds that the paternalistic form of government is inevitable and is in the best interest of all because the alternative is chaos. For the same reasons, the philosophy is vulnerable to straightforward attacks by assertive rhetoric. Ms. Bishop has at her service such emotive terms as "grassroots" and "walking the precincts" and can speak of her opponent as living in a "cocoon," not necessarily ignorant of the general interest of ordinary people, but ignoring it so as to serve better the special interest of developers and builders. Notice that in making such attacks, she steps around the defense that in technical task-oriented discourse there is no practical way in which everyone can take part in the decision, and turns from a discussion of the issue (the nature of representation) to an assult on the persons, by questioning their motives.

Her opponents have no alternative but to make an immediate attack on *her* motives. They drop the "technical impossibility" argument and turn on her, once rather wildly by volleying the back-room accusation word for word (and to the mayor's indignation associating him with the charge) and then talking of "political gimmicks." In such a discourse the word "political" no longer means "conducting the affairs of the polis" but rather ignoring or even subverting the best interests of the polis so as to gain electoral support for oneself. Ms. Bishop, her opponents argue, is seeking attention for herself, preventing the council from getting ahead with the development of Oceanside, and thus exhibiting her "gusto and proclivity for disruption."

The greater part of this case apparently yields to the tools of analysis outlined in earlier chapters. The fundamental issue is whether Oceanside should have an elite or an arena council. Only the populist side (Melba Bishop) can afford to keep this issue assertively on the front of the stage. Given that open elitism is out of fashion, her opponents can make only an indirect defense and attempt to screen off the issue of representation by emphasizing the task and its technical complexities. At the same time they launch a diversionary attack by claiming that Ms. Bishop is "naive" (that is, cannot use the sophisticated code required to solve the city's problems) and is in fact destroying the general interest by putting considerations of her own electoral advantage first.

What residues remain? Everyone parades a civic self: everyone is serving the public interest. They even appear to agree broadly what this interest is and they attempt to reduce their differences to questions only of means: "It's a difference in methodology. Melba is very concerned with participatory democracy." But the difference at this level is precisely not one of methodology. It is a fundamental disagreement over values. The main issue is popular participation, and the development question is the means by which that main issue gets a hearing and a testing, and appears to result in irreconcilable differences. The apologist, speaking of methodology, has presented as secondary what is in fact primary.

Given that there is at this level such a fundamental difference, we would expect to find—and do—a resort to assertive rhetoric, to displays of passion, faces flushing crimson, voices rising, bushy moustaches twitching, and gavels being slammed down. We also find, predicatably, the argument shifting from the issue (the proper role of an elected representative) to the motivation of persons: they are using "political gimmicks" or dealing in back rooms, and thereby, unlike Lloyd George, forgetting that they should be "one of the people."

What then is left? One feature appears in this example that has been absent until now. The style and the self are not always those that are "officially" linked with the purpose, as may be the case with Elizabeth Worthington's kisses. Melba Bishop's opponents defend their elitist position assertively, but

233

not in the form of assertive rhetoric: rather they use a sophisticated code to present arguments about technical feasibility.

Ms. Bishop herself, despite having at her disposal a normative theme that can be advanced in plain and open assertive rhetoric (which she uses—"walking the precincts," encountering "cocoons," which are places that provide warmth and comfort and nourishment without demanding work in return), goes further and makes use of what she describes as "rhetoric." In plain words she tells lies. But perhaps those words are too plain: the writer of the article calls it "hyperbole." Presumably he means by that "an exaggeration of the truth." The persuasive device appears to be one that we have met before (but with a difference). Ms. Bishop uses it to "underline" a philosophy, and the device resembles that use of models (that is, vivid examples) described elsewhere. General statements are given immediacy by particular illustration. Lloyd George does not content himself with saying that landlords are rapacious: in addition he presents an anecdote—"I know districts in Wales where a little bit of barren rock . . ." Enoch Powell evokes the notorious lone white Wolverhampton widow, persecuted by her colored neighbors, to make vivid black incivility (Smithies and Fiddick, 1969:41–42). In the same way Melba Bishop claims to be presenting deals in the back room as a metaphor representing paternalism.

But the accusation invites more than a metaphorical interpretation. The "little bit of barren rock" is clearly a token, metaphorically rather than historically and factually relevant. So also, perhaps to a lesser extent, is the lonely widow in Wolverhampton. But deals in back rooms in Oceanside between councilmen and developers are different: the statements look like matters of substance and fact rather than like tokens. Nor do they signify paternalism, but its corruption into material self-interest. They appear, inevitably, to be manifestations of the evil itself, rather than a mere rhetorical device intended to create feelings of immediacy. But the lady herself "admitted there probably are no 'back-room deals' shaping Oceanside's future." She claims that she made the accusation to draw public attention to her colleagues' paternalistic philosophy. One can speculate about reasons that might have prompted this

234

confession (even if it is qualified by "probably"), but to do so would be a digression. What stands out, and what first aroused my interest in the story, is the apparently casual manner in which the admission was made and an evident assumption that the newspaper readers would contentedly classify this as "rhetoric" (a proper part of the political game) rather than as deceit. (Powell, however, insisted to the end that his story about the widow was historically accurate, although he declined to give the evidence—see Smithies and Fiddick, 1969:59–60.)

Thinking about that assumption, one begins to suspect that one is witnessing in this case little more than a process of domestication, made possible by a genuine agreement on the manner in which differences of opinion should be kept short of total breakdown. Moustaches may twitch and faces flush crimson, but their owners elsewhere remark that Ms. Bishop is new on the council and "naive in the real world," and in doing so they proclaim her exclusion; but it has the air of a temporary exclusion. She will not always be new. Already she gives "fair hearings" to developers, unlike other newcomers who failed to stay the course. From her side, she makes robust accusations but seems to know that these statements will be taken as "hyperbole" and indulged as just one more stage through which the naive councillor must go on her way to maturity. There appears to be a great deal of noise and fury and Ms. Bishop is given a rough time and it sounds very serious and very deadly. But they can make fun of themselves: they know how to play.

> A former Oceanside city manager, Bagley had found himself playing part-time referee from his middle seat on the dais.
> At Wednesday's council meeting, Bagley even donned a black-and-white referee's shirt when temperatures started to rise during a council discussion of beach erosion. The mayor threatened to throw a yellow penalty flag for "mouths illegally in motion."

Let us suppose that the council's tacit task, for the moment, is the socialization of a new member. Given a fundamental disagreement on substantive values about the proper role of a representative, the form of discourse becomes, as we would expect, assertive rhetoric and pseudo-cerebral rhetoric. But there are clues that suggest that just as Elizabeth Worthington may front bids for power with kisses, so also, in this example of the Oceanside City Council, the forms of assertive rhetoric, the diversionary tactics, and the instances of outright deceit are facades behind which the antagonists conceal fundamental procedural agreements (about how to quarrel and how to domesticate a new member), which may eventually allow them to find a similar agreement in matters of substance. At that point Ms. Bishop could find herself inside the "cocoon." Alternatively, like some of her populist predecessors, she may be out of the council altogether.

At first sight it is difficult to reconcile these carryings-on with Simmel's insistence that there can be no society that is not "based on [a] teleologically determined non-knowledge of one another." At least, if they do not know everything, nothing of what they know seems to fall into the category of the "unmentionable." There are deals in the back room. There is an unscrupulous and destructive search for publicity, a ready sacrifice of the general interest for the purpose of grabbing votes. Ms. Bishop admits to perpetrating "rhetoric." Waves of emotion (anyway, displays of emotion) shiver the timbers of Oceanside's small ship of reason.

Overheated hearts seem to be in fashion and cool heads are left in the closet. All this behavior conforms very satisfactorily with the ethic of open democratic government. The people, as the journalists are fond of saying, have a right to know; to know not only what is going on in the back rooms but also, it seems, what is going on in the psychological nooks and crannies of every public person. *Pace* Simmel, there is a "teleologically determined" prurience—a morbid curiosity that insists that everything—public, private, even the most highly personal— should be known to everyone; that ensures, it is supposed, a wise choice of representatives and a high level of public accountability.

If the Oceanside case seems to be out of line with our own and Simmel's analysis, there are reasons that might explain why this should be so. City councils proceed by bureaucratic rules but they are at the same time political arenas in which competition is the norm. They are that marginal form of bureaucracy which I earlier called an arena committee. At this point we can put Simmel back on one of his thrones. To keep secrets, he said, is to avoid subjection. Therefore to broadcast another person's privacies is to be on the way to subduing him—hence the "gusto" with which the councillors hang out in public what they claim to be their rival's dirty washing.

But is there nothing below the line? Let us first recall that our model does not require it to be the case that what is "unmentionable" is never mentioned, only that those who do mention it are penalized—or at least they fail to make their definition of the situation dominate.

By this reckoning Ms. Bishop has two failures. One concerns the "back-room deals": that is not allowed to become a major issue, despite appearances. There is no talk of judicial investigations or prosecutions. Ms. Bishop withdraws the accusation, in the end, saying that she had made it only in order to draw attention to the elitist tendencies of the council. That constitutes a second failure. No one else accepts this as a definition of the council or as an issue that requires discussion. In short, she fails to persuade and she gets herself into hot water.

Her opponents have one failure—or so it appears from the published account. The argument about the need for privacy in negotiating "a complicated, multi-million-dollar real estate transaction" is never pressed home. Instead they prefer personal attacks, making charges of irresponsible vote-grabbing, and even return to the "back-room deals" (which, if anything, one would think would be in the category of "unmentionable").

What could account for the following features? First, the argument about complicated transactions, which could have been, it seems to me, trenchantly prosecuted and rendered indisputable, is quickly abandoned. Second, Ms. Bishop's attempt to bring out into the open the issue of the proper style of representation is thwarted and presented merely as a question of "methodology." Third, there is an undercurrent of tolerance: Ms. Bishop is said to be "naive" but is showing the right tendencies. Fourth, Ms. Bishop backs away from the charge of corruption, which, if pursued, might have led to the law courts.

Earlier I used these features to deduce that possibly we were witnessing not a fight with no holds barred but a process of domestication by which Ms. Bishop was herself being drawn into the cocoon. Now these same features suggest that what is "unmentionable" (albeit mentioned in fact) is the existence of this cocoon. By its very nature, if it is to function at all, a city council requires privacy and a lessening of competitive electoral pressures, in order to make possible the use of a sophisticated code. This does not, of course, necessarily mean that the people are corrupt. It means only that arena conditions tend to inhibit task-oriented activity.

Since elitism, in Oceanside's culture, is considered the opponent of open democratic government, and since the latter is the theme normatively dominant, elitism must be kept behind the facade (so far as possible with such ebullient people). That is what lies below the line: to bring it out into the open and tie it to an action or a person is to perpetrate an abomination. Properly domesticated councillors—those who are no longer "naive"—collude in keeping out of sight the inevitability of elitism.

Our second example is entirely free from such populist tendencies: in it elitism rules.

It is an episode taken from a chapter in that same novel in which Elizabeth Worthington appears (le Carré, 1977:165–189), and since it is a *novel,* I shall begin with some remarks on its standing as ethnography, and at the same time make clear once again what I mean by "our culture."

That phrase refers to the culture of political behavior mainly in a bureaucratic setting in the English-speaking parts of the world, especially England and the United States. We derive our knowledge of a culture mainly from informants. Even when they do something different from what they say they do (as in the case of the Tuareg, quoted earlier), we can still rarely find out what they do unless we can so design our questions as to get the appropriate answers. Our knowledge of a culture comes more from what we are told than from plain observation bereft of commentary.

But the category of informants contains more than speakers. There are also the culture's products: historical writings, my own observations of what people say and do (which is of the same genre as history), newspaper reports, poetry, and fiction. All these provide data from which we may infer the rules in that culture.

Le Carré's book is especially appropriate because, like Snow's *Search,* it is offered as a realistic novel. Of course it has, like most works of fiction, allegories coded into the narrative, but it is not offered as fantasy. There are no river creatures messing about in boats, no nursery toys adventuring in the forest, no Hobbits or Lilliputians or rabbits on a long march to freedom. The novel is realistic: it convinces to the extent that its characters remain within cultural expectations and therefore remain comprehensible to the reader.

Of course it is still that particular author's view of the culture, just as what the anthropologist learns from an informant is that informant's view of the culture. But it is still a window on the culture. Certainly it is secondhand, filtered through the lattice of his facade. But the facade is not his alone: it is also mine and that of his readers—otherwise he would have no readers. Certainly for me—coming from the same culture—there is nothing unfamiliar, nothing that rings false, in what the characters do and say.

Now let us go to the story. It is a chapter that describes the meeting of an intelligence steering group. They supervise the work of a unit that is called the Circus. The head of this unit is George Smiley.

The Circus is in disarray and in some disgrace, for it has contained within its senior ranks a Russian agent, Haydon. This man's role was uncovered, and by the time the novel opens he is already dead. But the Circus has lost all its agents, its bases of operation abroad have been closed, and it has been denied funds for any activity other than documentary post mortem research.

The intelligence steering group turns out to have the form of an arena committee, not in the sense that the various members are elected to represent constituencies, but in that they come from the various government departments that are concerned with espionage. One of these departments is the Cabinet Office, and its man is Lacon, for whom the Circus has been a power base and who, of all those present at the meeting, comes nearest to being its patron. A second interest is that of the Foreign Office, from which come Endeby and Martindale. The Foreign Office and a third interested party, the Commonwealth Office (formerly the Colonial Office), are now joined as the Diplomatic Service, but there are evident enmities between the two departments. The Commonwealth Office has responsibility for relations with former colonial territories and for the management of the few remaining colonies. Its contingent is headed by Wilbraham, supported (and somewhat disastrously) by an aggressive "youth" and (more effectively) by "a lady in brown." These three units (Cabinet Office, Foreign Office, and Commonwealth Office) together with Smiley are the protagonists. In addition there is an occasionally vocal chorus of other departments: the Treasury, Defence, and security experts from the Home Office. They have the air of "seconds" in a duel of which they disapprove.

The meeting is called to consider a document, prepared by Smiley, on evidence for Russian espionage in Hong Kong. Specifically he has discovered that a large sum of money, coming ultimately from Moscow, has been placed in trust in a Hong Kong bank through the agency of a prominent Hong Kong citizen, Mr. Ko. Hong Kong is still a colony and therefore within the domain of the Commonwealth Office. But its continuation as a colony depends upon maintaining good relations with Red China, and anything that happens in Hong Kong clearly is relevant to Britain's relations with China, and therefore a concern for the Foreign Office. Given the bad relations between the Russians and the Chinese, Russian espionage in Hong Kong is a delicate matter for Britain.

There are two other actors, presences without being present at the meeting. One, obviously, is Russian espionage, known as the Centre. The other is the United States and its equivalents to Smiley and his Circus are referred to as the Cousins. The Cousins are ubiquitous and well endowed, and evidently disdainful of British espionage after the disaster of the Haydon affair.

The meeting takes place in conditions of maximum security. The members assemble in a room adorned with a printed notice warning them against discussing confidential matters. They may do so only when they have entered a makeshift room suspended inside the building and elaborately proofed against electronic listening devices. The facilities otherwise exhibit the meager squalor supposed to be characteristic of the British Civil Service. Coffee spills stain the green baize table; the air conditioners from time to time are excessively noisy or fail to extract tobacco smoke. An attendant explains that they ordered the new parts nearly a year ago: "Still, you can't blame delay, can you, sir?"

They sit around the table in a fashion that symbolizes their parts in the drama. Enderby (F.O.) takes the head of the table, his aides beside him. Wilbraham (C.O.) sits at the opposite end with his "youth" and the "brown lady." Smiley and his aide sit alone at one side. Opposite them sit the chorus from the Treasury, the Ministry of Defense, and the Home Office. Lacon, the patron of the Circus, sits himself "apart from everyone, for all the world the person least engaged." Each of them has a copy of the eighteen-page report that Smiley had prepared.

Lacon has called the meeting, and he is invited to "start the bowling." "You shoot first" says Enderby, with both those metaphors signaling an attack on Smiley; and that is how Lacon begins. He complains that they have not been given enough time for preparation; he says that he is embarrassed to be the link "for a service which has rather cut its links of late." Smiley's thesis is "momentous," hard to swallow, and—in an oblique reference to the Circus's recent disgrace—"it also comes at an awkward time." He then summarizes the report:

"A prominent Hong Kong citizen is under suspicion of being a Russian spy." Smiley, "talking to his hands," pulls Lacon back from the extreme conclusion: "He is known to receive very large Russian subventions." The questions continue, and each time Smiley answers in the same way, stating the facts rather than the conclusion that might be deduced from them, adding the cautionary phrase "to the best of our knowledge."

At this Wilbraham (C.O.) pounces, asking how good their knowledge is and remarking, in a way that is anything but oblique, "Hasn't been too good in the past, has it?" His lady "in Church brown" adds, less maliciously, that they would need far more corroboration.

Smiley agrees, adding with deceptive mildness, "So would we," and then says that their object in asking for permission to proceed is exactly in order to obtain corroboration.

That ends the first episode—"round," as Smiley's aide says. The points clearly go to Lacon and Smiley. Lacon begins, from the neutral chairman-like position he has set for himself in taking a seat apart from the rest, by voicing the hostility and the skepticism that are the sense of the meeting, not even shrinking from an indirect reference to the recent Haydon disgrace. He is not a partisan, not an advocate for Smiley—at least, that is what his words and manner say: he is in a position from which he can recognize the facts and the truth when they appear. But at the same time, whether by design or not, he sets up Wilbraham and allows Smiley to perform that most satisfactory feat of argument: using the other man's words to make convincingly precisely the point that was being denied. Smiley makes no counterassertions: he accepts his opponents' statements and draws from them a conclusion that denies their case.

A similar pattern, but more strongly marked, appears in the second episode. The protagonists are still Lacon, Smiley, and Wilbraham. Lacon returns to the attack on Smiley, underlining the weakness of his submission. There is no evidence that Ko goes in for subversion; he is not trying to get the Hong Kong sterling reserves withdrawn from London; he is not trying to drive the British off the island; he is not a rabble-rouser; he is not demanding effective trade unions or an effective parliament for the Chinese.

In the course of doing this, while apparently maintaining his studious and entirely rational concern for the facts, he indulges in language, when describing the Colony's institutions, that Wilbraham finds offensive. He affects not to know the names of the representative bodies in the colony and calls them "tame assemblies." This is too much for Wilbraham, who snaps out the names, asserts that they are anything but tame, and, evidently excited, openly seals himself in a position that reveals that he is not searching for the facts, but knows them already: "They've got it all wrong. It's a goose-chase." Once again there is no counterassertion and Lacon ignores the intervention. But he then goes on to describe Mr. Ko (still apparently asserting the implausibility of Smiley's theses) as a "Hong Kong prototype: Steward of the Jockey Club, supports the charities, pillar of the integrated society, successful, benevolent, has the wealth of Croesus and the commercial morality of the whorehouse." This draws from Wilbraham: "I say, that's a bit hard!" But he is again ignored by Lacon, who continues his praises for Mr. Ko, saying that there could hardly be a less appropriate person for "harassment by a British Secret Service, or recruitment by a Russian one."

Once again the stage has been set for Smiley: "In my world, we call that good cover."

The argumentative device that crowns this episode is the same as that used in the first. Smiley is allowed to take the statements of his (ostensible) opponent, accept them, and then draw from them the opposite conclusion. "*Touché!*" says Enderby, applauding the coup.

The strategies are also similar. Smiley maintains his posture of disinterested rationality, of letting the facts speak for themselves. Lacon, in refusing to notice Wilbraham's interjections, is similarly objective and rational, but at the same time with his references to "tame assemblies" and to the "commercial morality of the whorehouse" is provoking and irritating the contingent from the Commonwealth Office.

Lastly, Wilbraham—and he was destined to mismanage his

hand in this way almost throughout the meeting—allows himself to be rattled by disrespectful references to his protégés, and is maneuvered into very obvious use of a rhetoric against persons (the disgrace of the Circus in the first episode and the "goose-chase" in the second) when by the conventions of such meetings he should be seen to be addressing himself rationally to the facts. The breach of custom is obvious enough to allow Lacon the advantage of—presumably in a sorrowful fashion—taking no notice, sticking to the task, and refusing to allow the discussion to descend to an *argumentum ad hominem*.

The same pattern continues in the next episode. It begins with an apparent diversion. The man from the Treasury objects that Smiley has used the post mortem funds secretly granted him for quite other purposes. He does not go on to say that these purposes are obviously to rebuild the Circus: that remains an unspoken item on the agenda until it is jerked out of Wilbraham's "red-haired boy," who turns out to be even less subtle than his master. But Enderby closes down the man from the Treasury: the point is not that "George has been a naughty boy" but whether he has squandered the money or made a cheap killing. This small episode serves to remind the reader that this is very much a task-oriented occasion, to be encumbered neither by the morality of personal relations within the committee nor by conventional moralities of right and wrong conduct: they are in the world of espionage, where naughtiness counts for little beside effectiveness.

Enderby then invites Wilbraham to speak—"time the Empire had its shout." The "shout," made from "below the salt," turns out to be a good point badly made. All they know about for certain is the money. There is a lot of complexity and subterfuge and the methods of delivering the money seem to have changed. He doesn't understand why, but "we'll take your word for it." Could Smiley explain? Smiley does (apparently the explanation is already in the document): it makes sense to vary routine in such matters.

Somewhat patronizingly Enderby addresses Wilbraham, saying that this was what they called "tradecraft." That is a small clue to the direction in which the episode is moving: espionage is a business for experts, and Wilbraham is not an expert.

But Wilbraham first manages to make his good point. All they know about so far is the money, and the money is in trust: it does not belong to Mr. Ko. The beneficiary could be anyone. So what do they have against Ko?

There is no immediate answer. Instead Enderby asks Smiley about thumbprints, for apparently the beneficiary is identified on the document by his left thumbprint. Smiley, as usual with "about as much emotion as a speaking clock," explains that it is a custom surviving on the China coast from the days of widespread illiteracy. When his discourse is finished, Enderby speculates that it may be Ko's own thumb on the document; Wilbraham says there is no evidence for that. Then the "red-haired boy" speaks up: "*You* say Ko is on the Russian payroll. *We* say that it's not demonstrated . . ." and so on for several sentences, using the same antithetical form of *you* and *we* (thus inadvertently signaling attention to the persons rather than to the issues) and winding up with "You're talking about guilt. Whereas *we* say Ko's done nothing wrong under Hong Kong law and should enjoy the due rights of a Colonial subject."

They pounce on this. "Guilt doesn't enter into it in the least degree. We're talking about security." The young man evidently does not understand the sophisticated code. Again we pick up the point that was made at the beginning of this episode: to be naughty is nothing, to be effective is everything. This is immediately underlined when one of the Treasury men remarks that under Hong Kong law they can do what they like to Ko, steam open his mail, tap his telephone, "suborn his maid, or bug his house to kingdom come." Enderby, saying nothing about morality or about legal rights, remarks that they no longer have the local facilities, and without these facilities they might do it clumsily enough to give the game away. But Wilbraham's young man is still fresh and innocent in his indigation: such measures, he says, would be "scandalous."

Wilbraham and his colleagues are apparently seeking to stay within the bounds of rational argument. They assert again what they said at the beginning: that there is not enough cor-

roboration to justify an investigation of Ko by the Circus.
Smiley could still say that without an investigation there can
be no further evidence, but he keeps silent. There is evidently
no rational way in which to settle that particular issue: it is like
refusing to reimburse the would-be traveler until he produces
the ticket, which he has no cash to buy until they reimburse
him.

The discourse about thumbprints serves to undermine Wilbraham's claim to rationality. First it gives Smiley, still with
"Oriental self-effacement," the opportunity to demonstrate his
expertise, and to do so with detachment and without emotion.
The others, in particular Wilbraham, are ignorant. But worse
is to come: not merely do they lack knowledge, they also cannot stay with the appointed task, but slide off into questions of
right and wrong. Three times the group is reminded that neither morality nor legality is its concern: Smiley's "naughtiness" in spending the money in unauthorized ways is beside
the point; guilt is not the issue, only security; whether or not
practices are scandalous does not matter if they are effective. In
short, if Wilbraham has made a "good point," it has been
blown away on the breeze of Smiley's quiet parade of knowledge and on the gale of the young man's aggressive
moralizing.

The fourth episode opens with Wilbraham walking—indeed, thrusting his way into—a trap set for him by Enderby.
Enderby asks whether the governor of Hong Kong should be
told about the Ko crisis. Wilbraham has argued that there is no
such crisis. Of course the governor should be advised, he insists: the colony's government has the responsibility—
"They're self-administering." No one remarks on the
inconsistency of this position and the denial of a crisis. The
rest hang back, and it is left to Smiley to make the running.

He does so in the style maintained throughout the meeting;
carefully and even ostentatiously dealing with facts and avoiding both personalities and speculation. But this time there is a
difference: he picks up the line of tactics set first by Lacon and
then by Enderby.

He remarks that no one could object to the governor's being taken into confidence, but then he asks might it not be too much for him? To Wilbraham's puzzled expostulation he replies by listing what the governor would have to do, behaving as if he had only just thought of the implications. Since his staff could not be involved ("That's asking too much of anyone"), the governor would have to brush up his coding abilities. Then there is an ethical question. If he continued to entertain Ko at his official residence, would he not be acting as an *agent provocateur*? "Some people take to it quite naturally," he adds, innocently.

Wilbraham is suitably outraged. Suppose Ko is a spy and the governor innocently "commits some minor indiscretion" over the dinner table. It would be "damned unfair. It could ruin the man's career. Let alone what it could do to the Colony! He must be told!"

Wilbraham has led with his chin. "Well, of course, if he's given to being indiscreet . . ." Smiley murmurs. In this short passage Smiley has succeeded in impugning the governor's intelligence, his morals, and his discretion.

But the provocation is all delivered in the quiet voice of reason. Enderby is anything but quiet. In a cheerful voice he paints a lurid picture of the "Queen's representative" entertaining "Moscow's ace spy" and giving him a medal. Then he asks brightly, what medal Ko has so far received for his public services. Not a knighthood? Someone answers that it is an O.B.E. Enderby commiserates with the absent Ko and says that he is surely on his way and will work his passage to the top "same as we all do."

That, it turns out, is a piece of playful malice. Enderby already has his knighthood; Wilbraham is still "stuck in the bulge," and like Mr. Ko is waiting for that higher recognition.

Throughout the episode they play upon Wilbraham's weakness: that he cannot subordinate his loyalty toward—his moral concern for—the colony, its citizens, and above all its officials. They do not confront him with the obvious contradiction of his position: if, as he maintains, there is no crisis, then nothing

need be said to the governor. Instead Smiley is allowed to reason his way "meekly"and with apparently no less concern for
the welfare of the governor than that displayed by Wilbraham—toward stating the governor's incompetence, managing
yet once again to use Wilbraham's own words to draw the
unwelcome conclusion. Wilbraham makes no answer. Still less
can he afford to answer the boyish taunt about being "stuck in
the bulge," for the taunt is so outrageous in those circles as to
be instantly deniable by an apology for such an inadvertent
indiscretion.

The undermining of the position into which the Commonwealth Office contingent has fortified itself continues in the
next episode.

First there are signs that the Treasury people have been won
over to the idea of further investigation. Nothing direct is said:
no one, in this affair, readily lays his cards on the table—
except Wilbraham, who loses each time he does so. The Treasury men want it agreed that if the Russian money should fall
into British hands, it should be at the disposition of the Treasury and not simply "recycled" through the Circus. Smiley
agrees, without drawing attention to the implications of this
claim.

Then Smiley is allowed to make a further demonstration of
his expertise. Someone asks about the difference between
"above-the-line" and "below-the-line" espionage. The former
is carried out by those who have a legitimate presence in the
country—diplomatic personnel, businessmen, those who work
for airlines or tourist agencies, and so forth—and who therefore enjoy a degree of official protection. "Below-the-line"
people are those without such protection, who can, if caught,
be "denied." Since, in deference to Peking, all Russian representation had been excluded from the colony—diplomatic,
commercial, news agency—they would have no choice except
to go the below-the-line route. The ground was being laid by
Smiley for a change in tactics: the use of what Lacon calls "the
panic factor."

But once again the Commonwealth Office contingent is

given an opportunity to overreach itself. Someone asks what the Russians have done in Hong Kong, since they have been driven below the line. It seems a good occasion for the colony to have its trumpet blown, and the "youth" leaps at the chance of demonstrating that Hong Kong can deal with Russian espionage effectively and without the aid of outside agencies. He "reeled off a bunch of boring instances": the Orthodox priest from Paris who attempted to suborn members of the White Russian community in Hong Kong; sailors who tried to foment discontent among dock workers; and so forth. Each time they were arrested, given much publicity in the press, made to look ridiculous, and Peking was duly gratified. Then "thoroughly over-excited," thinking he has conclusively demonstrated the colony's ability to keep its own espionage house in order, he says the unsayable: ". . . the Circus is doing a special bit of pleading in order to get its nose back under the wire!"

Wilbraham "looked more embarrassed than anybody." Smiley, with a pressure of his hand, restrains his aide from making a protest. Once again the rebuke is allowed to take the form of an embarrassed silence at such a breach of custom.

The spoken rebuke comes at another level. "Sounds more like *smoke* to me," says Enderby, addressing Wilbraham. But Wilbraham is at a loss, and it has to be explained to him that the Russians are "waving their sabres where you can watch 'em" and meanwhile getting on with the undercover work elsewhere. Smiley "concedes" that he thinks that is the case, and delivers the coup de grace by remarking that Haydon (the traitor) had always been keen to insist that the Russians had washed their hands of Hong Kong. He adds, in a mild rebuke, that "actually" he has said so in the document before them.

Then they break for lunch, which is delivered from a van, on plastic trays, and the partitions are too low and the custard flows into the meat. Even the food, it seems, needs to trespass across categorical boundaries.

Throughout these five episodes the pattern is unchanged. Smiley and the Commonwealth Office contingent are the protagonists. Lacon, as patron of the Circus, and Enderby (partly out of hostility toward the Commonwealth Office and partly for other reasons that emerge elsewhere in the story) are covert supporters of Smiley.

Smiley's tactics remain the same throughout.

> I speak not to disprove what Brutus spoke,
> But I am here to speak what I do know . . .

Smiley speaks always in a tone of rational disinterest. He shows his expertise when called upon to do so, and he concentrates on the issue of Russian espionage in Hong Kong. He disregards suggestions about (and certainly himself never refers to) the possibility that out of the present affair may come the resurrection of the Circus.

The Commonwealth Office tactic is also mainly to deal with the facts: that there are none to prove Smiley's case. But Wilbraham and his colleagues are not successful. First they are several times shown to be naive about the world of espionage: they do not know about "tradecraft" and they fail to recognize an obvious case of "smoke." Second, they fail to anticipate that (on three occasions) Smiley will be able to use their own statements to undermine their conclusions and support his own. Third, they, especially the "youth," become excited and indignant and violate the required image of being cool and collected. Finally they attack the person rather than the issue. They are *seen* to be deflected into rhetoric. Lacon does not make the same mistake: his rhetorical provocations ("the morality of the whorehouse") are ostensibly directed at outsiders and ostensibly support Wilbraham's case. Enderby, with his outrageous gibe about knighthoods, also occludes the possibility of Wilbraham's taking open umbrage or even of an unspoken accusation of bad taste. In short, traps are set for them, and they fall into these traps. They do so because they are pushed into feeling and displaying emotion, and because they are forced to operate in a variety of sophisticated code (that concerning espionage) which they do not know how to handle.

In the "torpor" that follows lunch, Smiley seeks "to entrench in the meeting a sense of logic behind a Soviet presence in Hong Kong." The phrase the novelist chooses is interesting for its verb: "entrench" (like "implant" or "instill") connotes something more than reasoned agreement. Rather it suggests the kind of conviction that will accept inadequate evidence. Smiley describes the difficulties that the Russians encounter elsewhere in setting up espionage against China, and elaborates upon the natural amenities of Hong Kong for that purpose. Sooner or later the Russians have to come to Hong Kong. The form of his persuasion is entirely one of reasoning from accepted premises to likely conclusions, but the purpose of the discourse is not so much to make people think as to make them feel. Smiley is, to use Lacon's phrase, seeking to raise "the panic factor."

He succeeds. Martindale, Enderby's second string, takes up the questioning. He, and then Lacon, and then the man from the Treasury all plead with Smiley to speculate and draw conclusions—"kick a few ideas around for us." Smiley refuses. "Like scared patients they were appealing to him for a diagnosis."

Recall Mark Antony at Caesar's funeral.

> But here's a parchment with the seal of Caesar.
> I found it in his closet; 'tis his will.
> Let but the commons hear this testament,
> Which (pardon me) I do not mean to read,
> And they would go and kiss dead Caesar's wounds
> And dip their napkins in his sacred blood. . . .

Thus did Mark Antony tickle plebeian greed, speaking of the will "which (pardon me) I do not mean to read." In a manner more subtle and more indirect, befitting his audience, Smiley is playing a similar game, teasing out their apprehensions and withholding the substance.

Then the Commonwealth Office has its one success. The "colonial lady in brown," taking exactly Smiley's tone and style, elicits from him admissions that there are some features that do not make sense in his thesis. Funds are set aside for

agents less readily by the Russians than by other espionage services, but there are precedents. It is, however, unprecedented
that they should be banked in the territory concerned. Usually
they are kept in Moscow or, in rare cases, deposited in a neutral place, such as Switzerland. Furthermore, it seems strange
that funds began in small quantities and have only recently
been brought up to the very large sum involved. How does
Smiley account for that? But Smiley refuses to speculate, to
the evident discomfort of his aide.

Smiley, at the opening of the next episode, is "saved by the
bell." The "bell" marking the end of that round and the beginning of the next is a diversionary question put by Enderby.
What shall they tell the Cousins (the espionage service of the
United States)?

It is an effective diversion, for the question probes at the
open hostility that this group customarily feels for the Americans. (We are led to suspect later that several of them are already colluding with the Americans, but that remains below
the line.) Wilbraham, as we have by now come to expect, reacts immediately and explosively. How could they think of
telling the Americans when they do not intend to take the
governor of Hong Kong into their confidence? Hong Kong is
British territory, for one thing; for another, Ko is a British subject; and the Americans, as they have done elsewhere, "would
go clean overboard." With the Americans "ten deep crawl-
ing over his house with microphones," the governor would
certainly find out, and feel obliged to "turn in his badge."
Wilbraham would certainly do that, and he is sure that Enderby,
once an ambassador, would do the same.

This vehemence produces a "strained silence" broken by
play, in which Enderby and Lacon collude. "Be a brave man
who diddled you on that one," says Enderby, addressing
Wilbraham.

For once they seem all to be in genuine agreement. Then
Smiley, maintaining the same low key and the same reasoned
tone, says something that provokes from Wilbraham "You're
putting a pistol at our heads, man!" Smiley points out that if
they refuse to let him proceed with the investigation, as he has

been told is the likely outcome, then he will be obliged to share what information he had so far gained with the Cousins. If he is not to do that, then he will require instructions "in writing"—a phrase that signals that the gloves have come off. Their information about Ko includes operations in territories that come under the domain of the Cousins: it is not confined to Hong Kong alone. Not only do they have a bilateral agreement with the Cousins, but Smiley himself has a "standing instruction from this committee" to mend the connections with the Cousins that have been damaged by the Haydon affair. He reminds Enderby of the phrase that has been used: "get us back to the top table." His threat, he is in effect saying, comes not from Smiley himself, but has been visited by the intelligence steering group upon itself.

Once again Wilbraham has served as the trampoline. His argument against admitting the Cousins has a thin coating of rationality in the implication that by coming in "ten deep" they will surely make a mess of the affair. But the sentiment of keeping others off one's own patch is clearly a primordial one, and his vehemence seems to catch a sympathetic response from the rest of the committee. Against this resonating emotion Smiley can more effectively sound the cold "facts-and-rules" presentation of his threat.

The air conditioners go wrong and they learn that the parts have been on order for a year. Tea comes in paper cups and leaks onto the green baize. Everyone is sulky.

Then, in the fnal episode, Lacon takes control and asks what Smiley wants. Smiley remains stolid. "Enthusiasm would have been fatal." He makes his requests: to proceed with the investigation, both in Southeast Asia and in the United Kingdom (there is a brief protest from the Home Office people); to be funded, as set out in his memorandum; and, finally, to be allowed to reopen the Circus residency in Hong Kong. The last item is greeted with "a stunned silence"; then a clamor; and then Smiley adds that if the residency is denied, they should be allowed to operate below-the-line agents in the colony, with the protection of London.

Smiley and his aide are sent from the room, the aide gloomily reflecting on the impossible nature of the residency request, and deciding, "Poor old sod: finally past it." He asks the silent Smiley how he feels and gets the reply, "It's not a matter of feeling."

When they return to the room, they are denied the request to reopen the residency, and the aide spies a "gleam of victory" in the eyes of Enderby and the Treasury man. Smiley formally registers his reluctance to accept that decision. Then, with certain small safeguards, they are told that everything else for which they have asked is granted.

It is hard not to conclude that Smiley has made this monstrous demand for the reopening of the residency only so that the committee can have something apparently big to refuse him.

Walking later in the park, they hear Enderby "applauding Smiley's victory." He says: "Nice little meeting. Lot achieved. Nothing given away. Nicely played hand . . . Pity about old Wilbraham. He'd have run India rather well."

In the world of espionage, those agents who work below the line are genuinely secret agents, and if detected may be denied by their sponsors. Those who work above the line have a degree of official protection and are relatively transparent; but not, of course, entirely so—in that case it would not be espionage. This distinction between above the line and below the line provides yet another analogy for classifying persuasive devices and persuasive tactics. Those that lie below the line are "unmentionable."

The same distinction can be made for issues and agendas, and for the conventions that are to govern the deliberations. In the case of the intelligence steering group, above-the-line items are: that this is an elite group; that it has before it a task; that this task is broadly defined as security and specifically defined as the Ko affair in Hong Kong; and that reasoned discussion will enable them to reach the correct decisions. To put it another way: since they all have a common interest and a common understanding of both goal and procedures, this is an occasion for the exercise not of political skills but of administrative expertise; a time not for rhetoric but for the use of sophisticated codes.

Below-the-line expectations and assumptions are different. Everyone knows what they are, but no one should *openly* admit that they know. First, Smiley has other interests. The charitable view would be that the successful management of the Ko affair would help to reestablish the fortunes and the reputation of the Circus. The cynical argument would be that Smiley has manufactured the Ko crisis so as to get his "nose back under the wire." Second, Wilbraham and the contingent from the Commonwealth Office have priorities that are different from those of others present. The first concern is not security in general, but the welfare of their subjects and their officials in Hong Kong. Wilbraham has, for example, a moral concern for the governor of the territory; the others are more inclined to look upon him as a mere instrument. Third, beneath the urbanity, the use of first names between senior people, and the posture of familiarity and cooperation, there is a generalized lack of trust. The Foreign Office people look down on the Commonwealth Office contingent; some suspect that others are already in collusion with the Cousins; not Smiley alone, but everyone has his own ax to grind.

This particular encounter is won by Smiley and lost by Wilbraham. If one asks why Smiley has won, the obvious answer is that he threatened to break ranks and tell all to the Cousins. But that, if correct, is also a meager answer and we shall put it in its place later. Meanwhile let us say that we learn more if we ask not why he has won, but what he has done in order to win. The brief answer is that he has made appropriately *covert* use of below-the-line items and used the correct below-the-line persuasive devices (successfully cross-matching form and purpose, as when he uses the cool voice of reason to provoke anger), whereas Wilbraham has either remained above the line, playing his cards openly, or else made clumsy use of below-the-line items (failing to conceal the purpose behind the facade of an acceptable form).

Smiley makes no direct reference to any of the three below-the-line items: not to his own hidden agenda, not to the

Commonwealth Office priorities, and not to the underlying enmities and rivalries among those present. He restrains his aide when the latter is moved to attempt a riposte to the "red-haired youth." But he makes use of these items, especially of Wilbraham's moral concerns for the governor of Hong Kong. He does not do so openly by saying, for instance, that the parochial concerns of Hong Kong must take second place to the nation's security. Instead, he indulges himself in an indirect *argumentum ad hominem,* hinting at but never explicitly stating the governor's incompetence.

Second, Smiley maintains throughout the deliberations a posture that indicates concern for the task in hand—what should be done to maintain security in the face of Soviet espionage in Hong Kong. He does this in several ways. First he gives a presentation of his own expertise, but only when invited to do so. In this he is abetted by both Lacon and Enderby, and enabled, without using direct indicative statements, to show that Wilbraham lacks this expertise. The only occasion on which Smiley is rattled is the intervention by the "colonial lady in brown," who uses the same code and style of presentation to show that there are gaps in this expertise.

Third, on no occasion does Smiley display emotion. He looks down at his hands when he speaks; he pretends to be thinking things out as he goes along; he speaks "meekly"; he ignores provocation and does not allow his aide to be provoked; when somewhat cornered by the "colonial lady," he does not struggle but remains "courteous," even managing "a small smile"; when making his presentation of demands, he knows that "enthusiasm would have been fatal." All this indicates an absence of personal concern and an interest exclusively in "the facts." To show enthusiasm or anxiety would be to open the trapdoor on his hidden concern: the reestablishment of the Circus. Even when raising the "panic factor," he shows a studious lack of intensity. To do otherwise would be to suggest to the others, "Smiley is in a panic," or, worse, "Smiley is deliberately trying to stampede us." This is an example of *suggestio veri*: not thrusting a point at others, but leading them to draw their own conclusions.

Lastly, there is an almost total suppression of the self, in any form. The tactical self is not allowed to appear, still less the moral or the silly self. Only at the climax, when he produces the threat to involve the Cousins, does he parade a version of the duty-bound civic self. For the rest of the time he is present as nothing more than a disinterested instrumental intelligence.

Wilbraham's performance is for the most part the opposite of Smiley's. What do he and his helpers do to make them lose? By adroit provocation they are trapped into bringing below-the-line items—both their own and others'—out into the open. Their competence to handle the task is put in doubt, both because they are shown to lack the necessary knowledge and becase they reveal that they have the wrong priorities—too much concern for people in Hong Kong and too little for the nation's security. They make direct reference to below-the-line items, first (and possibly acceptably) by a reference to the recent Haydon affair ("How good's their knowledge? Hasn't been too good in the past, has it?") and then (quite outrageously) by accusing Smiley of trying to push his nose back "under the wire." When Smiley's civic self reminds them that it will be his duty to pass information on to the Cousins if they do not allow him to continue the investigation, Wilbraham rips the mask away: "You're putting a pistol at our heads, man!" He gains nothing by it. Lastly Wilbraham, and especially his "youth," allow themselves to become "thoroughly over-excited." As in the game of the dozens, they lose by doing so: vehemence, intensity, and displays of emotion in this particular arena are signs of ineffectiveness.

In brief, like Pritt at the Royal Society's committee and like Ambedkar (on the occasion of that one outburst, but not otherwise), they show themselves to be without guile. They state the truth as they see it, and the result is not applause and approbation, but a verdict of "naive."

Those who meet in the "safe room" in London conduct their deliberations in a manner that contrasts markedly with the reported deliberations of the Oceanside City Council. One contrasting quality is urbanity: delicate fencing conducted under sharply pointed rules rather than slugging it out with clubs. When the red-haired youth openly refers to Smiley's nose getting under the wire, the gaffe is so obvious and so horrendous that it is best answered by a pained silence; when Melba Bishop talks about back-room deals, there is an uproar of counteraccusation.

What can be said about this difference? First, it is made the more obvious by the narrative form and by the skills of the novelist in comparison with the rather raw selected-highlight-with-commentary of journalistic reporting. But, making allowances for that, we are clearly faced with two different political cultures. How then should one account for the difference?

First it may be remarked that one institution lies within the frontier culture of western America, raw and honest and blunt, while the other is graced with that supreme urbanity for which the English in the higher reaches of their bureaucratic and academic creations are supposed to be famous. Americans are direct and robust; the upper-class English are devious and prefer delicate (if sharp) insinuation to plain speaking. There is surely some truth in that. The political cultures—those parts that provide devices for persuasion and procedures for reaching decisions—are different in Oceanside from what they are in Carlton Gardens. But that is only a beginning: there is more to be said.

Second, it might be pointed out (as I have done), that Oceanside's is a political committee. It might then be argued that the intelligence steering group is an administrative unit. This, too, has some explanatory value. Oceanside's City Council members must maintain the facade of an arena committee, and behave as if they were immediately accountable to their electors. The intelligence steering group has no electors and the members certainly have a frankly elitist outlook on the world. But the distinction does not much advance the inquiry, for it does not take account of what is below the line. The account of below-the-line realities for the intelligence steering group clearly shows arena-like rivalries and conflicting loyalties (not to constituents but to departments). Below-the-line

Oceanside knows that some elitism is inevitable. The one difference is that in the case of the intelligence steering group these conflicts are firmly located below the line; in Oceanside there is at least the shadow of a debate about elitism above the line (but, as I have shown, it did not get off the ground). That alone, however, cannot account for the striking lack of delicacy with which Oceanside's deliberations are, it seems, conducted.

A third argument might be that the members of elected bodies may have a short civic life and need not be too nice to one another, because they cannot assume that they will be together very long. On the other hand, tenured civil servants are around one another for a long time, know that they need to be allies on another occasion even if rivals on this one, and consequently are careful not to tread too heavily on one another's toes. The use of first names (in a culture that is quite sparing in that respect) suggests that this might be true for the intelligence steering group's senior members. This does not, of course, mean that they must be genuinely considerate of one another. They need only appear to be so above the line, meanwhile peppering their discourse with sly allusions to knighthoods not yet achieved.

Oceanside inverts the picture. The political audience and its expectations inhibit urbanity. In the open the members are doughty fighters for the interests they represent, never more triumphant than when they can expose each other's hidden iniquities. Covertly, however, we suspect the presence of that genuine mutual consideration which characterizes the members of an elite committee.

Let us repeat these descriptions in the form of rules.

The first rule accords with common sense: items above the line—call them directive principles—may be openly used for putting pressure on others. The most blatant example is Smiley's threat to tell all to the Cousins. He quotes back at the intelligence steering group its directive to him. He signals "above the line" by insisting that any departure must be authorized "in writing." Notice, however, that this above-the-line theme derives its potency from a below-the-line item——hostility toward the Cousins. Also, as we shall see shortly, there are below-the-line rules for timing and sequencing, which affect potency. It is as if above-the-line items are a mere skeleton; the muscles and the nerves are provided from below the line. Notice also that Smiley is using "reason" to provoke emotion (the panic factor) on this occasion, just as he did when he explained why the Russians should find Hong Kong irresistible as a basis for espionage.

If the potency comes from passions lurking below the line, we should ask how they may be used. This produces a second rule: no below-the-line item may be used *directly* as a persuasive device. Those who do so lose points. For example, Smiley's interest in rebuilding the Circus is below the line. The youth's phrase "nose under the wire" is a gaffe that embarrasses even his own superior. For a second example, recall the generalized rivalries and hostilities between the segments of the intelligence steering group. These are kept below the line. The youth's phrasing "you . . . we" violates this rule in indicating, albeit inadvertently, these cleavages.

The third rule is that below-the-line items may be used *indirectly*. Indirection has two modes. The first is when an opponent is provoked into violating the second rule and making direct use of below-the-line items. For example, the youth, in making use of an *argumentum ad hominem* against Smiley, and asserting that the Ko crisis is manufactured to serve Circus interests, has allowed his excitement to lead him openly below the line.

A second mode of indirection occurs when an opponent is manipulated into revealing himself unqualified for the task. Wilbraham is shown to lack expertise in espionage. He does not know the meaning of "good cover" and fails to recognize an obvious case of "smoke." At the same time Smiley gets the opportunity to show his own expertise. The excitement—not to say passion—that the Commonwealth Office people are provoked into displaying (except for the lady in brown) serves the same purpose: it signals an inability to reach the required high level of rationality.

What is the ontological status of these rules? Certainly they are not merely statistical statements about what most people are seen to do. As with any rule there is a teleology involved—an end toward which behavior is directed, an intention, a purpose. They are directive.

If they are directive, they must be in the minds of the actors. But what is the sense of that phrase "in the minds"? It might be said that in taking my example from such a severely intellectualized novelist as le Carré, I am presenting an overrationalized—even Machiavellian—picture of behavior which does not at all accord with the way people actually behave. Very rarely does anyone think it all out beforehand. Moreover, in that particular example, we know both from this and from other novels that George Smiley is a man with deeply troubled emotions, and these emotions can hardly fail to furnish unconscious motivations for the way he conducts himself in meetings as well as out of them. Of course this is true. I have said elsewhere that people cannot check in their entire personalities at the door when they enter a conference room. But the criticism is misdirected. We are not talking of emotions—of some inner psychological reality—but of cultural rules that identify *displays* of emotion, tell you how to recognize them, and link the displays with contexts and predict their consequences. Smiley's ostentatious calm may indeed be related to some inner emotional turmoil that can be traced to his private life. For us that is not the point: our task is to say what is the tactical significance of a studied lack of enthusiasm in this kind of meeting.

Where, then, are these rules located? There are two answers. The first is that a rule is in the mind of anyone who consistently puts it into practice, even if he is not able to say what that rule is. (There is an obvious analogy with rules of grammar.) The second answer is Durkheim's: these rules are collective representations (not implying, of course, that everyone shares equally in the knowledge of them).

To say that a rule is a collective representation is to say that it is part of a particular culture. The rule that tells you on no account to draw attention directly and openly to a colleague's covert interests belongs in the culture of Carlton Gardens but not in the culture of Oceanside. In neither political culture is straightforward cock-of-the-walk competition allowed (as it is in the case of the dozens): personal antagonisms must always be worked out behind a facade of concern about issues or principles. In short, to know the rules in one political culture is not to know all such rules.

Are there, then, any universal rules concerning persuasion—rules that are found in every political culture? Perhaps that question goes too far and it is enough to be able to ask what rules one might expect to provide a framework of inquiry in the next culture visited. Certainly I would anticipate finding the distinction between overt and covert, between the mentionable and the unmentionable (the latter being nevertheless available for use). The framework appears to offer the possibility of constructing a universal rule, such as: Bring up the unmentionable only in ways acceptable in that culture. But this tells us little until we know what, in that particular culture, is unmentionable and what are the acceptable ways of adverting to it. In fact, the rule appears to be universal only because it can be directly deduced from our axiomatic definition of culture—that it has overt and covert sectors. So, as we would expect, there are no universal rules (about displaying emotions or using rhetoric) that have substance in them. Even such a rule as "Don't be caught faking it" remains empty until we also have cultural rules about relevant contexts and about how to recognize a fake. That every culture has the idea of "fake" (which we have identified as the failure to camouflage suitably an item from the covert sector of the culture) is, of course, axiomatic.

Finally, let us consider what meanings should be attached to "power" in the course of investigating passion and reason. We have talked several times of the penalties and sanctions that are visited upon those who commit abominations in trying to be persuasive. They fail because their audience cannot take them seriously. But, it might be said, there have been not a few very powerful men whose utterances, like those of Sam

Goldywn, have become classical examples of foot in mouth. How is it that they were nevertheless exceedingly persuasive?

There is a variety of possible answers. One is that the foot goes into the mouth only when one discourses on matters of no great moment. In a paradoxical way the gaffe becomes part of the persuader's image, his ethos, his way of commending himself to his audience. Another answer would be that the abomination is a purely verbal thing and the audience is able to discern without difficulty what is really meant. But why should they bother to find out what an unintentional comedian really means? That question brings us to the hard answer: that he has power quite independent of his capacities as a persuader.

One can imagine a case in which a person has such power outside the arena of discourse that he will get his own way no matter how ineptly he conducts himself inside the arena. Indeed, this could happen (although it must be pointed out that he must at least have the communicative skills to convey what it is he wants). I suspect, however, that such animal force is rarely exercised in its pure form, that is, in such a way that persuasion has no part whatsoever in the outcome. More likely is the opposite extreme: a person who has no power outside the arena is nevertheless able, by skilled use of the tactics of persuasion, at least to influence the decision, even if not to control it.

Most cases will lie somewhere between these extremes. Let us go back to that most elaborately unanimal arena, the intelligence steering group. One might argue that the only piece of information one needs in order to predict the outcome of the meeting is that Smiley holds the trump card: he can talk to the Cousins. He holds, as Wilbraham says (breaking the conventions yet another time), "a pistol to [their] heads." That may be so. But why should he wait six or seven rounds before producing the weapon?

The answer may lie in timing. Like a trump card, the threat is more effective if it is produced at the right time, and it can be wasted if it is played too early. There is a long preparatory process in which negative feelings are directed away from Smiley and the Circus and allowed to focus on the Commonwealth Office. Then the panic factor is introduced and given time to work on them all. Only then is the threat effective. In other words, the ploy is not really like a trump card; rather it is the final push that topples the tree after a lot of hard work has been done to sever the roots.

The answer may also lie in the curiously persuasive properties of indirection. Smiley's position is perilous not least because he runs the risk of creating an abomination by appearing simultaneously as a supplicant and a dominator. In the interests of preserving a facade of orderliness for the committee members, Smiley must keep his dominance covert. He is very careful to present a civic self: someone intent upon carrying out the duties that the intelligence steering group itself has laid upon him. We have come back to Elizabeth Worthington's kisses. The facade must be kept intact: the intelligence steering group is in control; Smiley is a supplicant; except for the egregious Wilbraham, they collude in the pretense that nothing else is afoot.

This is, I think, a special instance of a more general feature of persuasion, which we have already noticed, *suggestio veri:* that people accept more completely a conclusion that they make for themselves than one that is thrust upon them. It is, I suppose, because they see themselves to have penetrated the facade and to have reached "reality" (which we see as the covert sector of culture). When a statement of the same substance is openly thrust upon them, however, it is weakened in two ways. First, being someone's assertion, it will appear to be part of a facade; second, it overtly and directly asserts what should be left unasserted because to assert it openly is to shake the foundations, to give the lie to "life's lie."

Is there, then, as Oxenstierna suggested, only a little reason involved in governing the world?

To govern is to cause things to be done, to make people act. If there is to be action there must be an end to questioning. Action requires faith, however momentary that faith may be, and faith is the suspension of reason. Therefore government by reason alone is an impossibility.

But it does not therefore follow that reason has no part to play, or even that it always must have a little part. Generalized statements about quantity do not make sense. But at least one can separate one situation from another, or one antagonist from another, by the relative prominence of a sophisticated code.

We have been seeking, throughout this discussion, those occasions on which reason triumphs and the tactics that make such triumphs possible. "Nicely played hand," says Enderby, walking in the park. He means by that (among other things) not that everyone has been rational and that no one has been moved by emotion, but that reason has been used to manipulate emotions and to capitalize on the resulting displays.

Reason, in the end, derives its *persuasive* strength from its high standing in our overt culture. It has that standing because that culture embraces two contradictory propositions. One is that we have in our culture all we need to know to cope with the world and other people. The other proposition asserts that this is a facade, psychologically necessary, but in fact so distorted that if one follows its directions, disaster must ensue. Behind the facade is the "real" reality, accessible, albeit imperfectly, only to reason. This real world, of course, includes other people's irrationalities.

References

Amis, Kingsley
  1954 *Lucky Jim.* London: Gollancz.
Aronoff, Myron J.
  1977 *Power and Ritual in the Israeli Labor Party.* Amsterdam: Van
         Gorcum.
  1980 "The Use and Abuse of Power and the Creation and Cor-
         ruption of Civil Religion in Israel." Paper prepared for
         Burg Wartenstein Symposium, no. 84.
Avard
  1962 *Panchayat Raj as the Basis of Indian Polity.* New Delhi:
         Avard.
Bailey, F. G.
  1963 *Politics and Social Change.* Berkeley: University of California
         Press.
  1965 "Decisions by Consensus in Councils and Committees" In
         Political Systems and the Distribution of Power. London:
         Tavistock.
  1976 "'I-Speech' in Orissa." In *Language and Politics,* ed. W. M.
         O'Barr, and Jean F. O'Barr. The Hague: Mouton.
  1981 "Dimensions of Rhetoric in Conditions of Uncertainty." In
         Politically Speaking, ed. R. Paine. Philadelphia: ISHI.
Barbu, Z.
  1960 *Problems of Historical Psychology.* New York: Grove Press.
Brecher, Michael
  1959 *Nehru: A Political Biography.* London: Oxford University
         Press.
Caro, Robert A.
  1974 *The Power Broker.* New York: Knopf.

D'Andrade, Roy Goodwin
    n.d.   "Cultural Meaning Systems."

Dumont, Louis
    1970   *Homo Hierarchicus.* Chicago: University of Chicago Press.

Durkheim, Emile
    1957   *The Elementary Forms of the Religious Life.*London: Allen &
        Unwin (first published 1915).

Eco, Umberto
    1976   *A Theory of Semiotics.* Bloomington: Indiana University
        Press.

Evans-Pritchard E. E.
    1940   *The Nuer.* Oxford: Clarendon Press.
    1951   *Kinship and Marriage among the Nuer.* Oxford: Clarendon
        Press.

Fest, Joachim C.
    1975   *Hitler.* New York: Random House.

Fox-Davies, Arthur Charles, ed.
    1913   *The Book of Public Speaking.* London: Caxton.

Fried, Albert, ed.
    1974   *Except to Walk Free.* New York: Anchor Books.

Goffman, Erving
    1961   *Asylums.* New York: Anchor Books.

Hirschman, Albert O.
    1977   *The Passions and the Interests.* Princeton: Princeton Univer-
        sity Press.

Jenkins, Roy
    1968   *Sir Charles Dilke.* London: Fontana Books (first published
        1958).

Larrabee, Harold A., ed.
    1952   *Bentham's Handbook of Political Fallacies.* Baltimore: Johns
        Hopkins Press.

le Carré, John
    1977   *The Honourable Schoolboy.* New York: Knopf.

Lévi-Strauss, Claude
    1963   *Structural Anthropology.* New York: Basic Books.

Mackintosh, John P.
    1962   *The British Cabinet.* London: Stevens.

Mandler, G.
    1975   Mind and Emotion. New York: Wiley.

Marriott, McKim
    1968   "The Feast of Love." In *Krishna: Myths, Rites, and Attitudes,*
        ed. M. Singer. Chicago: University of Chicago Press.

REFERENCES

Masters, John
  1956   *Bugles and a Tiger*. New York: Viking.
Milano, Euclide
  1925   *Dalla Culla Alla Bara*. Borgo S. Dalmazzo: Bertello.
Misra, B.R.
  1956   *V for Vinoba*. Calcutta: Orient Longmans.
Morris-Jones, W. H.
  1957   *Parliament in India*. London: Longmans.
Murphy, Robert F.
  1971   *The Dialectics of Social Life. New York: Basic Books*
Perelman, Chaim, and L. Olbrechts-Tyteca
  1971   *The New Rhetoric*. Notre Dame: University of Notre
         Dame Press (first published as *La Nouvelle Rhetorique* [Paris:
         P.U.F., 1958].
Polanyi, Karl
  1968   *The Great Transformation*. Boston: Beacon Press (first pub-
         lished 1944).
Rainwater, Lee
  1970   *Behind Ghetto Walls*. Chicago: Aldine.
Rhodes James, Robert
  1969   "The Politician." In *Churchill Revised: A Critical Assessment,*
         by A. J. P. Taylor, Robert Rhodes James, J. A. Plumb, Ba-
         sil Liddell Hart and Anthony Storr. New York: Dial
         Press.
Rickman, John
  1957   *A General Selection from the Works of Sigmund Freud*. New
         York: Doubleday (first published 1937).
Schaffer, Bernard
  1973   *The Administrative Factor*. London: Frank Cass.
Simmel, Georg
  1969   *The Sociology of Georg Simmel*. Trans. and ed. Kurt H.
         Wolff. New York: Free Press (first published 1950).
Smithies, Bill, and Peter Fiddick
  1969   *Enoch Powell on Immigration*. London: Sphere Books.
Snow, C. P.
  1956   *The Masters*. Harmondsworth: Penguin Books (first pub-
         lished 1951).
  1960   *The Search*. New York: Signet Books (first published 1934).
Thomas, Dylan
  1954   *Quite Early One Morning*. New York: New Directions.

University of the South Pacific
  1975 *Reports*. Suva: University Printing Unit.
  1976 *Reports*. Suva: University Printing Unit.
Weber, Max
  1957 *From Max Weber*. Trans. and ed. H. H. Gerth and C. Wright Mills. London: Routledge & Kegan Paul (first published 1948).

Index

Library of Congress Cataloging in Publication Data

Bailey, F. G. (Frederick George)
    The tactical uses of passion.

    Bibliography: p.
    Includes index.
    1. Power (Social sciences) 2. Emotions—Social aspects. 3. Rhetoric—Social aspects.
    4. Reason—Social aspects. 5. Culture. I. Title.
    HM136.B22   1983   303.3   82-22074
    ISBN 0-8014-1556-X